Risk and Cultural Theory:

A Management Consultancy Approach

For Meg and Felicity

Steve

June 2020

Steve Frosdick

Published by Paragon Publishing, Rothersthorpe, UK

First published 2006

ISBN (10 digit) 1-899820-27-2

ISBN (13 digit) 978-1-899820-27-6

British Library Cataloguing-in-Publication Data

A catalogue record for this book is available from the British Library

Book design and layout by IWI Associates

Production management by Into Print (www.intoprint.net)

Printed and bound in the UK and USA by Lightning Source

TABLE OF CONTENTS

FOREWORD BY GERALD MARS II

ABOUT THE AUTHOR.. III

ACKNOWLEDGEMENTS... IV

GLOSSARY OF ABBREVIATIONS.. V

LIST OF FIGURES VI

LIST OF TABLES.. VII

INTRODUCTION 1

CHAPTER ONE: THEORIES OF RISK 5

CHAPTER TWO: APPLIED THEORY & METHODS 49

CHAPTER THREE: REFLEXIVE HISTORY... 79

CHAPTER FOUR: PUBLIC ASSEMBLY FACILITIES RISK – PART I............. 93

CHAPTER FIVE: PUBLIC ASSEMBLY FACILITIES RISK – PART II 119

CHAPTER SIX: POLICE PROJECTS RISK – PART I 155

CHAPTER SEVEN: POLICE PROJECTS RISK – PART II.............................. 193

CHAPTER EIGHT: CONCLUSION 235

REFERENCES 267

APPENDIX A: CASE STUDY PROTOCOL/CODING FRAME............................ 295

INDEX 301

FOREWORD BY GERALD MARS

This is an unusual and useful book. It is unusual because it demonstrates how effective theory, when applied with intelligence to concrete data, can illumine what was previously confusing and only partially understood. This is not a common combination.

Dr Frosdick has skilfully combined ideas of risk derived from Cultural Theory to the very real problems faced by managers and management consultants. He guides us – with the aid of a series of fascinating case studies – to appreciate how different perceptions of risk and very different views of the world bedevil or can be used to empower the relationships within and between organisations. He then shows us how a management consultant, by following relatively simple guidelines, can forecast the values and attitudes that govern behaviours. We learn for instance, what conditions predispose to enterprise, to dependence on rules, to apathetic acceptance or to paranoid suspicion. We learn what makes for compatibility and what makes for conflict.

Having developed a battery of successful strategies and techniques, Dr Frosdick shows how, once the bases of these structural cleavages are understood, they can be adapted to advantage. His case studies demonstrate how the parties themselves can – and should – come to understand the sources of their standpoints and perceptions. His examples demonstrate how effective change can grow and develop as a result.

This book is not only unusual; it is therefore also extremely practical. This is in part because it is based on ten years sound experience and because it is so clearly written.

Professor Gerald Mars

University College, London

ABOUT THE AUTHOR

Dr Steve Frosdick has been Director of IWI Associates Ltd since 1996. He has two postgraduate degrees (MSc and PhD) and is a Registered Practitioner of the Higher Education Academy. He is a Registered PRINCE 2 Project Management Practitioner, a Founder Member of the Football Safety Officers' Association and is a Member of the International Institute of Risk and Safety Management.

Through IWI Associates, Steve has completed a wide variety of consultancy, research and training projects. His strategic risk management experience includes programme and project management, strategic and change management, corporate governance, safety and security at sports grounds, events management, policing, community and race relations, information security, general business risk and benefits management. Clients have included various police and criminal justice organisations, the football authorities, conference organisers, universities and publishers.

From 1979 to 1995, Steve worked as a police officer in a wide variety of operational and support posts. Operationally, he served as patrol officer, custody officer, shift manager and operations manager. In other roles he gained experience in corporate strategy, project management, the management of risk, information management, quality improvement, performance measurement and cognitive assessment. He retired following a career break during which he successfully developed a consultancy and academic career.

Since 1991 he has been involved in academia and from 1998 to 2006 worked with the Institute of Criminal Justice Studies at the University of Portsmouth. Steve has an international reputation as an expert in risk management, particularly in the stadium environment. He has taught and given conference presentations in the UK, US, France, Portugal, Switzerland, Italy and Mauritius. He has published three previous books and over 50 articles, book chapters and other papers. He is a frequent contributor to 'Stadium & Arena Management' magazine and has spoken at six of the annual 'Stadium & Arena'/ESMA conferences since 1998. He is also the editor of the UK football authorities' Training Package for Stewarding at Football Grounds. Although now a Southampton season ticket holder, he is a lifelong fan of Brentford.

ACKNOWLEDGEMENTS

I would like to thank the representatives of the football authorities and the many members of the Football Safety Officers' Association who have supported my work. I am also grateful to my many clients within police and criminal justice organisations, who are not named here to preserve the anonymity of the case studies. Thank you for the research access you have afforded me and above all thank you for your business.

Particular thanks are due to Gerald Mars, who saw the academic potential in a young police officer whilst walking on Hampstead Heath in 1992 and who has stuck with him (or at least been unable to shake him off) ever since. Thank you for your encouragement, patience and wise counsel.

I have benefited from the advice of several academic friends and colleagues who commented on earlier drafts of the work which underpins this book. So thank you to Carol Hayden, Les Johnston, Tim Meaklim and Alan Wright. I am similarly grateful to David Weir.

Thanks also to Steve Savage and again to Les Johnston in the Institute of Criminal Justice Studies at the University of Portsmouth. I am very appreciative of the two periods of sabbatical leave you have granted me for my research and for the university's financial contributions.

Acknowledgements are due to the publishers of my previous work, various extracts from which are included in this book. These are indicated in footnotes throughout. Similar acknowledgements are due to Gerald Mars, Andy Odell and Nick Capon, co-authors for the extracts indicated in the footnotes.

Finally I am thankful for my wife Alison, who has patiently put up with my frequent absences – visiting football grounds and other venues, travelling on business or 'just popping into the office for a few minutes' to study and write.

Steve Frosdick

October 2006

GLOSSARY OF ABBREVIATIONS

PAFs	Public Assembly Facilities
ACPO	Association of Chief Police Officers
ALARP	As Low as Reasonably Practicable
APM	Association for Project Management
CCTA	Office for Government Commerce (old acronym)
CCTV	Closed Circuit Television
COTASS	Club-Oriented Ticketing and Authorisation System for Stadia
CPSMR	Centre for Public Services Management and Research
CRAMM	CCTA Risk Analysis and Management Method
FLA	Football Licensing Authority
FMECA	Failure Modes and Effects Criticality Analysis
FSA	The Football Supporters Association
FSADC	Football Stadia Advisory Design Council
FSC	Federation of Stadium Communities
FSF	Football Supporters Federation
FSOA	Football Safety Officers' Association
GG-CT	Grid Group Cultural Theory
HAZOPS	Hazard and Operability Studies
HMIC	Her Majesty's Inspectorate of Constabulary
HSE	Health and Safety Executive
ILGRA	Interdepartmental Liaison Group on Risk Assessment
IPCC	Independent Police Complaints Commission
ISE	Institution of Structural Engineers
NASUWT	National Union of Schoolmasters and Union of Women Teachers
NFFSC	National Federation of Football Supporters Clubs
NSPIS	National Strategy for Police Information Systems
OGC	Office for Government Commerce
PAGIT	Home Office Police Advisory Group IT
PID	Project Initiation Document
PITACSA	Police IT and Communications Suppliers Association
PRINCE2	Projects Run in a Controlled Environment
QRA	Quantified Risk Assessment
SCIF	Sound and Communication Industries Federation
UEFA	Union of European Football Associations

LIST OF FIGURES

Number	*Title*	*Page*
1.1	The Risk Archipelago	6
1.2	The Stadium as a System of Zones	17
1.3	Fault Tree Analysis	18
1.4	Different Risk Perspectives	29
1.5	Cultural Theory Grid-Group Matrix	34
1.6	Business Continuity Planning	39
2.1	Four Views of Nature	55
2.2	Cultural Theory in an Organisational Context	63
2.3	The Cultural Web of an Organisation	65
4.1	The British Stadia Safety Industry	107
5.1	Framework For Cultural Theory Analysis	122
5.2	Management of Risk Framework	147
5.3	Example of a Hazards Register	148
5.4	Example Risk Evaluation Matrix	149
6.1	The NSPIS Programme and its Projects	161
6.2	Explaining Cultural Theory	170
6.3	Risk Matrix	185
6.4	Risk Evaluation Decision	185
6.5	Risk Management Decision Tree	187
7.1	Management of Risk Model for Case Study 'Bluegrass'	227
8.1	Pre-Coded Risk Evaluation Matrix	250

LIST OF TABLES

Number	*Title*	*Page*
1.1	Seven Contested Areas of the Risk Management Debate	42
1.2	The Management of Risk and Uncertainty	46
4.1	Disasters/Incidents Involving British Stadia or Supporters	96
4.2	Disasters in Football Grounds Outside Britain	98
4.3	Data Sources for the PAFs Risk Research Setting	104
4.4	Organisations Involved in the British Stadia Safety Industry	106
5.1	Organisations Typically Comprising a PAFs 'Safety Culture'	121
5.2	Indicators of Cross Organisational Collaboration	121
5.3	Aspects Concerned With the 'Grid' Dimension	123
5.4	Aspects Concerned With the 'Group' Dimension	124
6.1	Association for Project Management Body of Knowledge	156
6.2	Adverse Outcomes for a Police Programme	158
6.3	NSPIS Local Applications	160
6.4	Case Study Descriptions	166
6.5	Stakeholder Analysis for Case Study 'Ranger'	172
6.6	Stakeholder Analysis for Case Study 'Bluegrass'	172
6.7	Stakeholder Analysis for Case Study 'Orange'	173
6.8	Stakeholder Analysis for Case Study 'Royal'	174
6.9	Key Areas of NSPIS Programme Risk 1996-1998	190
6.10	Action Plans Progress Status	191
7.1	Case Study Details – Sorted by Start Date	194
7.2	Risk Categories in Risk Log for Case Study 'Whisky'	198
7.3	Workshop Groups Design for Case Study 'X-Ray'	199
7.4	Review Workshop Participants for Case Study 'Quebec'	206
7.5	Numbers of Risks Raised By Groups in Case Study 'Yankee'	208
7.6	Participants in Case Study 'Zulu'	209

Number	*Title*	*Page*
7.7	Risk Review Group for Case Study 'Uniform'	212
7.8	Risk Assessment Design for Case Study 'Sierra'	216
7.9	Semi-Structured Interview Process for Case Study 'Ranger'	220
7.10	Predicted Risk Concerns for Case Study 'Amber'	222
7.11	Risk Identification Interview Sources for Case Study 'Uncle'	224
7.12	Risk Identification Interview Sources for Case Study 'Bluegrass'	227
7.13	Fourfold Risk Perspectives for Case Study 'Royal'	230
8.1	Case Study Details – Sorted by Start Date	235
8.2	Chronological Increase in Stakeholder Involvement in Case Studies	237
8.3	Case Study Details – Sorted By Days Effort	237
8.4	Days Effort and Stakeholder Involvement in Case Studies	239
8.5	Case Study Details – Sorted by Stakeholder Participation	240
8.6	Cultural Theory as a Heuristic and Stakeholder Participation	241
8.7	Examples of Probability Estimation Scales	245
8.8	Examples of Consequences Estimation Scales	245
8.9	Example Multiple Consequences Estimation Scale	246
8.10	Example Adverse Outcomes Frequency Analysis	248
8.11	Stakeholder Involvement in the Risk Management Process	251
8.12	'How to Manage Project Risk' Course Timetable	262

INTRODUCTION

SUMMARY

This Introduction sets the scene for the book. It begins by explaining what the book is about. It then outlines the broader context in which the research is set. The Introduction closes with an overview of the remainder of the book.

SETTING THE SCENE

The Book

This is an eclectic yet integrated book about four things. It is about risk theory. It is about British Public Assembly Facilities. It is about British police project management. And it is about grounded theory.

The book is about theories of risk and risk perception, particularly Cultural Theory. This is a theory of classification derived from social anthropology (see Douglas 1978, Thompson, Ellis and Wildavsky 1990) and is explained in Chapter One. Applications of Cultural Theory and their implications are then discussed in Chapter Two. As a theory of the 'middle range', Cultural Theory is ideal for empirical research because it is sufficiently close to the data to be included in research questions that allow empirical testing (Merton 1957).

Previous applications of Cultural Theory have tended to be conceptual and retrospective. This book, however, seeks to apply Cultural Theory in two different 'live' research settings – British Public Assembly Facilities and the British police service. Emerging from and grounded in the history, outputs and outcomes of the empirical research undertaken in these two settings, the book concludes by offering seven theoretical propositions. Derived from these are two new Cultural Theory-based methodologies for consulting and training in the management of risk.

In summary, the aim of this book is to assess the practical application of Cultural Theory in a risk-related context.

The Broader Context

There are two settings for the research. First is the British Public Assembly Facilities (hereinafter referred to as PAFs) industry, with a particular focus on the management of risk in football grounds. Second is the British police service, more specifically the management of police programmes and projects. These are at first sight very different settings, yet they have at least three commonalities. They are both settings in which there is a history of things going disastrously wrong. They are both organisationally complex.

And they both involve a range of stakeholders with differing perceptions of risk.

Contemporary Britain since the early Thatcher years has seen a succession of what Ian Taylor (1991) has described as, 'disastrous breakdowns in public provision on the part of established institutions purporting to provide for, or, indeed, to 'look after' the citizenry'. These include the sinking of the Herald of Free Enterprise car ferry, the Kings Cross underground station fire, the Piper Alpha oil rig explosion and a long series of rail crashes from Clapham Junction in 1988, through Southall and Paddington in the mid 1990s, to the recent disasters at Selby, Hatfield and St Albans.

This general history of disastrous failings is mirrored in British PAFs, the most well known examples being the Bradford fire in 1985 and the crush at Hillsborough in Sheffield in 1989. The history is also apparent in British programmes and projects. Writing about the new Bath spa (four years late and three times over budget), Edwards (2004) notes that,

> 'like the Millennium Dome, Portcullis House, the Millennium Footbridge, Chelsea Barracks, the British Museum Grand Court and the Channel Tunnel rail link, [the new Bath spa] is yet another example of modern Britain's inability to build grand public projects properly, on time and within budget. Last month, for example, it was revealed that the troublesome £500 million British Library, which was opened only six years ago, is already in need of major repairs and upgrading.'

Similar comments have been made in respect of failures in information technology and public sector procurement projects (for example see National Audit Office 2001; 2003; Royal Academy of Engineering and British Computer Society 2004).

These disastrous histories are set out in more detail in the introductions to Chapters Four and Six. The issues of organisational complexity and risk perception are also fully addressed in the analysis of the two research settings (see Chapters Four and Five for PAFs and Chapters Six to Eight for police projects).

OVERVIEW OF THE BOOK

Following on from this Introduction, Chapter One reviews literature on theories of risk and risk perception, including a full explanation of Cultural Theory. The Chapter explores the diverse character of risk and the reasons why it has to be managed. It examines the processes of risk identification, risk estimation, risk evaluation and risk management, giving an overview of the most common and important techniques, together with a discussion of the most relevant areas of debate. Finally, the Chapter argues that the techniques of risk assessment and risk management are insufficient in themselves. Practitioners need to draw on theories of risk and risk perception for evidence to support what they do. Cultural Theory provides the best way of predicting how risks will be perceived and explaining how risk management decisions should be negotiated.

Chapter Two deals with applied theory, research methods and the research problem. The Chapter opens by briefly discussing the very qualitative grounded theory approach adopted for this book, together with relevant ethical issues. It then reviews the various applications, implications and criticisms of Cultural Theory. Developments in Cultural Theory and risk theory are discussed and the research problem is affirmed. The methods used in the two settings are then discussed. Finally, the usefulness, significance and originality of the research are assessed.

Because of the highly personalised nature of the research, Chapter Three then sets out the personal context within which the research has evolved. The research has involved extensive participant observation, 'action science' case studies and the consequent discovery of grounded theory. The researcher has been integral to the research process, thus a reflexive 'natural history' of the research is an important part of the data and analysis to be presented in this book.

Chapters Four and Five present a Cultural Theory analysis of the British PAFs industry. After introducing the research setting, the analysis begins by outlining the history of PAFs disasters and regulatory responses. Chapter Four then justifies the significance of the setting for research and discusses the impact the research has had on the setting. The Chapter continues by using Cultural Theory to analyse empirical data from and literature relating to risk in British PAFs. The analysis reveals the conflicting risk perceptions of individualist clubs, hierarchical regulators, long suffering fatalist spectators and their more egalitarian colleagues in supporter and local resident pressure groups.

Chapter Five uses Cultural Theory to propose the indicators for a fourfold categorisation of 'safety cultures'. The analysis reveals the four contrasting, viable and archetypal models of organising the cross-organisational collaboration required for managing risk in PAFs. The Chapter goes on to look at PAFs as systems and draws out the different types of hazards perceived in each of five zones by each of four different groups of stakeholders. Owners and operators are concerned with threats to their revenue streams. Spectators wish to view and enjoy events staged in comfortable surroundings. Regulatory agencies seek to enforce safety and security rules and the community want their environment disrupted as little as possible. The Chapter then uses a worked example to tentatively suggest how the grounded theory might emerge through a practical management of risk approach. Finally, the Chapter draws conclusions from the analysis and makes the link to the second research setting.

Mirroring and then building on the structure of Chapters Four and Five, Chapters Six to Eight presents a Cultural Theory analysis of programme and project risk case studies within British police management. Chapter Six opens by introducing the research setting, justifying its significance for research and discussing the impact which the research has had on the setting. It then gives an overview of the 41 case studies which form the data set for this setting. The Chapter shows how Cultural Theory has been applied in the case studies to disaggregate the stakeholders to be found in the police setting. It then suggests how Cultural Theory might be used to analyse project organisational cultures. Going beyond what was achieved in the PAFs setting, the Chapter closes with an extended case study. The 40 remaining cases are then presented in Chapter Seven.

Chapter Eight opens with the cross-case analysis which provides the second set of data required for a grounded theory approach. It continues by considering the theory that emerges from and is grounded in the research data and offers seven theoretical propositions. Finally, the Chapter sets out new Cultural Theory methodologies for consulting in and training on the management of risk.

CHAPTER ONE: THEORIES OF RISK[1]

SUMMARY

This Chapter reviews the literature on the management of risk, a concept which comprises both the analysis or assessment of risk and also is its actual management. The Chapter is presented in nine main sections. The first two sections explore the diverse character of risk and the reasons why it has to be managed. The next four sections examine risk identification, risk estimation, risk evaluation, and risk management. Each of these sections includes an overview of the most common and important techniques, together with a discussion of the most relevant areas of debate. The next section sets out a detailed explanation of Cultural Theory. The concluding sections examine recent developments and argue that the techniques of risk assessment and risk management are insufficient without an understanding of the areas of debates within risk theory. Practitioners need to draw on theories of risk and risk perception for evidence to support what they do. Cultural Theory provides the best way of predicting how risks will be perceived and explaining how risk management decisions should be negotiated.

INTRODUCTION

The Risk Archipelago

The concept of risk is extremely diverse, complex and the subject of considerable debate. In their 1996 collection of essays on contemporary debates about risk and its management, Hood and Jones (1996) observe that, since the mid 1980s, public interest in risk has given rise to a huge number of books and papers on the subject. This burgeoning literature has further fuelled the risk debate in which three fundamental problems remain unresolved.

> 'First, there is no clear and commonly agreed definition of what the term 'risk' actually means. Secondly, research on risk remains highly compartmentalised, fragmenting the subject into many relatively isolated subfields and specialisms. ... Thirdly, there is the continuing controversy over what-to-do issues - the 'practical philosophies', principles or doctrines concerning how the different major components within the 'risk environment' are best managed.' (Hood and Jones 1996:2)

---

[1] This chapter is derived from the publications listed in the references as Frosdick (1997l) and Frosdick (1999b).

We shall look in more detail at the meaning of risk and at the debates over doctrines of risk management later on in this Chapter. But first, let us be clear that there is (as yet) no single unifying theory of risk. On the contrary, risk is a sea containing what the Royal Society Study Group on risk (1992:135) refer to as the islands of 'the risk archipelago' (see Figure 1.1).

Figure 1.1: The Risk Archipelago

(Source: Frosdick 1999b)

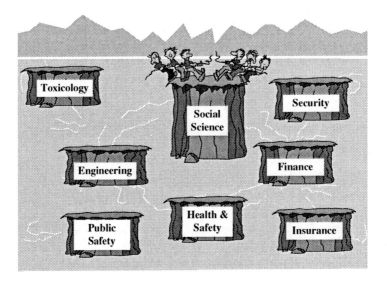

A helicopter tour of just some of these islands would find us visiting toxicologists trying to work out acceptable levels of human exposure to various substances and so, for example, to tell us whether it is safe to drink the water. There would be engineers seeking to establish the impacts of component failures and thus, for example, to inform us that there would only be a fire in the Channel Tunnel once every 10,000 years. We would find a pop concert being organised with crowd safety in mind and health and safety professionals seeking to reduce working time lost through accidents. There would be security specialists seeking to prevent and detect crime. Elsewhere we would find financiers assessing whether to grant loans and insurance brokers setting premiums commensurate with exposure to losses. On another island we would find social scientists researching people's perceptions and, as we shall see later, arguing among themselves about their findings.

Turner concludes that 'we are now in a situation where no single view of risk can claim authority or is wholly acceptable' (Turner 1994:148). Whilst Smallman warns,

> 'There is a very real danger that rather than it being drawn together into a coherent whole, risk management will continue to develop as a fragmented ill-defined gathering of theory and practice. Preventing such 'balkanization' requires informed and intelligent debate, agreement between various practitioner groups and communication with 'customers'.' (Smallman 1996:257)

Both Hood (1996) and Smallman (1996) advocated a move to more cohesive, inclusive, participatory and 'holistic' approaches to the management of public risk. And towards the turn of the millennium, some evidence of a 'new risk management' (Power 1999) began to emerge. Power argued that companies were starting to integrate the management of risk function across their whole business.

This trend may be seen in two ways. First, it may be seen as a response to the Turnbull rules on corporate governance (ICAEW 1999). Second, the trend has been accentuated by what has been described as 'the movement towards punitive regulation' (Baldwin and Anderson (2002:34). However, the islands of the risk archipelago are so diverse and dispersed that Hood and Jones' picture of 'an exceptionally broad, diverse and yet compartmentalised field of study' (1996:5) seems likely to endure a while yet.

Why Manage Risk?

Notwithstanding the difficulties in establishing what risk actually is, nevertheless we do have to manage it. Recent years have seen a host of natural or environmental disasters. For example, during 2003, Swiss Re reported that, 'almost 20,000 people lost their lives in just under 350 catastrophes around the world' (see Muspratt 2003). Human behaviour can wreak havoc through terrorism or crime, the most extreme example being the terrorist bombings of the World Trade Centre in New York. And many large-scale disasters, such as the Chernobyl nuclear melt-down or the Bhopal chemical explosion have resulted from the failure of complex technical or sociotechnical systems. These 'man-made disasters' (Turner 1978, Turner and Pidgeon 1997) happen because accidents are normal (Perrow 1984). As Weir puts it, 'all complex sociotechnical systems tend to operate in degraded mode' (Weir 1996:116).

More colloquially, Weir refers to the truism of Murphy's Law, which provides that 'if a thing can go wrong, it will'.

THE CONCEPT OF RISK

The Meaning of Risk

The various inhabitants of the risk archipelago – engineers, scientists, academics and others involved in studying the uncertain business of risk – employ terminology which is itself marked by some uncertainty. Even, or perhaps especially, the term 'risk' can be the subject of much debate. For such a little word, 'risk' is a very complex concept. Its meaning has evolved over the years and is now the subject of considerable disagreement.

Distinguishing 'Hazard' and 'Risk'

As Hood and Jones (1996) point out, 'It is notable that, instead of converging on agreed definitions of basic terms, the contemporary literature abounds with contradictory statements about what the words 'hazard' and 'risk' mean' (Hood and Jones 1996:2). Natural scientists tend to favour the term, 'hazard', whilst social scientists and mathematicians use 'risk'. Hood and Jones distinguish the terms by arguing that hazards give rise to risks, thus hazard management is a subset of risk management. 'The term 'hazard' generally denotes a phenomenon or circumstance perceived to be capable of causing harm or costs to human society. ... 'Risk', by contrast, is a broader and more diffuse concept.' (*ibid.*)

Historical Background

The development of the concept of risk from the seventeenth century to date has been outlined by Mary Douglas (1990). The idea of risk originated in the mathematics associated with gambling in the seventeenth century. Risk referred to probability, for example to the chance of throwing a six on a dice, combined with the magnitude of potential gains or losses. In the eighteenth century, the idea of risk was employed in the marine insurance business. Risk was a neutral idea, taking account of both gains and losses. Insurers would work out a premium based on the chance of a ship returning home laden with riches against the chance of it sinking with the loss of all its hands and cargo. In the nineteenth century, ideas of risk emerged in the study of economics. People were considered to be risk averse, therefore entrepreneurs needed special incentives to take the risks involved in investment.

Engineering and Science Definitions

The twentieth century has seen the concept of risk move on to refer only to negative outcomes in engineering and science, with particular reference to the hazards posed by modern technological developments in the offshore, petrochemical and nuclear industries. The Royal Society Study Group (1983 and 1992) definitions began with risk as 'the probability that a particular adverse event occurs during a stated period of time, or results from a particular challenge' (Royal Society Study Group 1992, p.2). Acknowledging the needs of engineers and scientists who specialise in risk studies, the 1992 Report also included definitions from British Standard 4778. This defines risk as 'a combination of the probability, or frequency, of occurrence of a defined hazard and the magnitude of the consequences of the occurrence' (British Standards Institution, 1991).

For the information technology industry, risk has been defined as 'the probability of exposure to the adverse consequences of future events' (Scarff, Carty and Charette 1993:88). These definitions suggest that a risk has three components: a future event or hazard, the chance or probability that the hazard will occur and the adverse consequences if it does occur.

Distinctions also need to be drawn between individual and societal risks, because of the differences in perception to which these give rise. For example, we are more horrified by the deaths of 300 people in one plane crash than we are by the deaths of 300 people in individual car crashes. Individual risk has been defined by the Health and Safety Executive (HSE) as 'the risk to any particular individual, either a worker or a member of the public, [that is] anybody living at a defined radius from an establishment, or somebody following a particular pattern of life' (HSE 1988, para. 52). Societal risk represents the risk to society as a whole and has been similarly defined as 'measured, for example, by the chance of a large accident causing a defined number of deaths' (*ibid.*)

As Warner points out, 'Scientists and engineers use these definitions because they provide the basis from which they can carry out their practical work' (Warner 1993:45). This work is mainly concerned with putting numbers on risk through the calculation of probabilities and the use of data bank information on failures and reliability.

Perspectives from the Social Sciences

These ideas of risk are not shared by social scientists, for whom

> 'there are serious difficulties in attempting to view risk as a one-dimensional concept [when] a particular risk or hazard [means] different things to different people in different contexts [and] risk is socially constructed' (Royal Society Study Group 1992:7).

However, within the behavioural sciences themselves there are disagreements; between psychologists, such as Slovic (1991), who view risk as an individual construct influenced by factors such as familiarity and dread, and anthropologists, for whom, according to Warner, risk is 'threat or danger whose perception will depend on the prevailing culture in which there are

four major groups: hierarchists, egalitarians, fatalists and individualists'
(Warner 1993:45). This debate about risk perception is central to the
theoretical underpinning of this book and is examined in more detail both
later in this Chapter and in Chapter Two.

Risk as Blame

Since the 1980s, the concept of risk has moved on from probability and
consequences, and from threat or danger, real or perceived, to also
encompass the idea of risk as accountability, or risk as blame and liability,
even without fault. This view has emerged from the idea that the world is a
more individualist place. This shift from hierarchy to individualism may be
evidenced, for example, by developments in criminal justice policy. Ryan
(1999) has argued that the deferential ordinary person excluded from policy
making by the elite has been replaced by the active citizen driving a (media-
led) populist approach to policy.

Douglas (1990) shows how, in a more individualist world, risk has become a
tool of the legal system. Previously, the world made rules to protect itself
from individuals. Now, individuals need to be protected from the effects of
the world. The reduced influence of the Church has had implications for the
ability of sin and taboo to constrain behaviour. When society was more
hierarchical, being in sin or breaking taboo meant the individual was out of
line with society. In a more individualist global culture, being at risk means
that society is out of line with the individual, whose rights are in need of
protection. As Douglas puts it, 'A generalised concern for fairness has started
us on a new cultural phase. The political pressure is not explicitly against
taking risks, but against exposing others to risk' (Douglas 1992a:15).

Other writers have linked risk with the law of tort in America and highlighted
the increase in both litigation and liability for risk. Priest observes that 'the
principal function of modern civil law is to control risk' (Priest 1990:209).
Emphasising the link with accountability, he goes on to argue that

> 'the more precise statement of the first principle of civil liability
> today is that a court will hold a party to an injury liable if that party
> could have taken some action to reduce the risk of the injury at a cost
> less than the benefit from risk reduction'(*ibid.* p.216).

Fairlie goes further, arguing that, 'the prevailing attitude in America is that
people should be safeguarded against not only negligence but also bad luck'
(Fairlie 1989:).

It may be argued that the United Kingdom has followed a similar route. The
newspapers carry almost daily stories of large payments being awarded in
civil damages for injuries sustained. Many such cases appear to be settled out

of Court, thus there is a suspicion that ability to pay is as important an issue as negligence in any pre-trial discussions about liability. Lowi summarises the development of tort in America,

> 'from individual responsibility to interdependence, from individual blame to distributional balance, from liability to risk, and from negligence defined as 'no liability without fault' to the dropping of negligence altogether in favor of ability to pay, spread through insurance and customer markup, toward the concept of 'social costs'.' (Lowi 1990:30)

Whilst public liability insurance can provide the requisite ability to pay in actions for negligence, it is not now just a matter for the civil law (Wells 1996; Walley 1997). In December 1994, British legal history was made. An outdoor activities company and its managing director were convicted of manslaughter following the deaths of four teenagers during a canoeing trip in Lyme Bay in Dorset. The managing director was jailed for three years, later reduced on appeal to two years. But he went to jail. And so did the school teacher who organised the school trip to the Lake District in 2003 which ended in the drowning a ten-year-old boy.

There is a clear trend here and other companies and individuals will no doubt find themselves facing criminal prosecution under new legislation. This is notwithstanding that the Law Commission's original proposals (1996) on corporate killing have been somewhat toned down (Becket 2003). The proposed legislation was eventually included in the government's legislative plans for New Labour's third term and finally brought forward in July 2006.

Whilst 'risk as blame' delivers the risk society's demands for accountability, it comes at a price. Referring to the government response to the Lyme Bay tragedy, the politician and former athlete Sebastian Coe commented that,

> 'New regulations and insurance requirements were put in place to protect young people from bad practice in a few outward-bound courses. Since then good courses have closed because the regulations have become suffocating and the insurance costs too heavy to bear and a generation of youngsters will never experience the controlled challenge of the mountainside or wave.' (Coe 2000)

Responding to the increasing threat of civil and criminal liability arising from school trips, the National Union of Schoolmasters and Union of Women Teachers (NASUWT) has advised its members not to participate at all.

> 'It is highly regrettable NASUWT has been forced to advise members against taking school trips. In recent high-profile cases teachers have been heavily penalised. Some have lost their jobs as a

result of alleged misjudgements. In an increasingly litigious society which no longer appears to accept the concept of a genuine accident, our first responsibility must be to protect our members' interests.' (NASUWT 2004)

Thus school children are deprived of the excitement, enjoyment and controlled risk-taking which should be part of their growing up.

There is some recent evidence that the tide is turning against the concept of risk as blame. A May 2004 report by the UK Government's Better Regulation Task Force noted that 'It is a commonly held perception that the United Kingdom is in the grip of a "compensation culture"' (BRTF 2004: 4). Reviewing the evidence, the report went on to conclude that the Courts were very good at sorting out dubious claims and that the compensation culture was in fact a myth. Nevertheless, the report was clear that the costs of dealing with the myth and the burdens it placed on behaviour were very real.

The Royal Society

The Royal Society is an institution of the British scientific community and an authorised voice of the establishment. It has been an influential player in the risk debate, with its three major contributions since the 1980s mirroring the shifts in the understanding of risk. Its first report, (Royal Society Study Group 1983), 'saw risk as non-problematic, but as a concept which needed to be explained clearly to the public and especially to those in charge of hazardous operations' (Turner 1994:148-149). Thus the scientific experts knew best. The public might claim that a particular road was dangerous to cross, but the engineers would point out the low death toll to 'prove' that the road was safe. The scientific community was thus deaf to any attempt by the public to explain that the death toll was low because people were too scared to cross the road.

In response to the emerging debate about the importance of risk perception, which we shall discuss in more detail later on, the Royal Society Study Group commissioned a second report (1992). This was supposed to bridge the gap between the 'objective risk' determined by scientists from statistics, and the 'subjective risk' assessed by the public according to their experience and perception of the world. But the effort failed.

'Rather than being a collaborative discussion of risk, the 1992 report consists of two sections, written from different viewpoints which in part flatly contradict one another. Chapters one to four are the work of engineers, statisticians and natural scientists. They cling to the notion that objective and perceived risk are distinct, and that the public's perception of risk is flawed.' (Hinde 1997:18)

Chapters five and six were written by social scientists and set out the rather different view that risk was socially and culturally constructed and that its management was an inherently political process. Unable to resolve the differences of approach, the Royal Society published the report, 'not as a report of the Society, but as six independent chapters attributed to those listed, as a contribution to the ongoing debate' (Royal Society Study Group 1992:iii). Thus the report became known as 'four chapters good, two chapters bad' (or vice versa, depending on whom you asked).

Five years later, in 1997, the Royal Society organised a one day discussion meeting in a further attempt to bring the two sides closer together (Royal Society 1997). The organiser, Dr John Ashworth, was reported by Hinde (1997) to consider that renewed discussion was essential. Ashworth said that, 'There needs to be a dialogue between social scientists and pure scientists. Both at least need to know why what the other does is seen as contentious. There has been a dialogue of the deaf until now' (Hinde 1997:19).

Adams (1997) argued that some of the heat could be taken out of the debate by distinguishing between three different types of risk. First are the directly perceptible risks, such as climbing a tree or riding a bicycle. These are obvious to everyone, but attempts to manage them are thwarted by people insisting on exercising their own judgement.

Second are the risks perceived through science, for example structural stresses or quantified estimates of dose-response, where the scientists agree and the results are widely accepted. This is the difficult middle ground but, in general terms, these risks are capable of objective measurement and the scientists can provide useful information about them.

The third category of virtual risks are those where the scientists either do not know or else cannot agree about the risk, and where the public responds to the uncertainty by imposing meaning upon it. Global warming and the beef scare are good examples of risks which are virtual and thus culturally constructed.

Again mirroring developments in risk theory, the Royal Society have also acknowledged that risk is about forensic blame and liability. In a response to a Government consultation document proposing a code of practice for scientific advisory committees, the Royal Society commented that 'The Office of Science and Technology may wish to take advice on the liabilities of members who give advice and take decisions in good faith' (Royal Society 2000:4).

A Royal Society spokesperson was cited as saying,

'There is a feeling that we are going more and more the way of
America, where lawyers have a field day. We believe it is
unfortunate that we are facing a litigation culture like the States.
Unless there is protection, you won't get anyone to sit on any of
these scientific advisory committees if it means that their homes and
families are in jeopardy. No one is asking for an indemnity for doing
something in bad faith; it is not for people who do sloppy work. But
what has happened in the States is that the courts have sometimes
decided that, even though there is no statistical evidence of a link
between a vaccine and various diseases, they will nevertheless decide
that there is a causal link according to legal standards of proof.'
(Cracknell 2001)

The Meaning of Risk Analysis and Risk Assessment

Notwithstanding the report title, 'Risk: Analysis, Perception and
Management', the working definitions employed by the Royal Society Study
Group (1992:3) do not include the term 'risk analysis'. Neither do the further
definition headings in the report taken from British Standard 4778.
According to the Study Group, *risk estimation* is comprised of identification
of the outcomes and estimation of both the magnitude of the consequences
and the probability of those outcomes. The addition of *risk evaluation*
completes the process of *risk assessment*. British Standard 4778 considers
risk assessment to refer to analysis of inherent risks and their significance in
an appropriate context. It therefore seems possible to conclude that *risk
assessment* and *risk analysis* are synonymous terms.

Other definitions, however, suggest that risk analysis or risk assessment go
beyond evaluation to include some of the decision making processes of *risk
management.* This confusion over terminology is not surprising, given what
Silbergeld (1991) calls the uneasy divorce which seeks to seperate the
supposedly objective science of risk assessment (or risk analysis) from the
political values of risk management.

Notwithstanding the confusion, for the purposes of this book, *risk analysis* or
risk assessment will be deemed to be the sum of the processes of risk
identification, estimation and evaluation.

The Meaning Of Risk Management

The Royal Society Study Group consider that risk management is 'the
making of decisions concerning risks and their subsequent implementation,
and flows from risk estimation and risk evaluation' (Royal Society Study
Group 1992:3). Much of the literature on risk, however, uses the expression
'risk management' with two different meanings, depending upon the context.

For example, British Standard 4778 distinguishes between the risk management *concept* and the *term* risk management. The former describes 'the overall subject area concerned with hazard identification, risk analysis, risk criteria and risk acceptability' (British Standards Institution 1991). Whilst the latter describes 'the process whereby decisions are made' (*ibid.*).

Such dual use carries with it the possibility of ambiguity and confusion for the reader. The Office for Government Commerce[2] offers a neat way of avoiding this, adopted in this book, by distinguishing between *risk management* and *management of risk*. The former 'refers to planning, monitoring and controlling activities which are based upon information produced by risk analysis activity,' (Scarff *et al.* 1993:2). Whilst the latter, 'is used to describe the overall process by which risks are analysed and managed' (*ibid.*). Hence this Chapter is a review of the *management of risk* rather than of *risk management*.

RISK IDENTIFICATION

An Overview Of Techniques In Risk Identification

The techniques of risk identification are facilitative tools, intended to maximise the opportunity of identifying all the risks or hazards inherent in a particular facility, system, or product. The tools may be categorised under the broad headings of intuitive, inductive and deductive techniques.

Brainstorming (see Osborn 1953) is the main intuitive technique, involving a group generating ideas 'off the top of their heads' with a philosophy of 'nobody is wrong – lets get the ideas on the board'. Although quick and simple, it lacks the comprehensive approaches of the more sophisticated techniques. Inductive (what if?) techniques include preliminary hazard analysis, inspections, checklists, human error analysis, Hazard and Operability Studies (HAZOPS) and Failure Modes and Effects Criticality Analysis (FMECA). The benefits of hindsight inform the deductive (so how?) techniques of accident investigation and analysis. Event and fault trees, although primary tools in risk estimation, can also be employed in a purely qualitative way, event trees as inductive and fault trees as deductive tools.

---

[2] The Office for Government Commerce was previously known as the Government Centre for Information Systems and before that as the Central Computing and Telecommunications Agency (CCTA). It continued to use the acronym CCTA to identify itself until the late 1990s. References to either CCTA or to OGC are therefore to the same organisation.

Specific Risk Identification Techniques

Inspections

In its leaflet, 'Five Steps to Risk Assessment', the Health and Safety Executive (2003) advises that the first step is, quite simply, to look for the hazards. Thus the simplest of all risk identification techniques is to walk round with a clipboard looking for things that might cause someone harm.

Checklists

Rather than starting with a blank sheet of paper, risk identification may be informed by the use of checklists. These will vary depending on the type of hazards being studied. For example, in a health and safety at work context, the list might include slips/trips, falls, chemicals, fire, machinery, vehicles, noise, etc. Whilst in computer security, there might be a list of common hazards which can result in data unavailability to users, data destruction, unauthorised data modification or unlawful data disclosure.

Hazard and Operability Studies (HAZOPS)

The HAZOPS technique was originally devised by ICI Ltd for use in risk identification in chemical plants. The HAZOPS is a structured brain-storming exercise in which a multidisciplinary team of experts systematically consider each item in the plant, defining its intention and using guidewords such as 'not', 'more' and 'less' as cues to identify possible deviations from the intention. Such deviations can then be investigated to eliminate as far as possible their causes and minimise the impact of their consequences.

The HAZOPS approach is flexible and can be used to identify potential hazards in buildings and facilities of all kinds at all stages of their design and development. For example, a HAZOPS could be carried out on the detailed design drawings for a new plant and any hazards identified designed out before the plant is built. Alternatively, a review of contingency plans at an existing facility could be more comprehensively informed by a HAZOPS exercise, which could identify hazards not previously planned for.

Failure Modes and Effects Criticality Analysis (FMECA)

Unlike the HAZOPS, FMECA studies are usually carried out by an individual expert with a thorough understanding of the particular system under investigation. The FMECA is a step by step procedure for identifying failure modes or design weaknesses and the criticality of the consequences of failure. The technique can be either hardware oriented, concentrating on potential equipment failures, or event oriented, where the emphasis is on functional outputs and the effect of their failure on the system. Complex systems are often analysed using a combination of these approaches.

The system under investigation is converted into graphical form by the preparation of logic block diagrams depicting its functional components and sub-systems. Take the example of the stadium, which can be depicted as a system of zones and sub-zones, as shown in Figure 1.2.

Figure 1.2: The Stadium as a System of Zones
(Source: Frosdick 1998:67)

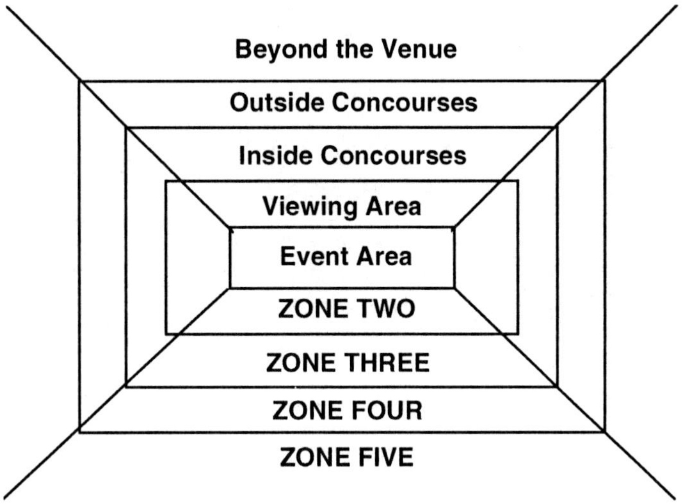

A similar approach might be taken for a project, broken down into its component stages, progressing both in series and in parallel. Whether a stadium, project, plant or other facility, every component of the system is considered and each mode of failure identified. The effects of such failure are then considered at both sub-system and overall system levels.

Fault Tree Analysis as a Qualitative Tool

A fault tree depicts the way in which a particular system failure might occur (see Figure 1.3 on the next page). The failure mode, for example a house fire, forms the top event of the tree. Working downwards through the branches, using 'and/or' logic gates, the analysis reveals the combination of events which themselves cause the top event to occur. Thus the components of a fire would be fuel *and* oxygen *and* a source of ignition. The source of ignition could be an electrical fault *or* a discarded cigarette, etc. The tree stops when no further analysis is practicable or necessary.

Figure 1.3: Fault Tree Analysis
(Source: Frosdick 1999b:19)

Such an analysis informs an understanding of how the failure could occur and what effect design modifications might have. In qualitative terms, the preparation of a fault tree analysis for each of the failure modes or deviations identified through a HAZOPS or FMECA, ensures that the possibilities of failure have been thought through and designed out as far as is reasonable and practicable.

Event Tree Analysis as a Qualitative Tool

Whereas a fault tree depicts the causes of a particular failure, an event tree shows its consequences, asking sequential questions to which the answer is either 'yes' or 'no'. Taking our house fire as the event, one might ask, 'are there smoke alarms fitted?' 'Do they work?' 'Are there people at home?' 'Are the fire brigade contacted quickly?' and so on. Following the alternative answers through the tree will lead to a variety of consequences ranging from minor damage with no injuries to severe damage and possible fatalities. In same way as a fault tree, the event tree has qualitative value as a comprehensive thought process, enabling attention to be paid to eliminating those paths which lead to the more severe consequences.

Accident Investigation and Analysis

Official Inquiries, such as that conducted by Lord Cullen into the Piper Alpha fire in the North Sea, carry out retrospective analysis of the causes of disasters and produce recommendations designed to avoid a recurrence. The comprehensiveness of such analyses can be improved through the use of techniques such as the Schematic Report Analysis Diagram, a type of fault tree designed by Toft and Turner (1987) to summarise the causes of the failure and link the evidence with recommendations for change.

Issues in Risk Identification

Learning the techniques of risk identification is not, however, sufficient in itself. The techniques rely on hindsight, from which lessons are often not learned, and which cannot in any case predict the future risks we face. The engineering paradigm is blind to the influences of cultural bias on risk perception, and problems of over arousal impact on risk identification in emergencies.

Hindsight

The techniques described above are reliant on hindsight to generate the hazard identification. The FMECA analyst uses their knowledge of what has gone wrong elsewhere as a predictor for the facility under examination. The HAZOPS team are doing the same thing, but should have more chance of success because they share the collective experience of a multi-disciplinary group. The Inquiry team seeks to apply the lessons learned from a particular disaster to prevent similar recurrences.

This reliance on hindsight exposes three main weaknesses in the techniques. First, there have been many occasions, for example the Kings Cross Underground Fire in 1987, when the responsible organisations have failed to turn the passive learning from previous non-disastrous events into the active learning necessary to prevent repetitions with potentially disastrous consequences (Toft 1992; Toft and Reynolds 1997).

Second, the learning that does take place is usually confined to similar system types, often within the same industry. Yet as Turner points out, there is a general principle that 'disaster equals energy plus misinformation' (1978:189) and 'many disasters and large-scale accidents display similar features and characteristics' (*ibid.* p.1). However, the opportunities for what Toft (1992; 1997) calls 'isomorphic learning' – the more universally applicable lessons – are lost. Toft cites in this context the collapse of an

Australian bridge and the closing down of nuclear power plants in America, both cases resulting from defects in the computer design software.

Third, hindsight cannot predict the new risks of which we are not yet aware. Kasperson and Kasperson (1991) discuss 'global elusive' hazards such as acid rain and global warming, which have appeared as the unintended consequences of earlier human activity. In their discussion of how risks are hidden, Douglas and Wildavsky conclude that, 'there must be substantial dangers to life and limb that are hidden from us still, dangers we have not found out about yet' (Douglas and Wildavsky 1982:26).

Cultural Bias

In their review of rival theories of risk perception, Cultural Theorists Wildavsky and Dake conclude that cultural biases are the best predictor of risk perception findings because 'individuals choose what to fear (and how to fear it), in order to support their way of life' (Wildavsky and Dake 1990:43). Their research provides good supporting evidence for the theoretical approach adopted for this book (see Chapter Two). Their work also exposes a further weakness in the 'objective science' techniques of risk identification, in which there is no place for the very subjective issues in cultural biases. Risk blindness may occur because the analyst's cultural bias prevents them identifying the hazard. This may be because they cannot see it, because they see it and reject it or because they consider it inherently acceptable.

Thompson and Wildavsky (1986) have shown how different cultural biases in organisations result in information being rejected in different ways. Kasperson and Kasperson (1991) provide a further example in their discussion of 'ideological' and 'marginal' hazards. Some risks are hidden because they are embedded in a web of values that emphasise the benefits and denigrate the consequences. Other risks affecting minority groups pass unheeded by those in the mainstream of power.

The engineering paradigm is technical and quantitative. It follows that engineering analysts will be strong on the identification of technical failure modes, and less strong if not blind to failures in human communication or management systems. No engineering FMECA of a Boeing 737 aircraft would have been likely to throw up the risk of a pilot shutting down the wrong engine and then not be advised of his error because of the hierarchical social mechanisms in operation (see Weir 1996:118). Had it done so, the 1989 Kegworth air crash may have been prevented. Weir (1997) points out that the captains of large jets are expected to be autocratic leaders, not team players with good listening skills. At Kegworth, the passengers and cabin crew were aware there had been a fire in the left hand engine yet the captain insisted on shutting down the right hand engine.

Problems of Arousal

Risk blindness may also result from over arousal. In his analysis of the Staines aircraft disaster, Toft (1993) discusses Easterbrook's hypothesis, which demonstrates how an individual becomes more aroused as the number of cues to which they are exposed increases. At the point of maximum arousal, the optimum number of cues can be accommodated. If more cues come in, the individual becomes over aroused and begins to reject some of the cues. This theory illustrates the need not to lose your temper when fighting or you'll be floored by the unidentified risk – the unseen punch.

RISK ESTIMATION

An Overview Of Techniques In Risk Estimation

The identification of hazards is an essential prerequisite for using the techniques of risk estimation. These are quantitative methods of assessing the probability of the hazard or failure occurring and the consequences if it does. The techniques of risk estimation are part of the discipline commonly referred to as 'QRA' (Quantified Risk Assessment). Component reliability is a key element within probability assessment. Reliability block diagrams and network analysis can be used to depict systems in a graphical form from which failure probabilities can be worked out. Quantification of fault and event trees provide further means of calculating the probability of the variously defined events occurring. The assessment of consequences from a trigger event can be quantified using a combination of either computer modelling techniques, testing or expert value judgements.

Specific Risk Estimation Techniques

Reliability Estimation

Component reliability may be defined as 'the probability that a component will perform a required specified function' (Royal Society Study Group 1992:16). Engineering statistics on the occurrence of component failures provide data, derived from many instances, from which the probability of systems failures can be calculated. There are a considerable number of reliability data banks providing data, classified according to various characteristics, on a wide range of systems and equipment in diverse industries (see Royal Society 1992:18). In the absence of such data gained through experience of the component in service, engineers may either undertake some kind of simulation modelling or testing to generate the data.

Alternatively, it may only be possible to make a 'best guess' estimate of the failure probability.

An analyst can model a system using block diagrams showing the network in which the various components are connected, whether in series or in parallel. Armed with the component failure data, the overall probability of a system failure may then be calculated mathematically. For example, let us imagine a system with three components which have known failure probabilities of 0.2, 0.3 and 0.5 respectively. If the three components are arranged in parallel, and all three have to fail for the system to fail, then the overall probability of a system failure is the three individual probabilities multiplied together (0.2 x 0.3 x 0.5 = 0.03). Of course most engineering systems, for example a chemical plant, involve a far more complex combination of series and parallel networks, and the more complex the system, the more complicated the mathematics.

Quantification of Event and Fault Trees

Both types of trees contain a number of different paths leading either to (fault tree) or from (event tree) a particular failure mode. The probability of each individual step along the path can be calculated, using either reliability data, testing or expert judgement. In the case of a fault tree, the probability of the failure mode occurring because of the particular combination of steps along that path can be calculated as the product of the probabilities of each step. Similar principles apply to the quantification of event tree paths.

Consequence Modelling

Reliability analysis will seek to calculate the probability of, for example, the explosion of a pressurised vessel containing a hazardous chemical. Using data bank information or judgement about such matters as quantity or duration of the release, dispersion characteristics, dose-effect etc, the consequence modeller then estimates the consequent probability of harm to a human population.

Issues in Risk Estimation

As with risk identification, there are reasons why the techniques of risk estimation are insufficient in themselves. First, there are differing definitions of probability. Second, the reliability of the data upon which quantified estimates are based is open to question. Third, different expressions of quantified risk impact upon the way in which the risk is subsequently perceived. Fourth, risk is a subjective social construct and the scientists claims of neutral objectivity in risk estimation cannot be sustained.

Probability Theory

What is the probability of throwing two sixes with two dice? The answer depends on the definition of probability. According to Pidgeon (1992), probability is about uncertainty and is itself an uncertain concept.

> 'Lay beliefs about probability are multi-faceted and reflect the confusion in the literature regarding the precise nature of uncertainty. To ask the question, 'What is uncertainty?' of a group of students in any discipline is likely to elicit a range of responses associated, primarily, with conceptions of probability; for example, uncertainty is something to do with games of chance - it is a frequency, a degree of personal belief, a likelihood and it is just plain luck!' (Pidgeon 1992:169)

Pidgeon outlines three main definitions of probability. Classical probability dates from sixteenth century studies of gambling and is a ratio derived from equally probable outcomes. Thus classical probability would hold that the chance of throwing a double six with two unbiased dice is 1 in 36, i.e. the number of ways a double six can be obtained (one) divided by the total number of equally likely outcomes (36).

Because the theory of classical probability often doesn't work in practice, for example because dice are sometimes biased, nineteenth century mathematicians developed relative frequency probability, which is the basis for most statistical theory. Here the ratio is calculated from the number of observed outcomes over an infinite series of identical trials. Thus if an experiment shows you get four double sixes in 100 throws of the dice, relative frequency probability holds that the chance of a double six with that set of dice is one in 25.

The third main definition is of subjective or Bayesian probability, which is a degree of confidence or belief that a particular event will occur – in other words a 'guesstimate'. If one of the dice in our experiment were replaced by a new dice, which might or might not be biased in a particular way, we would have to repeat the experiment to determine the relative frequency probability. But since one of the original dice still remained, we might choose to take the middle line between the classical one in 36 and the relative frequency one in 25 and settle on a subjective probability of one in 30.

Problems with Reliability Data

The Royal Society Study Group acknowledge that the use of event and reliability data banks is 'not without considerable problems [because] there is a great variety of practice in categorization and allocation' (Royal Society Study Group 1992:19). Toft (1995; 1996) questions the extent to which reliable historic data is in fact available to estimate the risk probabilities. He notes the Royal Society's (1983) point that data on the frequency of unwanted events is in short supply and that because the events are rare the techniques used for sampling do not provide sufficient data. If the 'objective scientific' data upon which a probability estimate is based is in fact unreliable, the value of the whole estimate is called into question, since, as Toft concludes, 'the level of uncertainty regarding the validity of any conclusions will be extremely high' (Toft 1996:104).

Expressions of Estimated Risk

There are a number of different measures which can be used to express estimated risk. These include individual mortality rates, societal mortality rates, fatalities per million, loss of life expectancy and death per unit measure of activity (Royal Society 1992:24-25). As Slovic (1991) points out, the range of different ways in which risk estimates can be presented has been shown to have marked effects on the ways in which a risk is subsequently perceived during the evaluation process. Whether by accident or design, the risk analyst has the opportunity to manipulate perception through their selection of the expression of estimated risk.

The Myth of Scientific Objectivity

The two strands to this myth are neatly summarised in two chapter headings used by Douglas and Wildavsky (1982); namely 'assessment is biased' and anyway, 'the scientists disagree'.

Schrader-Frechette (1991a) argues that the 'naive positivists' efforts to reduce risk estimates to objective scientific calculations go wrong for a number of different reasons, principal among which is their erroneous belief that science can and should be free of value judgements when the reality is that all facts are laden with values. Her view is supported by Toft (1996), who questions some implicit assumptions on which quantitative techniques are based. First, how can risks be treated as concrete physical entities which can be precisely defined and unambiguously measured when Douglas and Wildavsky (1982) argue that risks are not objective but socially constructed?'

Second, how can risk modelling be considered a neutral objective activity giving rise to an unbiased independent quantitative assessment when the assumptions adopted by the analyst and their choice of data have such a strong effect on the numerical outcome? As Schrader-Frechette points out, notwithstanding standardising legislation passed by the US Congress, 'quantitative risk assessment is still practised in somewhat divergent ways' (Schrader-Frechette 1991b:6). Thus Schrader-Frechette makes the obvious statement that, 'even for the same hazard, risk analyses often do not agree'

(Schrader-Frechette 1991b:7). Douglas and Wildavsky discuss the scientific debates about drinking water quality, carcenogenic chemicals and cancer in children living near nuclear installations to demonstrate their proposal that, 'scientists disagree on whether there are problems, what solutions to propose, and if intervention will make things better or worse' (Douglas and Wildavsky 1982:63).

RISK EVALUATION

An Overview Of Risk Evaluation Techniques

Having identified a hazard and estimated both the probability of its occurrence and the magnitude of its consequences, the third step in the process of risk analysis or risk assessment is that of evaluating the tolerability or acceptability of the risk. The various techniques for risk evaluation are derived from the different approaches of engineering, economics, politics and the various strands of the behavioural sciences.

At its extreme, the engineering position has been described as assuming that, 'risk assessment is a field of objective, scientific analysis that can be divorced from political values that are part of the subsequent management of risks' (Mayo and Hollander 1991:93). Less extremely, engineers acknowledge that, 'risk perception depends very much on beliefs, feelings and judgements [and] has a major influence on the tolerability or acceptance of risk' (Strutt 1993:7). Nevertheless, the engineering paradigm is one of quantification because 'it is necessary for them to quantify what is an acceptable risk in particular circumstances to have a target for their risk assessment exercise.' (Royal Society Study Group 1992:15). Engineering techniques are therefore based on quantified comparisons. Economic techniques similarly rely on quantification of potential financial gains and losses.

An opposite view would acknowledge that risk perception is a dominant issue affecting both how the acceptability of risk is evaluated and how subsequent risk management decisions are made. Therefore the boundary between risk evaluation and risk management is very blurred. Psychological approaches to risk and cognitive techniques in the psychometric tradition reveal more qualitative characteristics of risk evaluation. Similar qualitative processes are found in the more participative or 'democratic' approaches to risk evaluation.

Specific Engineering Risk Evaluation Techniques

Risk Criticality Matrices

These matrices are the outcome of a Failure Modes and Effects Criticality Analysis (FMECA). Having identified each failure mode, its probability can be determined and its consequences in terms of fatalities modelled using data bank reliability and event data. Where such fully quantitative methods are not practicable, a semi-quantitative approach allows expert subjective judgements to be made. For example, probability could range between 'a highly improbable occurrence' and 'a frequent and regular occurrence'. Consequence could range between 'negligible injuries' and 'multiple fatalities'. The two dimensions are then plotted against each other on a two by two matrix, on which top right represents the greatest risk and bottom left the least.

The evaluation exercise is one of noting the relative position on the matrix of the variously identified risks, prioritising and establishing the acceptability threshold, through use of the ALARP (as low as reasonably practicable) principle (HSE 1988, 1996). Similar techniques may be used to evaluate the relative riskiness of the paths within event and fault trees.

The ALARP Principle

The setting of tolerability thresholds requires a baseline against which comparisons may be made. In this context, engineers rely on guidelines provided by the HSE (1989:vi). Maximum tolerable individual risk is deemed to be one in 1,000 for workers and one in 10,000 for the public. At the lower level, negligible risk is deemed to be one in 1,000,000, which represents the annual risk of death in a fire at home.

Having established that a risk is more than negligible, the analyst examines whether additional risk reduction measures can be identified. If they can, the costs of providing the measures are balanced against their risk reduction effect. If the additional precautions are reasonably practicable, they should be adopted. If additional risk reduction measures cannot be identified, the question is whether the risk is within the maximum tolerability threshold. If it is, the workers or public will have to live with it. If it is not, the activity must be stopped or curtailed immediately.

Specific Economic Risk Evaluation Techniques

Market Mechanisms

The resolution of issues in the market place was a cornerstone of Conservative economic philosophy during the 1980s and 1990s. Some reports have suggested that successive Governments have been planning to abolish a number of health and safety measures in the interests of 'cutting red tape'. Given increasing deregulation, the acceptability of risk could be determined in the market. Within bounds allowed by the insurance industry, which Beck (1992) argues has become the final arbiter of tolerable risk, increased risk exposure could be accepted as the corollary of reduced prices.

However, it is hard to see how deregulation could be extended into hazardous modern technologies such as the nuclear industry. Indeed, as society becomes increasingly focused on risk and blame, the tendency seems to be towards greater rather than less regulation, with new Government Inspectorates for food safety and the protection of people in care.

Cost Effectiveness and Cost Benefit Analysis

Where the budget is limited, cost effectiveness refers to the lowest risk which can be achieved within budgetary constraints. The doctrine of BATNEEC ('best available technology not entailing excessive costs') provides an example of the cost effectiveness approach to risk reduction. For example, in a computer security risk assessment which I carried out for a charitable organisation, the client rejected a number of the recommended countermeasures generated by the software tool on the grounds that they were simply too expensive. More cost effective solutions offering a lower level of protection were chosen instead.

Cost benefit analysis is an appraisal technique which has been widely used since the 1960s. According to Pearce, the technique 'retains its strength because of its ability potentially to identify optimal expenditures (where net benefits are maximized) and to secure a well-defined project ranking' (Pearce 1985:165).

In the context of risk evaluation, cost benefit analysis informs the ALARP process. Here there are no theoretical limits on the budget. The issue is whether the cost of the risk reduction measure is less than the value of the benefit achieved. If it is, then the reduction measures should be implemented. If it is not, then it need not be, however an alternative which does deliver the cost benefit will need to be found. Given the concept of risk as blame, failure to implement measures which deliver cost benefits creates issues of accountability and liability.

Specific Cognitive Theories of Risk Evaluation

Risk/Risk Comparisons

In his discussion of individual risk acceptability, Rothschild (1978) suggests that an index of risks should be produced, centred around the 1974 figures of the one in 7,500 risk of being killed in a car accident and the one in 18,000 risk of death from influenza. This, he argues, would help you 'decide above what level – road fatalities, perhaps – you should get into a panic; and below what level – death from influenza – you should relax. (Rothschild 1978:718). His argument is that risk should be simply expressed as a probability over a given period of time. Given this information, risk acceptability becomes a matter of personal choice.

Risk Homeostasis or Risk Compensation Theory

According to Wilde (1982), individuals balance possible risks against potential gains. This is a kind of subconscious cost benefit analysis in which an individual's level of acceptable risk is a qualitative issue determined by both personal and situational factors such as personality, role, economic circumstances, peer group pressure and cultural background.

Wilde's ideas have been developed by Adams (1985, 1995). He argues that, 'The starting point of any theory of risk must be that everyone willingly takes risks. This is not the starting point of most of the literature on risk' (Adams 1995:15-16). According to Adams, we all have an internal risk thermostat set to our preferred level of risk-taking, which will vary from person to person. The Grand Prix racing driver likes it hot, whilst a little old lady named Prudence likes it cool. We have all evaluated the level of risk we want. Thus, 'Safety interventions that do not alter people's propensity to take risks will be frustrated by responses that re-establish the level of risk with which people were originally content' (Adams 1995:215). In other words, give me a car with ABS brakes and straighten out a dangerous bend in the road, and I will drive faster and brake later to keep the level of risk as it was before.

The Psychometric Approach

Psychologists from the psychometric tradition (see Royal Society Study Group 1992:101-107) argue that the 'expert' view of risk as the product of frequency and consequences is not shared by the layman, for whom risk is simply a matter of consequences. Some consequences are immediately observable and known to those exposed, others are newer and unknown risks, perhaps with delayed and unobservable effects.

On another dimension, some risks are controllable, voluntary and not dread, whereas others are catastrophic, uncontrollable and involuntary. Slovic (1991) describes these two dimensions or factors as 'dread risk' and 'unknown risk' and demonstrates, through references to his previous studies of individual's evaluations of the riskiness of a variety of hazards, how the more dread and unknown the risk, the more hazardous the risk is perceived to be. Take the simple example shown in Figure 1.4 on the next page.

Figure 1.4: Different Risk Perspectives
(Source: Frosdick and Odell 1996:27)

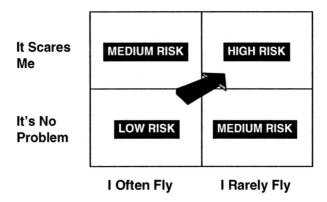

The matrix shows how, if we were to ask four different people to evaluate the risk of flying in an aeroplane, we might get four different answers, as follows. First, I often fly and it doesn't scare me at all – flying is low risk. Second, I often fly but it still scares me – flying is medium risk. Third, I rarely fly, but it doesn't bother me – flying is medium risk. Last, I rarely fly and the thought really scares me – flying is high risk. Thus for any one hazard, the risk may be evaluated as either high, medium or low, depending on who you ask. This is significant for the research in this book, since it implies that risk assessment should be undertaken as a group activity.

The Tolerability of Societal Risk

The HSE find that it is not possible to place an upper limit on the tolerability of hazardous events causing multiple fatalities. This is because,

> 'we commonly take large numbers of individual accidental deaths far less seriously than we do a single event killing a similarly large number of people. Any large scale accident raises questions of responsibility for safety and public accountability in a way that accidents to individuals do not.' (HSE 1989:28)

More Democratic and Participative Techniques

Here we begin to straddle the fuzzy boundary between risk evaluation and risk management. One of the seven areas of the risk management debate, which we shall be looking at later in this Chapter, is to do with the size and composition of groups involved in decision-making. According to Jasanoff, 'some European countries, notably the Netherlands, Sweden and West Germany, have already gone far toward institutionalised participation by major interest groups and the lay public in decisions related to the management of risk' (Jasanoff 1990:77). In the case of such approaches, evaluation decisions about the tolerability of risk blend into the political decision making processes of risk management.

Technical and Democratic Models

The technical model describes the evaluation process undertaken by a panel of experts, often relying on their own judgement rather than scientific fact. This is similar to ideas of peer review of a particular evaluation to validate its acceptability. Having outlined the model, Fiorino (1989) criticises it as elitist, preferring a more democratic and participatory model, involving both experts and lay persons and informed by the psychometric approach.

The Adverserial Model

Schrader-Frechette (1985) advocates a three stage process of risk evaluation and management. In the first stage, a tribunal of experts and members of the public debate the risk. Any conflicts generated by the debate are put forward to a panel of 'impartial' scientists and lay persons, who consider the issues and then make public their final decision about the risk. This approach is represented as a middle path between 'objective science' and 'cultural relativism', continuing to make use of QRA whilst incorporating in the process, 'the use of ethically weighted risk-cost-benefit analysis and the ranking of experts' risk perceptions on the basis of their past successful predictions' (Schrader-Frechette 1991b:12).

This approach finds no favour with Douglas (1992b), who castigates Schrader-Frechette for inventing artificial enemies to sustain her own sectarian position, and, since perceptions are informed by cultural bias, sees the debate about risk measurements simply shifting to disagreement about ethical weightings.

Schrader-Frechette's Adverserial model seems too unwieldly to be viable for anything except the major societal risks. The whole approach is egalitarian and thus tending to be risk averse. It overlooks the likelihood of non-participation by fatalists, and presupposes that the individualists and hierarchists will fall into line with egalitarian perceptions.

Issues in Risk Evaluation

The whole question of risk evaluation, blurring into risk management, is extremely complex and becomes increasingly intricate under more detailed examination. Nevertheless, it may be argued that the techniques of risk evaluation are inadequate in themselves if they do not allow for risk as something which is collectively, socially and culturally constructed. As Douglas and Wildavsky conclude,

> 'Acceptable risk is a matter of judgement and nowadays judgements differ. Between private, subjective perception and public, physical science there lies culture, a middle area of shared beliefs and values. The present division of the subject that ignores culture is arbitrary and self-defeating.'(Douglas and Wildavsky 1982:194)

Economic Approaches

The determination of risk acceptability through market mechanisms relies on the fallacy that decisions can be fully rational and informed by full information. Cost Benefit Analysis has been criticised (see Schrader-Frechette 1985) as failing to consider market fluctuations in price, the equitability of distribution of the risk and perceptions of the acceptability of risk.

Engineering Approaches

Our earlier discussion of the myth of scientific objectivity is also applicable here. But let us broaden the debate out to now include the overall contribution of QRA to risk evaluation. The Royal Society Study Group (1992:158-161) refer to this question as one of the seven areas of the risk management debate. An entire HSE publication (1989) is devoted to the matter and other writers have commented upon it.

Between the extreme positions of all or no quantification, the Royal Society Study Group report there are many who, 'would concede that QRA has limitations in practice and needs to be combined with other, broader forms of information and analysis' (Royal Society Study Group 1992:160). This point is reiterated throughout the HSE (1989) publication, 'QRA: Its Input to Decision Making'. It is argued that, 'predictions based on QRA are not hard and fast figures ... They are useful guides to policy making but their limitations must be made clear' (HSE 1989:iii). Thus, 'the numerical element must be viewed with great caution and treated as only one parameter in an essentially judgemental exercise' (HSE 1989:iv). This is because an evaluation process involving QRA is 'a process which is essentially economic and political though informed technically' (HSE 1989:2).

Referring to the contribution of QRA, Smallman argues that, 'Historical modelling is a valid and proven technique. However, it is too frequently used as a substitute for good management judgement. The holistic approach demands the use of 'intelligent' quantificationism' (Smallman 1996:258). Slovic (1991) draws attention to the limitations of risk assessment resulting from expert disagreements about techniques and terminology and the fact that the the assessments are based on assumptions and subjective judgements. Whilst Schrader-Frechette notes that, 'hazard evaluations often contradict one another, not only because scientists frequently dispute the relevant facts but also because policymakers and the public disagree about what responses to risk are rational' (Schrader-Frechette 1991b:7).

There seems to be broad agreement among many authorities that, although QRA has a role in risk evaluation, the whole process is far more complex than numbers alone, needing to take account of how risk is actually perceived, and the variations in the perceptions of experts and lay persons.

Criticisms of the Psychometric Tradition

We have seen the arguments of psychologists that risk is an individual construct derived from perceptions informed by factors such as familiarity, dread and the greater fear in which societal risks are held. Their views have been criticised by anthropologists as failing to take account of the cultural dimensions of risk perception. Douglas argues that, 'the profession of psychologists which has grown up to study risk perception takes the culturally innocent approach by treating political dissension as intellectual disagreement' (Douglas 1990:9).

Psychologists seek to emulate the engineers by the use of supposedly objective methods such as questionnaires to determine perceptions of risk. This can lead psychologists to support the view that the science of risk analysis should be separated from the political process of risk management (Daniels 1992). However, according to Douglas, 'the effort is skewed by the culturally innocent assumption that cultural bias is irrelevant for us at home, that culture is something that starts with the Wogs (*sic*), abroad' (Douglas 1990:10).

The Royal Society Study Group lend credibility to these criticisms in their acknowledgement that

> 'one of the major challenges to orthodox psychological approaches to risk perception over the past ten years has come from the grid-group 'cultural theory' proposed by the anthropologist Mary Douglas and her colleagues.' (Royal Society Study Group 1992:112)

Cultural Theory provides the principal theoretical underpinning for this book and is detailed in the next section. Applications of the theory and its implications for risk assessment are discussed in Chapter Two, which also looks at criticisms of and developments in the theory over the course of the research conducted for this book.

CULTURAL THEORY[3]

There has been substantial debate among scholars about the definitions of culture. Rather than getting drawn into this debate, Thompson, Ellis and Wildavsky (1990) have sought to clarify matters by distinguishing between three terms: cultural bias, social relations and way of life. They explain that,

> 'Cultural bias refers to shared values and beliefs. Social relations are defined as patterns of interpersonal relations. When we wish to designate a viable combination of social relations and cultural bias we speak of a way of life.' (Thompson *et al.* 1990:1)

Their book seeks to identify the viable ways of life and explain how these maintain themselves. Their 'Cultural Theory' is derived from social anthropology and founded on the work of Professor Mary Douglas (1978; 1982; 1985; 2003a). Cultural Theory has also been variously referred to as the 'Theory of Cultural Complexity (Mars and Frosdick 1997, Frosdick and Mars 1997) and as 'Grid-Group Cultural Theory' (GG-CT 1999; Mamadouh 1999). 'Cultural Theory' is used for the purposes of this book.

Although rooted in neo-Durkheimian traditions of collective analysis, Cultural Theory takes as its specific point of departure the grid-group typology set out by Mary Douglas (1978). This argues that there are two dimensions by which all cultures can be classified. The first is the *grid* dimension, which has been defined as 'the total body of rules and constraints which a culture imposes on its people in a particular context' (Mars and Nicod 1983:124), and as, 'the degree to which an individual's life is circumscribed by externally imposed prescriptions' (Thompson *et al.* 1990: 5). The Hindu caste system is an example of a high grid context, whereas the free and easy lifestyle of the American West Coast represents an instance of low grid. The second dimension of *group* 'emphasises collectiveness among people who meet face to face' (Mars 1994:24). The group dimension also, 'refers to the extent to which an individual is morally coerced by others,

---

[3] Some of the discussion of Cultural Theory in this section is derived from the publications listed in the references as Frosdick (1997h), Frosdick and Mars (1997), and Mars and Frosdick (1997).

through being a member of a bounded face-to-face unit' (Mars and Nicod 1983:125) and describes, 'the experience of a bounded social unit' (Douglas 1978:viii). Living in a total institution such as an army barracks represents high group, whereas being housebound alone in a tower block is an example of low group.

Considering the two dimensions together produces a fourfold typology of ways of life. These four social solidarities – individualism, fatalism, hierarchy and egalitarianism (also called sectarianism) – each reflect a cohesive and coherent cluster of attitudes, beliefs and styles of relationships. Thus each way of life is the product of a value system (the cultural bias) and a pattern of social relations, classified by reference to the relative strength of grid and group. These ways of life inform the perceptions of the participants, determine their behaviour and are used by them to justify the validity of their social situations. The four ways of life can be depicted on a simple grid-group matrix as an aid for understanding (see Figure 1.5).

Figure 1.5: Cultural Theory Grid-Group Matrix
(Source: Frosdick and Mars 1997:109)

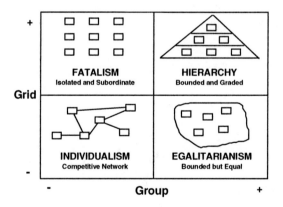

Where both dimensions are weak, we find an individualist way of life. Where both are strong we have a hierarchical one. These two types represent the conventional economic duality of the free entrepreneurial market at one extreme and the highly regulated Weberian bureaucracy at the other. Cultural Theory introduces a more disaggregated view of the world since there are two further ways of life to consider; egalitarianism (weak grid with strong group) and the more passive fatalism (strong grid with weak group). These categories can be brought to life through examples which illustrate features of each of the ways of life. Mars, for example, has used Cultural Theory to set out a classification of occupations and their associated deviance (1994), whilst Thompson *et al.* (1990) give outline vignettes of a Hindu villager, a communard, a self-made manufacturer and an ununionised weaver.

Thompson *et al.* introduce the possibility of a fifth way of life, that of the hermit, who withdraws altogether from social life. The hermit avoids both dimensions; refusing either to be controlled by others or to engage in any groupings with others. Since this book is aimed at underpinning the practical application of Cultural Theory in a social world from which hermits are absent, their existence may for present purposes be properly regarded as a theoretical distraction and we will move on.

The Impossibility Theorem: Four Viable Archetypal Ways Of Life

We have seen how the grid/group typology gives rise to four ways of life, each the product of a distinct combination of cultural bias and social relations. It is possible to conceive of other alternative ways of life. However, according to Cultural Theory, these four (ignoring the hermit) are the only four viable archetypal ways of life. That is, it is only these four ways of life that are able to sustain themselves so that they endure over time. This idea that there are only four viable ways of life is what Thompson *et al.* refer to as the 'impossibility theorem'.

They set out to substantiate this theorem in a number of ways. Summarising very briefly, the assertion is first grounded in the fact that Cultural Theory meets the logical requirements of classification, namely that the four types produced are both mutually exclusive and jointly exhaustive. The argument is then developed through a complex analysis of the social construction of nature, that is, what models do different people use to explain both physical nature and human nature. The argument then builds by examining the ways in which people manage their needs and resources in order to make ends meet, and the way in which adherents derive their preferences from their chosen way of life, including their preferred perception of risk.

Requisite Variety: All Must Be Present For Each To Survive

The impossibility theorem does not of course mean that the four archetypes are necessarily found in their pure form. Most social situations are found to comprise 'regimes' – combinations of these archetypes. Whilst there are only four viable ways of life, according to Cultural Theory they cannot exist independently of each other. The idea that each depends upon the survival of the others for its own continued existence is what Thompson *et al.* (following Ashby 1968) call the 'requisite variety condition'.

Implicit in this is the recognition that ways of life are inherently political (Douglas and Wildavsky 1982; Douglas 1992a), that is they are concerned to control resources, manipulate rhetoric and influence events. They are mutually competitive and define themselves not only by the distinctiveness of their coherent value structures (what we are) but also by their opposition to other ways of life (what we are not) (Mars and Mars 1993). As Thompson *et al*. put it (1990:96), 'it is only the presence in the world of people who are different from them that enables adherents of each way of life to be the way they are'.

This conclusion is argued through Thompson *et al*.'s analysis of surprises, that is, the way in which adherents look for an alternative way of life when they find a lack of satisfying fit between the world as they perceive it and the world as they actually find it. Whilst the world as a whole may be stable and coherent, its constituent parts are unstable, evolving and changing in response to surprises.

The adherents to each of the four ways of life do not recognise the existence of this requisite variety condition. As far as they are concerned, and until they are otherwise 'surprised', their own view of the world is the only right view. This ethnocentricity makes it difficult for adherents to perceive the reality and validity of the other three points of view, a significant feature which has particularly influenced this research.

RISK MANAGEMENT

An Overview Of Techniques In Risk Management

However problematic and difficult the risk analysis or risk assessment process may be, there comes the point where risk has to be managed. Put at its simplest, having identified all the things which could go wrong and determined which matter the most, risk management is all about putting in place the reduction and control measures needed to manage them out before they happen, or else to minimise their impact if they do happen. The techniques of risk management include risk avoidance and reduction measures, risk transfer and financing through insurance, risk retention, business continuity planning, and risk communication.

Specific Risk Management Techniques

Risk Avoidance

Some hazards may have been evaluated as posing risks so serious that they present only two possible choices; either they have to be eliminated altogether, or else the activity has to be stopped. For example, imagine a

North Sea oil rig where it has been assessed that it is very likely the divers will be killed if they go down into the sea today. Or else a nuclear power plant where a risk analysis shows that the failure of a valve would result in a massive explosion which would decimate the plant, kill most of the workers and contaminate the surrounding country for years to come. In the former case, it may be argued that diving would have to be halted, whilst in the latter, the valve would have to be made fail-safe.

Risk Reduction

Very commonly, risks will have been evaluated, by whatever means, as being not acceptable. Countermeasures, action plans or other reduction mechanisms will therefore have to be found to reduce the risk to a level which is 'as low as reasonably practicable', 'tolerable' or whatever other threshold has been set by the risk evaluation process.

The selected risk reduction measures will vary enormously, but will generally fall into two main categories: probability reduction and consequence reduction. Take the case of one of my clients and research subjects, a UK Constabulary which undertook a project to implement a new telecommunications infrastructure. One of the high risks identified was that the project might fail to secure the necessary funding. Here the probability was reduced by pursuing a dual funding route, both through the Public Finance Initiative and by securing the back-stop of a Home Office promise to fund the project conventionally if required. Another high risk was that there would be protests by eco-warriors if a green field site was chosen for the new command and control complex. Short of not choosing a green field site, even though this choice might prove to be the best business decision, there was nothing to be done to reduce the probability of such a protest. However, the training and other measures taken to enhance the Constabulary's ability to police such protests served to mitigate the various adverse consequences which might have ensued.

Risk Financing and Transfer

Whatever risk avoidance and reduction measures have been taken, some residual risk will still remain. Residual risks will include hazards evaluated as low risk and for which no countermeasures are considered necessary, or else risks which have been reduced but where the hazard has not been eliminated altogether. At this point decisions have to be taken about whether to insure against the risk.

The fundamental purpose of insurance is to provide indemnity. In other words, insurance is supposed to restore the policy holder to the same position they were in before the risk became a reality and the loss occurred. Thus the payment of the premium, which is a known cost, enables the policy holder to transfer some of the unknown costs of the risk to the insurer.

Insurance companies do not accept such risks without conditions other than the payment of the premium. They may require the implementation of risk reduction measures, for example the fitting of a burglar alarm. They may require the policy holder to retain some of risk by way of an 'excess' on the policy. In the event of a loss, they are entitled to require the insured to strictly prove both the claim and the cause of the loss. The insured is also bound by the doctrine of *uberrimae fides* (utmost good faith), which requires the insured to communicate to the insurer every fact and circumstance which may influence the insurer's decision to enter into the contract of insurance.

Insurers distinguish between pure and speculative risks. Pure risks have only negative outcomes, for example fires or crimes, whilst speculative risks refer to both gains and losses, such as buying stocks and shares hoping that the price will go up but knowing full well that the price could also go down. Only pure risks are insurable, and, notwithstanding the problems we have discussed in respect of hindsight, insurers use historical data and probability theory to infer what will happen in the future and thus determine the level of premium.

Some organisations self-insure either by establishing a cash fund from which to recover the costs of losses, or sometimes by forming a wholly owned subsidiary company, known as a 'captive', to underwrite the risks. Having accepted both the premium payment and the associated risks, insurance companies and captives will then protect themselves by laying off some of the risks through the re-insurance market. Finally, either as a matter of choice or after the purchase of insurance, some risks will still remain and thus be retained.

Business Continuity Planning

Hudson (1997) cites the Home Office publication on national disasters, which begins its section on business continuity planning by saying that

> 'Nearly every day there are many unpublicised disasters, man-made and natural, which devastate both private and public sector business units. Statistics indicate that 80% of companies which experience a computer disaster but which do not have appropriate plans go bankrupt within 18 months.' (Home Office 1994)

He argues that the

> 'acknowledged frequency of disasters and their impact on the business community underscores the management maxim 'Failing to

plan is planning to fail'. Business survival depends on planning, business continuity planning.' (Hudson 1997:95)

This involves all the steps used to assess and mitigate risks, contingency planning for things going wrong, response to crises, emergencies and disasters, continuing to operate through the incident and managing the process of returning to normal (see Business Continuity Institute 2001). The business continuity process is depicted in Figure 1.6.

Figure 1.6: Business Continuity Planning
(Source: adapted from Hudson 1997:97 & 99)

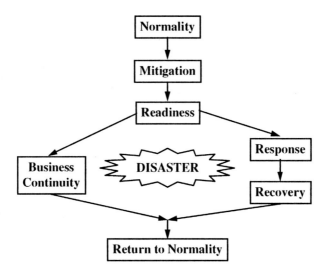

Risk Communication Techniques

The techniques of risk communication are all about informing the public about the risks relating to various hazards with a view to influencing the way people behave. For example, if nobody knows that smoking can damage their health, then there may be little health incentive to stop smoking.

The public management of health scares such as safe sex, mad cow disease, salmonella in eggs and the use of antibiotics to promote growth in chickens illustrate that one-way communication from the experts to the lay public represents the most commonly practised model of risk communication. This deficit or public dissemination model is founded on the assumption that the experts know best and that their findings are both objective and unequivocally correct. The lay public are seen collectively as a homogenous mass and individually as ignorant empty vessels waiting to be filled with knowledge. Once they have been informed about the risk, it is assumed they will change their behaviour and do what the scientists have advised.

Issues In Risk Management

Having assessed risk, simply applying the techniques of risk management is not enough. There needs to be awareness that risk management is a contested area of debate. Risk management decisions are political decisions. There is growing evidence of the need for dialogue and participation in decision-making, and it is not clear why the public and media are concerned with some risks but not others.

Issues in Risk Communication

According to Beck (1992), we have become a 'risk society', one where debates about the justice in the distribution of resources have been replaced by concerns about the equitable distribution of risk – i.e. exposure to danger or disadvantage. This 'risk society' has two main features. First, the hazards posed by modern science and technology are ever increasing and ever more global in their impact. Second, we ourselves have a greater awareness of the hazards and want more of a say in how they are managed. These features of the 'risk society', taken together with the myth of scientific objectivity discussed earlier in this Chapter, suggest that the one-way deficit model of risk communication is inadequate. The Phillips Report of the BSE Inquiry (Phillips 2000) was cited by the Royal Society as highlighting 'the clear need to improve communication of risk to Government and to the general public in advice and reports' (Royal Society 2000:3).

Risk managers need to engage in dialogue with the public and with public perceptions of risk if risk communication is to be effective. Irwin, for example, argues that

> 'the inadequate modelling of citizen understandings (e.g. the *tabula rasa* [clean sheet] assumption that the public are 'information poor' leads to initiatives which are limited in practical terms. Instead of attempting to engage with these citizen perspectives, top-down approaches tend to assume that an authoritative and scientifically validated (even if heavily simplified presentation will command popular attention.' (Irwin 1995:102)

The Royal Society Study Group (1992) noted that the one-way deficit model had been much criticised, and went on to outline three more sociological approaches to risk communication. The first of these stresses the importance of a two-way dialogue, whilst the second sets that dialogue within the cultural and institutional contexts in which messages about risk are exchanged. The third approach sees risk communication as an explicit part of the political process. These approaches suggest that risk management decisions are not best left in the hands of the scientific 'experts'. For example, Funtowicz and Ravetz note that environmental risks are increasingly novel, complex and variable, and argue that, 'For these new problems, science cannot usually provide well founded theories, based on experiments, for explanation and prediction' (Funtowicz and Ravetz 1996:173). They conclude that this suggests the need for broader participation in decisions about how risks are managed.

This view is supported by O'Riordan, who suggests that "expertise' is becoming devalued' (O'Riordan 1996:182). He notes the rise of a more participatory 'civic science', and argues that, in the case of 'virtual risk' (Adams 1997; 1999), 'there is a domain where 'good science' means interacting societal value judgements and ethical biases in the form of an extended dialogue' (O'Riordan 1997). O'Riordan has used Cultural Theory to work with focus groups to draw out perceptions of environmental risks and to discuss what should be done about them.

This suggests a changed role for science. Instead of telling both policy makers and the public what the risks are (as fact) and what should be done about them, the approach becomes one of participating in the public debate by giving a scientific opinion on risk to Government and, where appropriate, offering suggestions for policy.

The social amplification of risk
In 1996, the UK Government Interdepartmental Liaison Group on Risk Assessment (ILGRA) reported the urgent need to improve Departments' performance in respect of risk communication, noting particularly that, 'pressure groups and the media have tended to exaggerate insignificant risks, often at the expense of ignoring larger more common-place ones.' (ILGRA 1996:37).

In response, the Health and Safety Executive commissioned further research into the social amplification of risk. This is a theoretical framework which seeks to integrate work in the areas of risk perception and risk communication (see Pidgeon 1997). Why is it, for example, that public and media perceptions play down risks such as smoking and road traffic accidents, which seem more likely to cause more harm to more people. Yet at the same time, public and media perceptions play up risks such as mad cow disease, which seem to have a much lower likelihood of causing harm and then only to a small number of people.

Contemporary Debates in Risk Management

In our earlier discussion, we saw that the size and composition of groups involved in decision-making, and the contribution of QRA, were two of the seven areas of the risk management debate – the widespread disagreement about what to do – referred to by the Royal Society Study Group (1992). This debate is summarised in Table 1.1, which sets out what Hood and Jones describe as, 'seven commonly recurrent sets of opposing views about how risk management should be handled' (Hood and Jones 1996:8).

Table 1.1: Seven Contested Areas of the Risk Management Debate
Sources: Royal Society Study Group 1992:159; Hood and Jones 1996:9)

Doctrine	Justification	Counter-doctrine	Justification
Anticipation	Apply causal knowledge of system failure to ex ante actions for better risk management	Resilience	Complex system failures not predictable in advance and anticipationism makes things worse
Absolution	A 'no-fault' approach to blame avoids distortion of information and helps learning	Blamism	Targeted blame gives strong incentives for taking care on the part of key decision-makers
Quantification	Quantification promotes understanding and rationality, also exposes special pleading	Qualitivism	Proper weight needs to be given to the inherently unquantifiable factors in risk management
Design	Apply the accumulated knowledge available for institutional design	Design agnostism	There is no secure knowledge base or real market for institutional design
Complementarism	Safety and other goals go hand in hand under good management	Trade-offism	Safety must be explicitly traded off against other goals
Narrow participation	Discussion is most effective when confiend to expert practitioners	Broad participation	Broader discussion tests assumptions and avoids errors
Outcome specification	The regulatory process should concentrate on specifying structures or products	Process specification	The regulatory process should concentrate on specifying institutional processes

Referring to the table, Hood and Jones go on to point out that it is a simplification. Few people actually hold the extreme views expressed by the opposing pairs. It is more common for people to subscribe to a variety of combinations of paler versions of each position.

We have already covered QRA and institutional design, and our earlier discussion of risk communication in the 'risk society' suggests that there is little support for the hard science view that risk management decisions are best left to experts. The remainder of this discussion will therefore outline the remaining four of the seven areas.

Anticipationism versus resilience
One area of the debate involves the extent to which risk management should be concerned with proactively looking forward – anticipationism – rather than reactively bouncing back – resilience. The case for anticipationism has two main strands. First, the German *Versorgensprinzip* (precautionary principle), which has been influential in pollution control in Europe, argues that controls should be imposed just in case, even though the scientific evidence and cost/benefits are inconclusive (Tait and Levidow 1992). Second, socio-technical disasters might be better avoided if the lessons were learned from previous incidents (Toft 1992; Toft and Reynolds 1997). The case for resilience is based on the arguments that the future is uncertain and that proactivity can lead to a belief nothing will go wrong – a belief which can be paralysing in a crisis (the 'Titanic effect'). Risk management should thus focus on improving ability to respond when things go wrong.

Absolution versus blame
We have seen how the concept of risk might increasingly be seen as being about accountability, liability and blame. Trends in litigation and prosecution are driving risk managers to 'cover their backsides' rather than gather information and promulgate lessons learned. Absolutionism calls for the type of 'no-blame' culture involved in civil aviation, where pilots are encouraged to report their own near-misses so that others can learn from them. Johnston argues that,

> The designers of such risk-reduction systems are invariably convinced that action leading to individual blame or sanction will adversely interfere with the quality of feedback, ultimately leading to a decrease in total system safety.' (Johnston 1996:83)

Horlick-Jones (1996a) also advocates the benefits of 'no-fault' risk management. He concludes, however, that, 'organizations operate in social and institutional contexts, and the ability to maintain blame-free corporate cultures may be severely constrained by cultural and political factors' (Horlick-Jones 1996a:70).

Complementarism versus trade-offism
The next area of debate covers the question of whether safety and other goals can go hand in hand, or whether they have to be traded-off against each other. For the complementarists, Horlick-Jones (1996b) suggests that a quality management approach to risk management might provide a way to build safety into operations in accordance with the 'precautionary principle' discussed earlier. On the other hand, Foster (1996) argues that safety is but one of the important factors to be evaluated in decision-making. Economics and environmental impact also have to be weighed in the scales.

In the case of the PAFs industry, I have previously used Cultural Theory to argue that

> 'managers are faced with four competing demands. Commercial pressures require them to optimise the commercial viability of the venue and its events. Spectator demands for excitement and enjoyment require credible events staged in comfortable surroundings. Regulatory and other requirements for safety and security must also be met, whilst any negative effects which the venue and event may have on the outside world must be kept to a minimum.' (Frosdick 1998:66)

Successful management means striking a balance between these demands. It may therefore be argued that appropriate trade-offism can result in complementarism.

Outcome or process specification
The last area of debate is the question of whether risk management should specify changing either structures or else processes (and thus behaviours). In engineering and science, the emphasis lies on designing products, for example pharmaceuticals, and structures, for example stadia, which are 'safe' in the sense that risk has been reduced either 'as low as is reasonably practicable' or whatever other evaluation measure is used. On the other hand, quality management systems such as ISO9000 focus on risk reduction through compliance with organisational processes. Hood and Jones (1996) note that, 'this dimension of risk management is not characterised by sharp and explicit debate' (Hood and Jones 1996:193).

It is perhaps thus less a question of either structures or processes but rather finding a place for both. British stadia may today be much 'safer', having been substantially rebuilt and refurbished during the 1990s. But 'even the most modern ground could still be unsafe if the club cannot properly manage the safety of its paying customers.' (Frosdick and Sidney 1997:210). Thus the Guide to Safety at Sports Grounds (Department of National Heritage 1997) lays equal emphasis on both the physical condition of the ground and the quality of its safety management.

TOWARDS A UNIFIED THEORY OF RISK?

As we move toward the conclusion of this review of a very diverse, compartmentalised literature, we should note that the work of John Adams represents perhaps the first glimpse of a possible unified theory of risk. Building on his paper for the 1997 Royal Society discussion meeting (Adams 1997), Adams has further developed his arguments to distinguish between risks which are directly perceptible (cars), perceived with the help of science (cholera) and where scientists don't know and can't agree (mad cows) (see Adams 1999a; 1999b; Adams and Thompson 2002). He offers the conclusions set out in Table 1.2 on the next page, which are important because they seek to accommodate all the islands of the risk archipelago.

Psychological explanations of risk perception fit well with directly perceptible risks such as riding a bicycle. Here risk can indeed be seen as the product of familiarity and dread. Engineering and science quantifications of risk are valid and appropriate where science is accepted, for example the proposition that, if you smoke cigarettes, you are so many times more likely to develop lung cancer than if you do not smoke. The area of virtual risk is where Cultural Theory provides the tool for explanation. These risks are products of the imagination, perceived through the various cultural filters of the individualist, fatalist, hierarchical and egalitarian ways of life.

CONCLUSION

This discussion has highlighted the scope of the concept of risk and the divergence of expert opinion about its meaning. This wide debate raises the question of whether theories of risk have any relevance in practice. Thompson (1997) for example, reviews the Bhopal chemical explosion, the fire in the Channel Tunnel and the general trends in disasters to conclude that

> 'it is recognised that disasters – of all types – strike suddenly and unexpectedly.... Risk theories have little relevance to those with a practical role to play in such matters. What is crucial is that there are trained and equipped personnel ready to respond immediately to a disaster if and when it happens' (Thompson 1997:137).

Table 1.2: The Management of Risk and Uncertainty
(Source: Adams 1999b:44-45)

Where risks are directly perceptible,
- everyone takes risks; everyone is a risk manager;
- taking risks leads, by definition, to accidents; the pursuit of a world free of accidents is a futile exercise;
- it is important to distinguish self-risk (e.g., driving without a seat belt) from behaviour that puts others at risk (e.g., driving at 100 mph down a busy shopping street); the second is a legitimate area for regulation; the first is not;
- attempts to criminalize self-risk are likely to be worse than useless; they are likely to redistribute the burden of risk in ways that harm innocent third parties;
- everyone has a risk thermostat, and he may adjust it so that he has the risk level that he likes regardless of the experts' best efforts to decrease risk;
- institutional risk managers who do not take account of the reasons that people have for taking and balancing risks – the rewards of risk – will be frustrated.

Where risks are perceived with the help of science,
- science can reduce uncertainty by illuminating the connection between behaviour and consequence;
- science, effectively communicated, can defeat superstition and purely imaginary scares; but
- science cannot provide 'objective' measures of risk;
- risks come in many incommensurable forms that defy reduction to a common denominator;
- the act of measurement alters that which is being measured;
- risk is a reflexive phenomenon; in managing risks we are continually modifying them; in the realm of risk a Heisenberg principle probably rules.

Where scientists don't know or cannot agree,
- we are in a realm of *virtual risk* where plural rationalities contend;
- virtual risks are cultural constructs;
- they may or may not be real – science cannot settle the issue – but they have real consequences;
- the precautionary principle is of no help; different rationalities adhere to very different versions of the principle;
- virtual risks are a fact of life; science will never have all the answers;
- humility in the face of ignorance is a precondition for civilized debate about virtual risks.

Taking the contrary view, Hoare (1997) discusses high order, application and practitioner theories and their relevance to practice. He concludes that

> 'All practice started with somebody's theory of the best way to do things. To say that theory is irrelevant to the practitioner makes no sense. It assumes that only practitioner theories are valid. But examination of them may reveal that their genesis might not have been older and wiser practitioners but theoreticians from elsewhere. Ignoring theories other than your own is not likely to lead to best practice, and involvement in the creation of new hypotheses in the only real option for serious professionals. Theories have to be tested, modified, adopted or rejected' (Hoare 1997:135).

The climate of risk as accountability and blame, the media's love of scapegoating, the integrated and proactive 'new risk management' (Hood 1996; Power 1999) – these drivers all suggest that those who carry responsibility need to appreciate the nature of risk and know how to assess and manage it. Theories of risk need to be understood and then applied in practice. Whether in a safety, project or some other risk context, this means recognising risk as a multiplicity of perceptions about the source and level of threat or danger from future events or hazards and about the variety of adverse consequences, including legal liability, to which such events may give rise.

It does not mean reacting to every perceived risk, but it does require the exercise of practical management judgement, informed by a sound understanding of risk and risk perception. It means evaluating which risks have not been reduced to an acceptable level, determining what to do about them and doing it. It means knowing how to document actions and decisions to produce the evidence to show an insurance company, a Civil Court, the police, a Coroner's inquest or even the jury in a criminal trial, that everything that could reasonably be expected has been done. Practitioners need to draw on risk theory for evidence to support what they do in practice.

From our discussion of the risk perception debate, we have seen that there is considerable evidence from the behavioural sciences regarding the effect of risk perception on the techniques of risk assessment. The application of quantitative techniques, particularly where risks are products of the imagination, is fundamentally flawed because of bias and disagreement in assessment (Douglas and Wildavsky 1982). Individual risk perception is the product of individual psychology, whereas cultural bias – and thus Cultural Theory – provides the best way of predicting how risks will be perceived (Wildavsky and Dake 1990).

Many of the risks with which we shall be concerned in the two research settings for this book fall into the category of virtual risks (Adams 1997; 1999a; 1999b). Here again it is Cultural Theory which provides the explanatory power.

From our discussion of issues in risk management, we have seen that risk management decisions are inherently political. Knowing and applying the techniques in isolation is insufficient in itself. In the 'risk society', there is growing evidence of the need for dialogue and participation in decision-making in the making and communicating of such decisions. Successful risk management means striking an appropriate balance between the competing demands of different cultural constituencies.

The evidence from this review of theories of risk thus provides good support for the qualitative Cultural Theory approach adopted for the research reported in this book.

CHAPTER TWO: APPLIED THEORY & METHODS

SUMMARY

This Chapter deals with questions of research design, applied theory, problem and methods. The Chapter opens by briefly considering the differences between quantitative and qualitative research. It then discusses the very qualitative approach adopted for this book, together with relevant ethical issues. Moving onto theory, the next section reviews the various applications, implications and criticisms of Cultural Theory. Developments in Cultural Theory and risk theory are discussed and the research problem is then affirmed. The methods used for researching risk in two settings are set out in the next sections. These are followed by a discussion of some of the issues around the quality and usefulness of the research. Finally, the significance of the research is discussed and its original contribution to the body of knowledge assessed.

RESEARCH APPROACH

Quantitative or Qualitative?

The main types of social science research represent two opposing views. The positivist school of thought (following Comte) is that the methods used in natural science are also applicable to the study of man. This philosophy gives rise to a dependence on the quantitative methods which seek to measure the social world through the use of statistics. The phenomenological or interpretivist philosophy holds that social life has no meaning independent from that ascribed to it by the people involved. This gives rise to the qualitative approach which undertakes its measurement by providing plausible description of the phenomena concerned.

The important differences between the qualitative and quantitative research traditions have been set out by, amongst others, McCracken (1988:16-18), who identifies the main distinctions between the two approaches. Most striking, in his view, is the treatment of analytic categories. The more positivist researcher seeks to define categories before starting the research and then goes on to investigate the relationships between them using statistical tests. The softer, more anthropological approach is to get into the field, observe, muse and allow the categories to evolve throughout the research.

Rose (1982:117) summarises the distinctions between the two types. The ideal quantitative approach is seen as having pre-determined concepts which are theoretically tested through representative sampling of statistical data which is presented in tables, graphs, and so on. The ideal qualitative method, however, uses more purposive sampling of qualitative data, presented as author's summaries, quotations and illustrations, to build theoretical concepts as they emerge from the data. This latter approach has been the one adopted from the outset for this research.

A Qualitative 'Grounded Theory' Approach

The research design for this book has, from the very outset, been the qualitative approach of explanation through plausible reflection and of theory grounded in the explanation.

There are both theoretical and practical reasons for this choice of approach. First is that there is no question of the quantitative approach always being better than the qualitative. It is not that I was unable to devise appropriate statistical testing and so had to settle for description instead. As Alexander has argued, an over-emphasis on positivism has impoverished social science.

> 'By unduly emphasizing the observational and verificational dimensions of empirical practice, the positivist impetus has severely narrowed the range of empirical analysis. The fear of speculation has technicalized social science and driven it toward false precision and trivial correlational studies. This flight from generality has only contributed further to the inevitable atomization of social scientific knowledge.' (Alexander 1985:632)

It is simply that many theoretical concepts do not lend themselves very well to investigation using quantitative methods. The discussion of theory later on in this Chapter will argue that Cultural Theory (Douglas 1978; Thompson, Ellis and Wildavsky 1990), the application of which forms the nub of this research, is one such concept. From a theoretical perspective therefore, a qualitative approach was the best choice.

The second main reason for a qualitative grounded theory approach to this research has been practical, because the research process itself has been evolutionary rather than planned. The work has its origins in a 1993 study of the British risk in PAFs industry (Frosdick 1993a). Building and very substantially expanding on that original work, the book is an account of over ten years empirical research effort undertaken between 1993 and 2004 to investigate how Cultural Theory might be applied in practice as a risk consultancy tool.

The investigation has been highly personalised and grounded in an ongoing data collection and analysis process rather than the subject of one or more controlled experiments. As Whyte puts it,

'Often we have the experience of being immersed in a mass of confusing data .... The actual evolution of the research ideas does not take place in accordance with the formal statements we read on research methods. The ideas grow up in part out of our immersion in the data and out of the whole process of living.' (Whyte 1961:280)

This has been very much the experience of this research. Turner (1983) notes that, 'Qualitative social research generates large amounts of non-standard data which make analysis problematic'. He therefore advocates the use of 'grounded theory' for the qualitative analysis of organisational behaviour.

This research has therefore followed what Glaser and Strauss introduced in 1967 as the 'discovery-based' or 'grounded theory' approach. This offered a qualitative alternative to the more quantitative methods in vogue in the social sciences at that time. 'Grounded theory' is a 'means for systematic discovery of theory from the data of social research' (Glaser and Strauss 1967:3).

According to Jupp (1996:7), this evolutionary approach 'eschews any notion of an obligatory and unilinear transition from problem through theory to method'. The theory is grounded in the data 'because it arises out of and is directly relevant to the particular setting under study' (Frankfort-Nachmias and Nachmias 1996:294). The theory is grounded in the analysis because of the fundamental reflexivity of the research design. As Hammersley and Atkinson (1995) put it,

'We are part of the social world we study, ... there is no escape from reliance on common-sense knowledge and methods of investigation. All social research is founded on the human capacity for participant observation. We act in the social world and yet are able to reflect upon ourselves and our actions as objects in that world' (*ibid.* p.21).

Thus the analysis for this research has consisted of two distinct phases. First has been an ongoing process of reflection (as researcher) on the data collected (as agent), looping back into the shaping of the research ideas and to the subsequent data collection and analysis. This cycle is reflected on in the reflexive 'natural history' of the research set out in Chapter Three.

The second phase of the analysis was then very much a post-hoc rationalisation of the first phase, structured around the two sets of files needed for a grounded theory approach (see Turner 1983). The first set of files is more data and less analysis. In the PAFs setting this set is represented by the original field notes, interviews and documentary sources from which Chapters Four and Five are derived, whilst in the police setting it is the case study reports in Chapters Six and Seven. The second set of files is more analysis than data. In the PAFs setting this is represented by publications and by the written up argument in Chapters Four and Five. In the police setting it is the cross-case report in Chapter Eight.

Thus although the analysis draws on empirical research data, this book is a grounded theory rather than a primarily ethnographic study. It must therefore be made clear from the outset that there is less in the way of the detail and mess expected in a deep ethnography. The ethnography in this book is far more in the way of purposive sampling of examples from the empirical data to illustrate the analysis and substantiate the emerging grounded theory.

Participant Observation and Ethics

Given this evolutionary 'whole life' 'grounded theory' approach to the research, it follows that the principal method of data collection has been 'participant observation'. This refers to a set of techniques in which researchers immerse themselves in their research setting, gaining direct access to observe and experience the world of meaning of the social actors involved (see Jorgenson 1989). The research approach shows that I have been fully immersed in both the risk in PAFs industry and the police service. By virtue of my former police career and previous research, I had excellent access to my two research settings and was pre-socialised in them – I already knew their relevant patterns of social organisation and embedded values. I was well placed to participate, observe, reflect, analyse and report on what I experienced.

But the application of the technique was different in each setting. Raymond Gold (1958) identified four types of participant observation. First is the 'complete observer', whose presence is not known to the research subjects and who thus observes them covertly, not taking part in the activity. Second is the 'observer as participant' whose presence and role is known but who does not take part in the activity. Neither of these fit with my own very active involvement in the research settings. Third is the 'participant as observer', where the researcher does take part in activities and their role as a researcher is known. Thus the subjects' informed consent is implicit in their own continued participation in the activity. Fourth is the 'complete participant', who takes part in the activity but whose role as a researcher is not known.

'Participant as observer' clearly represents my role in the PAFs setting, and also in the police setting, where my clients and some other subjects were aware that my consultancy assignments would potentially provide data for my doctoral studies. But for many of those who participated in the many workshop sessions held during the course of the police project risk research, I was a 'complete participant' – in most cases they did not fully appreciate they were research subjects as well as contributors to a client's analysis.

It is important to emphasise that this lack of knowledge on their part did not arise from any deception on mine. Unless deception is necessary to gain access to closed research settings to expose the truth, such as in Holdaway's covert observation of the police service (Holdaway 1983), deception is generally regarded as unethical. I had not concealed my dual purpose from my clients and often introduced myself to workshops as 'doing a PhD in management of risk'. Nevertheless, there are clear ethical issues surrounding my role as agent in the police project risk setting.

According to Frankfort-Nachmias and Nachmias, 'The practice of ensuring informed consent is the most general solution to the problem of how to promote social science research without encroaching on individual rights and welfare' (Frankfort-Nachmias and Nachmias 1996:85). In many cases I did not have this informed consent. However Maurice Punch, who carried out participant observation on policing in Holland, has argued that obtaining informed consent is often impracticable (Punch 1986). Negotiating with each subject individually is long winded, problematic and would kill off many research projects. What does the researcher do in a group situation where half the group agree to participate and half don't? This would have destroyed my consultancy assignments and thus the research data.

The absence of full informed consent in the police project risk setting has therefore been dealt with by the removal of all identifiers from informants and the use of aliases for case studies.

THEORY

During the course of any study or research, we may well carry out observations on our chosen research setting and take detailed notes which describe what we have observed. But description on its own does not take us very far. Given that we have been able to *observe* and *describe* a particular social phenomenon (let's call it 'Y'), we will often want to be able to *explain* why it happens (let's call the explanation 'X'). We can then go on to *predict* that, if 'X' happens, 'Y' will probably happen too. This ability to predict then gives us an opportunity to try and *control* the effects of 'Y' by tackling its cause 'X'.

In developing our explanation of 'X', we are developing theory. A theory is an explanation – something that presents a particular view of the world. Without theory there can be no proper understanding. The development of theory, then, is an essential and integral part of understanding the social world. Thus if we want to understand more about the world of risk in PAFs or police project risk management, we will need to draw on a variety of theoretical explanations about, for example, the concept of risk, how risk is perceived and why.

Theory can range between a student's minor working hypothesis and the master conceptual schemes of 'grand theory', for example Marx on the development of Capitalism. Much of the body of theory is constructed between these two extremes and is referred to as 'middle-range theory' – theory which is sufficiently close to the data to be included in research questions that allow empirical testing (Merton 1957). Risk theory and Cultural Theory offer two such sources of 'middle-range' explanation.

Risk Theory

The need to understand the nature of risk and its management is clearly central to both the settings for this research. The literature review in the previous Chapter represents an extensive review of risk theory and argued that the techniques of risk assessment and risk management are in themselves insufficient without a sound understanding of theories of risk perception, and in particular of Cultural Theory. This research seeks to apply Cultural Theory as risk perception theory and as organisation theory in the two research settings.

Applications of Cultural Theory[4]

Cultural Theory has enjoyed a breadth of application, particularly as a political science research tool. Thompson *et al.* (1990:14) suggest that 'the test of any theory is its effectiveness: does it explain better than alternatives? A glance at the bibliography [that they append to their book] will confirm that many practitioners are convinced that it does'. Mars and I have argued that Cultural Theory 'has proved highly effective in evaluating organisational, that is structural, influences on attitudes and behaviours and particularly so in locating differing perceptions of risk' (Mars and Frosdick 1997:115). Thompson, Grendstad and Selle have highlighted the wide range of contexts in which Cultural Theory has been applied, noting that 'A scheme that can clarify and re-order fields as varied as [the long list of references they give] ... deserves a second glance' (1999:5).

What is key here is that all these applications of Cultural Theory have been as a research methodology. As Thompson *et al.* (1999:3) put it, 'The idea is to go into some specific setting ... and use the analytical scheme to sort out the

---

[4] Some of the discussion of Cultural Theory in this section is derived from the publications listed in the references as Frosdick (1997h), Frosdick and Mars (1997), and Mars and Frosdick (1997).

various actors according to how grouped and gridded they are'. But requirements for validity and reliability mean that such research is often a protracted process. The pace of organisational life does not necessarily allow for the timescales needed for a protracted research answer. The Pareto principle (Pareto 1971) or law of diminishing returns – 80% of the answer for 20% of the effort – are the watchwords of a world of perpetual change. Thus as well as delivering high quality findings, management research sometimes needs to be more timely and better value for money in order to be relevant.

Here we find the beginnings of my research question back in 1993. To what extent, I began to wonder, could Cultural Theory be applied as a lean consultancy method for risk assessment and management? Was there a way in which Cultural Theory could provide the theoretical underpinning for a timely, rich and cost-effective analysis which represented good value for the client?

The Implications of Cultural Theory for Risk Assessment

We saw in Chapter One that, in their review of rival theories of risk perception, cultural theorists Wildavsky and Dake (1990) concluded that 'cultural biases best predict risk perception findings', and that 'individuals choose what to fear (and how to fear it), in order to support their way of life'. To develop the analysis, let us draw on Cultural Theory's four views of nature (Thompson *et al.* 1990:26-29), each of which can be graphically represented by a ball in a landscape (see Figure 2.1).

Figure 2.1: Four Views of Nature
(Source: Thompson *et al.* 1990, p.27)

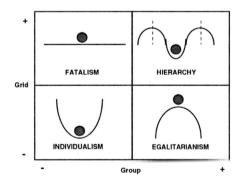

For the individualist entrepreneur, nature is benign. The ball will never come out of the cupped landscape and so there is an almost wilful disregard of risk in pursuit of short-term advantage. Disaster 'will never happen here'. If it does, the cause is either attributed to competitively induced treachery or else shrugged off as a random chance event. For the fatalist, nature is capricious and the ball thus rolls where it will. The fatalist may well be exposed to risk, but there is nothing he can do about it. Disasters are accepted as acts of God. For the hierarch, nature is perverse/tolerant. The ball will stay inside the cupped landscape only if it is not pushed beyond known limits. Risk is perceived as coming about if those limits are exceeded, usually by someone breaking the rules. Disasters are therefore blamed on deviance and rule breaking. Since nature is ephemeral, the egalitarian is concerned that the ball is precariously balanced on the landscape. Risk and potential disaster are an ever present threat from forces in 'the system' beyond the boundary.

The Royal Society (1992) report on risk, whilst failing to agree a cohesive approach, made the point that Cultural Theory could well have revolutionary implications for risk assessment and perception. Following Douglas (1990), Cultural Theory 'implies that people select certain risks for attention to defend their preferred lifestyles and as a forensic resource to place blame on other groups' (Royal Society Study Group 1992:112). Acceptance of this approach results in a scenario where no one measure of risk can represent the perceptions of the different cultural types. Cultural Theory holds that there are four different ways of life and correlated with these are four different ways of perceiving risk.

This idea of fourfold risk perception of risk has clear practical application (Frosdick 1997h:330; Frosdick and Mars 1997:113). The risk analyst needs to recognise that different people perceive risk in entirely different ways. There are, therefore, no right or wrong answers and nobody is wrong to perceive a particular matter as a risk. For risk consultants and their clients, therefore, it is important to ensure that a broad range of perspectives is adequately represented in any risk assessment exercise. Following Cultural Theory, this would be best accomplished by identifying representatives of each of the four ways of life and inviting them to participate in a process that would make their varied risk perceptions apparent not only to themselves but also to others engaged in the exercise. Most significantly, this means inviting those who oppose you to join in the exercise – they won't hesitate to articulate the risks you would prefer not to hear.

During the course of data collection and analysis in the police project risk setting, it was reassuring to find this approach reinforced, in political science research terms, by Thompson and Rayner's point that, 'the risk terrain is contested, and that progress lies not in our choosing one position on that terrain and rejecting those that are in contention with it, but in recognising and understanding all these positions and then finding ways of negotiating constructively between them.' (Thompson and Rayner 1998:144)

In the second part of the article, Thompson, Rayner and Ney affirmed the argument that risk was an inherently constructivist or subjective idea rather than any objective reality. They suggested that,

'To embrace constructivism, however, is not to reject science, not does it lead us into a relativistic morass in which anything goes. Plurality, on examination, turns out to be rather limited and quite well structured: just a small number of constructions ... each of which is supportive of a particular form of social solidarity and each of which is all the time defining itself in contradistinction to the others.' (Thompson, Rayner and Ney 1999:330)

In other words, operationalising Cultural Theory enables the political scientist to capture plurality and facilitate negotiation. Quite so; and it is this approach, applied as a consultancy method, which has provided the basis for this research.

Developments in Cultural Theory and Risk Theory

In view of the ten years which have elapsed since this research began, and the importance of both Cultural Theory and risk theory as the theoretical underpinning for the work, it has been important to keep abreast of developments over time. I have followed the evolving debate and literature on risk and used publication and papers (Frosdick 1995c; 1997l; 1998i; 1999b) as a method both of demonstrating my knowledge of contemporary risk theory and of gathering source material for the literature review in Chapter One.

I have kept abreast of Cultural Theory in three ways: by subscribing to the Cultural Theory e-mail discussion group; by relevant reading and by publications. In collaboration with my supervisor, I have had the opportunity of publishing three overviews of Cultural Theory (Frosdick 1997h, Frosdick and Mars 1997; Mars and Frosdick 1997). These have again served to demonstrate my knowledge of the theory and provided valuable source material for the book.

The e-mail forum was initiated by Mary Douglas in early 1997. The list was initially run from Vienna by Matthias Karmasin and later by James Tansey from the Sustainable Development Research Institute at the University of British Columbia. The active members have included distinguished researchers who have published seminal work on Cultural Theory, for example Michael Thompson, Gunnar Grendstad, Per Selle (see Thompson *et al.* 1999) and Steven Ney (see Thompson, Rayner and Ney 1999). During the course of 1999, the forum also set up a web site (GG-CT 1999[5]) which covered the basics of the theory and contains details of relevant readings and publications. Following the evolving debate and knowledge of who has published what has inevitably helped in maintaining relevant reading. Many of the exchanges on the list, particularly since 1999, have been a tad esoteric for one concerned with the practical application of the theory. Indeed Mary Douglas herself sent a contribution to the 'dear silent others who may be finding this discussion rather abstract, as I do too' (Douglas 2001). Nevertheless the experience has helped shape the research. Four matters have been particularly illuminating.

First has been the emerging consensus within the Royal Society and British scientific community on the usefulness of Cultural Theory within the wider body of risk theory (see Adams 1997; 1999b). In an exchange on the list during January 2000, Michael Thompson commented on how often he was now seeing Cultural Theory referred to in the literature reviews of risk-related publications. And in a contribution to the list in May 2003, Mary Douglas wrote that,

> 'Aaron [Wildavsky] used to say, "Cultural Theory is the best game in town. Pity nobody is playing it!". Now public policy is by far the most active part of the present practice of [Cultural Theory].' (Douglas 2003b)

So Cultural Theory has been commanding more widespread attention since the late 1990s, evidenced for example by the production of three journal special editions devoted to Cultural Theory (see Mamadouh 1999; Hoppe 2002; Ney 2003). The usefulness of Cultural Theory is particularly evident in settings such as this research. Here many risks may be seen as products of the imagination – perceptions of uncertainty – rather than as either directly perceived or else perceived through accepted science (see Adams 1999a; 1999b). Thus, notwithstanding the passage of time, this research may still be seen as timely, topical and relevant.

Second has been the growing realisation that there is a distinction to be drawn between the grid group framework and the theory itself. The theory is discontinuous, holding simply that there are four (or five if one includes the

---

[5] The Cultural Theory website fell into disuse following a change of host server at the University of Amsterdam and is no longer available online.

hermit) viable, mutually exclusive and jointly exhaustive social solidarities, whereas the grid group matrix implies that there is continuity from low (grid or group) to high on each of its two axis. Grid group is 'user friendly Cultural Theory' (Thompson *et al.* 1999:13) used both as a heuristic device for explanation and as a framework for analysis.

Third has been the idea that Cultural Theory can be applied at all levels of analysis, from the micro to the meso to the macro (Thompson *et al.* 1999:9). The grid group framework is rather like the letters in a stick of rock during manufacture. Wherever you cut the rock, whether at the fat end, thin end or anywhere else, the letters are always there. At whatever level you undertake an analysis – individual, household, community, nation state, and so on – the grid group lens is also always applicable. This is particularly significant for this research. The risk at sports grounds analysis uses grid group both at the macro level of the industry and at the meso level of the individual venue. The case studies of project risk in police management are drawn from levels ranging from the micro – individual projects in a single Force – through to the macro – the police service nationally.

Fourth has been an appreciation of the difficulties inherent in trying to test Cultural Theory using quantitative methods. Several researchers, for example Dake (1991; 1992), Marris, Langford and O'Riordan (1996; 1998) and Rippl (2002), have sought to so test Cultural Theory using social surveys. This work has been founded on the what Tansey and O'Riordan (1999) describe as the *stability hypothesis* – the assumption that different individuals always represent the same social solidarity, whatever the context, and therefore that this social solidarity can be revealed through carefully designed survey questions. But an alternative view suggests that different individuals can represent different social solidarities in different contexts – the *mobility hypothesis*. As Olli explains,

> 'Individuals, in this view, are no longer the carriers of particular cultural biases but the potential expressors of values and beliefs that are activated by a social context. Change the social context, and the individual's cultural bias will make the appropriate switch.' (Olli 1999:59)

Rayner argues that 'individuals may flit like butterflies from context to context, changing the nature of their arguments as they do' (Rayner 1992:108). Thus the same individual might conceivably work as a freelance consultant (individualism), live in a commune (egalitarianism) and chair the management committee of the local Horticultural Society (hierarchy). An extreme example perhaps, but as Thompson *et al.* (1999:13) neatly summarise the problem, 'you cannot interview a form of social solidarity'.

You may be able to interview individuals face to face and so clarify with them the relevant social contexts, but you certainly can't administer questionnaires.

This suggests that quantitative methods may be less appropriate than qualitative for investigations involving Cultural Theory, a point supported by Tansey and O'Riordan, who observe that 'The employment of extensive positivistic research methodologies is confusing and, for the most part, inappropriate for cultural theory' (1999:84). This all provides theoretical support for the highly qualitative approach adopted for this research.

Criticisms of Cultural Theory

The Royal Society Report (1992:113-114) notes that Cultural Theory has its critics and refers briefly to two main criticisms. First is the charge that the basic four types may oversimplify the complexity of social differences. One might argue that, on the contrary, having four (or even five with the hermit) types represents twice the complexity of conventional social science dualisms such as hierarchy and markets. But the key point is that four types are archetypes, illustrations of points on fields at varying levels of analysis rather than definitive descriptions of four fixed boxes. Cultural Theory analysis can also include discussions of antagonisms and alliances between the types, such as where egalitarian pressure groups recruit from fatalists.

The second criticism noted in the Royal Society Report is that 'as yet, the grid-group cultural theory has involved the generation of much less systematic empirical evidence than that gathered by psychologists in their work on risk perception' (*ibid.*). Reflecting on this criticism, Mars and I have commented that,

> 'Despite its effectiveness in [the areas of risk perception], (as well as its tested applications in many others), it is, however, still called upon to justify its claims with yet further examples of empirical support. Perhaps its origins, in an obscure field of scholarship considered more appropriate to the administration of so called primitive peoples, is responsible for its surprisingly reluctant acceptance. Or perhaps this is an area so vigorously guarded by its traditional champions, the hard headed figure-men from science and engineering, and their supporters, the psychologists, that interlopers have an even more difficult time than usual.' (Mars and Frosdick 1997:115)

The breadth and volume of applications of Cultural Theory and the growing recognition of its usefulness, both discussed earlier in this Chapter, suggest that this criticism may now be going out of date.

More substantial criticisms of Cultural Theory have come in papers by Friedman (1991), Boholm (1996) and Sjöberg (1997). These are to be welcomed since, as Tansey and O'Riordan note, 'It would be worrying if cultural theory was *not* the subject of criticism since this would imply that it was not considered a serious enough contribution to social theory to merit review' (Tansey and O'Riordan 1999:81).

Friedman (1991) offers four main criticisms. These are that individualism and egalitarianism are inseparable in modern society; that modern culture is not related to patterns of social life; that Cultural Theory ignores the influence of history on cultural preferences; and that Cultural Theory is not applicable outside contemporary Western politics.

These criticisms are refuted by Ellis (1993), who responds to each specifically, at length and in considerable depth. He argues that Cultural Theory does recognise what individualism and egalitarianism have in common – low grid i.e. relative freedom from constraints – but also shows where they are different – i.e. in strength of group. He acknowledges the difficulties facing any theory which seeks to link people's ways of life with their ideas, noting that a question for future work will be how people deal with different contexts, a point subsequently addressed by Olli (1999). He argues, however, that generations of social and historical theorists would be surprised at a position which argued no connection between how people live and how they think.

Ellis acknowledges that future research will need to look further at the interaction between historical context and cultural bias, but argues that Cultural Theory is not ahistorical. Neither, he argues, is it presentist, reviewing some of the evidence that Cultural Theory can be applied to non-Western and premodern settings. He concludes that, 'Whatever the inadequacies of Cultural Theory, it offers a much better understanding of preference formation than anything presented by Friedman' (Ellis 1993:82).

Boholm's (1996) critique was extensively reviewed and responded to on the Grid-Group Cultural Theory discussion forum by Perri 6 (see 6, 1997). According to 6's analysis, Boholm makes seven main points. First is that Cultural Theory is not clear whether social structure causes cultural bias or vice versa nor indeed how strong the causal links are. 6 notes that Cultural Theory does not privilege any direction, nor is it determinist. Second is that putting the 'grid' and 'group' variables on a scale is misleading, since they are too complex for a simple 'low' or 'high'. Well of course the grid group matrix is a simplification of complexity, originally designed by Douglas 'gently to push what is known into an explicit typology that captures the wisdom of a hundred years of sociology, anthropology and psychology'

(Douglas 1982:1). 6 observes that the real issue is whether grid group is a fruitful summary.

Boholm's third main criticism is of circularity – that Cultural Theorists claim to make predictions about how adherents will perceive etc. when in fact that perception etc. follows logically from the way of life. This is a fair criticism of sloppier Cultural Theory, says 6. Boholm's fourth criticism is around the empirical untestability of the mobility hypothesis discussed above and 6 agrees that Cultural Theory needs to do more here. Fifth is that Cultural Theory is poor at explaining social change, however 6 comments that 'it is not exactly straightforward to point to a body of sociological or anthropological theory that is doing strikingly better' (6, 1997).

Boholm's seventh point, with which my own analysis agrees, is that quantitative methods are inappropriate for Cultural Theory. Lastly, Boholm claims that 'promiscuously' applying Cultural Theory at every level of analysis results in crude stereotyping. 6 does not think this sticks for most applications of Cultural Theory and considers that, even where it does stick,

> 'there may be a case for a plea of mitigating methodological circumstances. After all, theory is supposed to be economical, to simplify, and to draw out similarities. If it turns out that the same biases and formations work (in some measure, with appropriate qualifications) at multiple levels, and if there are explanations for why this is the case, then that ought to be counted as a success' (6, 1997).

Sjöberg (1997) is dismissive of qualitative applications of Cultural Theory. He argues that such studies 'may be stimulating to read but they do not answer the question about the validity of the theory' (*ibid.* p.115). For Sjöberg, valid empirical investigation can only be about statistical testing. He thus takes a highly quantitative approach, reviewing previous quantitative studies and himself seeking to test Cultural Theory using data sets from Sweden and Brazil. He concludes that 'Cultural Theory explains only a very minor share of the variance of perceived risk and that it adds even less to what is explained by different approaches' (*ibid.* p.113). My earlier discussions around Cultural Theory's mobility hypothesis have argued that quantitative methods are far less appropriate than qualitative for Cultural Theory research.

Why Cultural Theory?

Given the wide choice of theories which might have been selected for deployment within this research, why should Cultural Theory have been chosen over other alternatives? There are four main reasons, three of which we have already covered. First, as we saw in Chapter One, Cultural Theory offers a more powerful explanation of risk perception than psychological explanations. To remind us, in their review of rival theories of risk perception, Cultural Theorists Wildavsky and Dake (1990) concluded that cultural biases were the best predictor of risk perception findings. Second, as we saw earlier in this Chapter in the discussion of the implications of Cultural Theory for risk assessment, operationalising Cultural Theory facilitates more democratic management of risk by capturing plurality and negotiating consensus (Thompson and Rayner 1998; Thompson, Rayner and Ney 1999). Third, and again as we saw in Chapter One, Cultural Theory provides better explanation than psychology and 'objective science' in the area of virtual risk, where perceptions of uncertainty are products of the imagination perceived through cultural filters (Adams 1999a; 1999b).

The fourth reason may be found in the deployment of Cultural Theory as organisation theory (see Figure 2.2.

Figure 2.2: Cultural Theory in an Organisational Context[6]

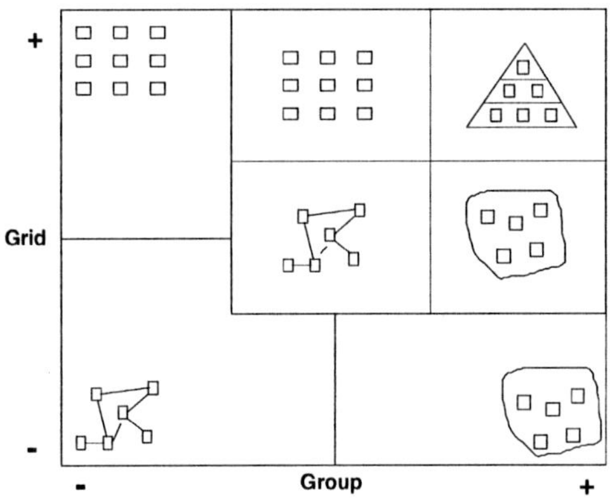

The use of Cultural Theory as organisation theory in this book takes place within an overall cultural context of organisational hierarchy. The analysis involves the application of Cultural Theory as a lens at both the macro level – to disaggregate the organisations within an industry setting; at the meso level – to analyse patterns of inter organisational relationships; and at the micro

---

[6] Adapted from Mars, G. Course Notes from Cranfield University MSc in Strategic Risk Management.

level – to analyse intra-organisational cases. Since all organisations, by definition, must have some degree of both grid and group, thus references within the analysis to low grid and low group mean that both grid and group are *relatively* weak when compared with the classic Weberian bureaucracy.

Cultural Analysis as a Management of Risk Tool

Many of the management philosophies developed in the 1990s represented a return to the classical approach to organisation theory. The acronyms for these new management theories abound. MBO (Management by Objectives), SBUs (Strategic Business Units), JIT (Just-in-Time Manufacturing), TQM (Total Quality Management), PRP (Performance Related Pay) and BPR (Business Process Re-engineering); each advocates a new universal management solution.

But, as Fons Trompenaars has argued, 'the fallacy of the 'one best way' is a management fallacy which is dying a slow death' (Trompenaars 1993:5). Strategies and ideas that work well in one organisation or country may lose effectiveness when introduced in another. Why should this be? Johnson and Scholes (1999) have referred to the cultural and political systems of an organisation and the importance of these issues for understanding the formulation and implementation of strategy.

Cultural analysis has an important role to play in the study of management in general, whether strategic management, risk management, disaster management or project management. Several writers have proposed various models as frameworks for such cultural analysis. Partly due to the popularity of their work as a set text for MBA students, the most familiar and enduring tool is probably Johnson and Scholes (1999) 'Cultural Web' of factors which sustain the core beliefs held within an organisation (see Figure 2.3 on the next page).

Elliott and Smith (1993) have shown the importance of understanding the cultural interaction of organisations in the context of disaster management. Referring to Johnson and Scholes, they highlight the need 'to look closely at the cultural web of the various organisations concerned and assess how this interacts with the crisis recipe that is in place' (Elliott and Smith 1993:210).

The recipe, or paradigm, is the set of subconscious basic assumptions and beliefs, shared by everyone in the organisation, which define 'the way we do things around here'. The paradigm is difficult to change because, it is surrounded by a protective web of cultural artefacts. The six factors in this 'Cultural Web' are: rituals and myths, symbols, power structures, organisational structures, control systems and routines.

Figure 2.3: The Cultural Web of an Organisation
(Source: Johnson 1992:207)

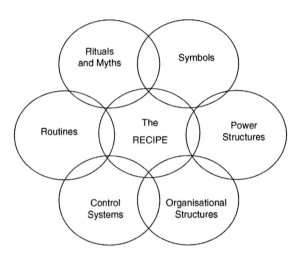

In workshops and seminars, the web is used as a heuristic device to enable managers to confront, perhaps for the first time, the culture of their own organisation. As Johnson points out:

> 'It is an exercise which is used frequently by the author to allow managers to 'discover' the nature of their organisation in cultural terms, the way it impacts on the strategy they are following, and the difficulty of changing it.' (Johnson 1992:208)

During the course of such an exercise, managers may be asked to draw a cultural web for their own organisation, perhaps using different sizes of circle to depict their perspective of the relative importance of each of the six factors. But for the would-be objective analyst there is a problem here. The cultural web accepts a definition of organisational culture which is ethnocentric both because it is top-heavy – only managers have participated in the definition – and because it looks on the organisation as a bounded entity rather than considering the social context in which it is set. Furthermore, because the web *surrounds* the core values – the paradigm – it cannot actually nail those values in to concrete forms of organisational structure.

Whilst use of the web allows members of an organisation to consider aspects of culture and assign value to them, perhaps through the relative sizes of the circles, it does not allow them to relate those aspects of culture to the structure of the organisation. Thus the 'Cultural Web' is *descriptive* rather than *analytical*. What is needed, then, is a model to disaggregate the different types of paradigm – for this research the risk paradigm – to be found within the web. And as we shall see in later Chapters, it is Cultural Theory which provides such a model.

THE RESEARCH PROBLEM

Given the difficulties already highlighted for the qualitative researcher in maintaining a strict distinction between problem, theory and method, it is perhaps unsurprising that the detailed research problem should in fact emerge rather untidily from the preceding discussion in this Chapter and from the reflexive 'natural history' of the research, which is set out in detail in Chapter Three.

In essence, however, the principal aim of the research has been to bridge the gap between theory and practice by testing the practical applicability of Cultural Theory. My research and consultancy interests were in two fields of risk; namely in PAFs and in the police. So it seemed entirely logical to adopt the objectives of seeking to develop a theoretically underpinned consultancy methodology for risk assessment and management and investigating whether it actually worked or not.

Given the user-friendly properties of the grid-group matrix, the research question can perhaps best be framed like this. This research is a study of whether Cultural Theory can be applied as a lean management of risk method through the practical application of grid-group: as a heuristic for explanation to clients; as a tool for stakeholder analysis and as a framework for disaggregated analysis.

The research began where my previous work left off, through participant observation and interviewing activities in the risk in PAFs industry. It continued through case studies of my consultancy assignments in the police project business. And to expose the emerging findings, I sought to publish the research as I went along. Of course one must accept that work gets published for a whole variety of reasons, not all of which are to do with its scholarly qualities. Nevertheless, it is the job of social science to make good sense of a problem, either by measuring it with statistics, or else by providing plausible explanation. It is hoped that the acceptance of ideas for publication by academic peers and practitioner colleagues offers some supporting evidence that the explanation offered in this book is plausible.

METHODS

Risk in Public Assembly Facilities

Between 1992 and 1994, I carried out 'participant as observer' activities at a quota sample of 35 football matches and eight other sporting and leisure events at 27 separate venues throughout Great Britain. The football matches were purposively sampled to include emotionally charged 'derby' and cup matches, all-ticket and likely capacity crowd fixtures, games being played at stadia under redevelopment and matches at ten football grounds identified as places where supporters felt threatened (Williams, Dunning and Murphy 1989a). The eight other events were an accidental sample which included a test match at Lords cricket ground and the 1993 British Formula One Grand Prix at Silverstone Circuits. Approaches ranged from single visits, through more involved case studies, to detailed ethnographies. In addition to the main participant observation activity, extensive networking resulted in meetings and discussions with over 100 informants from all levels of involvement in the risk in sports grounds industry. Finally, for the purposes of data triangulation, I gathered considerable quantities of supporting documentation during the course of the research, for example briefing notes, intelligence reports and operational plans.

My analysis of that part of the data set collected between 1992 and 1993 was set out in the dissertation submitted for my Masters degree at Cranfield (Frosdick 1993a). In view, however, of the external examiner's recommendation that the work was worthy of publication, I resolved to continue collecting data using accidental sampling as the opportunities presented themselves. Having joined the Centre for Public Services Management and Research (CPSMR) at Staffordshire University I then worked to refine the analysis in a form suitable for submission to learned journals (Frosdick 1995a; 1995b).

I then began to explore the ideas further and to suggest how Cultural Theory might be applied in a risk in PAFs context. I began to expose the research to scrutiny and to disseminate the ideas, submitting and presenting relevant conference and seminar papers (Frosdick 1995d; 1996a; 1996b; 1996c; 1996g; 1998a) and engaging in journalism (Frosdick 1996h; 1996i; 1997i; 1997j). The investigation was now clearly grounded in the identification of where Cultural Theory's four ways of life might be found in the risk in PAFs business (Frosdick 1995a; 1995b). The risk assessment problem for managers was that the three active social solidarities (individualism, hierarchy and egalitarianism) presented them with competing risk priorities. Individualist commercial pressures required them to optimise the commercial viability of the venue and its events. Regulatory and other hierarchical requirements for safety and security had to be met. Egalitarian spectator pressure groups demanded exciting, enjoyable and credible events staged in comfortable surroundings, whilst local pressure groups insisted that any negative effects which the venue and event might have on the outside world needed to be kept to a minimum (see Frosdick 1996h; 1997i; 1997j; 1998b; 1998c).

I continued my data collection, analysis and publication. My sampling for continued participant observation was accidental but purposive. Where I could get access, I was seeking to explore further the competing risk priorities of the active social solidarities. In terms of understanding commercial risks, I followed the trade journals and interviewed the Chairman of the Football League about his commercial plans (Frosdick 1998d). Over 18 months between 1996 and 1998, I became involved in organising and staging three commercial exhibitions held alongside the conferences of the Football Safety Officers' Association, of which I remain an active member. During 1997, I participated in work at a football club on striking an equitable balance between safety and atmosphere (Frosdick and Highmore 1997; Frosdick 1998e). I was able to draw on the findings from some environmental research on stadia (Rahilly 1996). And I looked at the tensions between safety, security, atmosphere, enjoyment and customer service inherent in various topical discussions. These included stadium design (Frosdick 1997e), pitch perimeter fences (Frosdick 1997k, Frosdick and Smith 1997), player behaviour (Frosdick 1997m), travelling away in Europe (Frosdick, Holford and Sidney 1997), the use of CS spray by police (Frosdick 1997n), integrated systems (Frosdick 1997o; 1997p), standing versus sitting (Frosdick 1998f) and alcohol in stadiums (Frosdick 1998g; 1998h).

I then sought to draw the research findings together through an edited academic book (Frosdick and Walley 1997). Here I was able to consolidate my work on historical and developmental context (Elliot, Frosdick and Smith 1997; Frosdick 1997a; 1997f; Frosdick and Sidney 1996a; 1996b). I was able to set out how I considered Cultural Theory could be applied in the stadium and arena environment (Frosdick 1997c; 1997d; 1997g). I followed the book up with a conference paper (Frosdick 1998b) and book chapter (Frosdick 1998c) which showed in more detail how the risk perceptions of the different social solidarities could be illustrated. Finally, in association with the Institute for Criminal Justice Studies at the University of Portsmouth, I designed and developed the materials (Frosdick 1999a; 1999b; 1999c; 1999d) for an academic course. The Certificate of Higher Education in Stadium and Arena Safety was grounded in Cultural Theory and risk theory. I worked the programme through to validation and it was delivered to students under my direction from April 1999 until October 2002, when it was subsumed within the Stadium and Arena Safety pathway of a full BSc in Risk and Security Management.

In my part-time academic career at Portsmouth, I continued to maintain my data collection, analysis and publication in this setting (see Frosdick 2001a; 2001b; 2001d; 2001e; 2002a; 2002b; 2002c; 2003a; 2004a; 2004b; 2004c; Frosdick and Vaughan 2003). I published two further books (Frosdick and Marsh 2005; Frosdick and Chalmers (2005). I was also involved in various knowledge transfer activities. I gave international conference papers and presentations (see Frosdick 2001f; 2001g; 2001h; 2002d; 2002e; 2002f; 2003b; 2003c; 2004d; De Quidt and Frosdick 2002; Frosdick and Newton 2004) and undertook consultancy work (for example see Frosdick 2003d). As well as teaching at Portsmouth (see Frosdick 2002g), I was a visiting lecturer for five years at the Université de Technologie Troyes in France (see Frosdick 2001c) and for three years at the University of Mauritius. I think I may fairly claim to be an expert on risk in PAFs – and that my expertise is underpinned by the application of Cultural Theory in this research setting.

Compromise in Research Design

During the course of 1996 and 1997 I sought to negotiate access to a Premier League football club where I had been collaborating with the safety officer and hoped to be able to carry out a detailed case study. I carried out several initial visits to matches, prepared a research proposal and was able to meet with senior managers at the club to discuss the details of the work. When presented with a Cultural Theory analysis of their stakeholders, they could clearly see how a risk assessment of their stadium operation would be richly informed by my suggested approach. Shortly afterwards, however, my principal contact changed roles within the club and a new Chief Executive was appointed. My research proposal was scuppered and I was never able to resurrect it.

Despite subsequent efforts, I was unable to negotiate similar access at another club. There are several reasons for this. First, as we shall see in Chapter Four, PAFs have become extremely highly regulated. Safety officers have the emergency services, the local authority, the Football Licensing Authority, the governing bodies of sport and a range of other regulatory bodies inspecting them and offering free advice on risk-related matters. They have no choice but to admit these organisations. It is thus difficult to persuade them to choose to let a researcher in to do something broadly similar. Second, safety officers are over-run with students wanting to research aspects of football, safety and security at sports grounds. Many of them simply ignore all such requests. I have had privileged access for other aspects of research and writing and have not wanted to spoil this by pressing my contacts too hard for other access. Third, stadium managers and safety officers are junior or middle managers of modest educational attainment who view risk from as a purely safety and security compliance issue. They don't, won't and can't think of risk in the more strategic terms suggested by a Cultural Theory analysis and laid out in the later Chapters of this book.

Only in May 2005, with the formation of the UK Stadium Managers Association, has a forum of more senior managers who might be more approachable on this matter begun to emerge. I was invited and seized the opportunity to address their inaugural seminar (see Frosdick 2005), but only ten managers attended and the relationships were insufficiently established for me to make any progress with access.

This lack of access is a great shame, since I had hoped to show how my consultancy method had its origins in a holistic approach to risk in PAFs, had then been further developed and applied in the police business, and finally reapplied in a major stadium. Whilst this was not to be, I felt that I had nevertheless achieved my research objectives in the first setting. Thus the data and analysis in Chapters Four and Five will show how Cultural Theory can be applied as a lean risk consultancy methodology through the practical application of grid group: as a heuristic for explanation to clients, as a tool for stakeholder analysis and as a framework for disaggregated analysis. But I have needed to test the theory in the real world environment to which I did have access, thus the further development of the research has had to be confined to the second research setting.

Risk in Police Projects

Within the police projects business, the research was methodologically more straightforward than in the area of risk in sports grounds. For the latter, the rather anthropological approach first adopted for previous research had almost inevitably continued on. My research question had rather untidily grown out of data collection and analysis built on my previous data set. The research question was much clearer by the time I embarked on my work on risk in the police business. The research approach was thus rather more active in foresight than apparent with hindsight.

Having been able to apply Cultural Theory for the first time in the police business in the context of the National Strategy for Police Information Systems (NSPIS[®7]), I took the opportunity to leave the police service, pursue my doctoral studies and embark on a consultancy career. I was seeking to

---

[7] NSPIS is the registered trademark of the Police Information Technology Organisation (PITO).

investigate my research question by selling consultancy rather than by organising an experiment. This was a multiple case study approach, but sampling was entirely determined by whom I could convince to take a chance on buying my relatively unproven Cultural Theory approach to risk assessment and management. My sampling of cases was therefore accidental, with access a matter of winning business. I had already published an early version of the NSPIS case study (Frosdick and Odell 1996; Mars and Frosdick 1997) and would now be looking to collect and analyse further cases.

My work within the NSPIS continued from early 1995 up until November 1999. This allowed me to further refine the case study over time. I was able to publish the revised case study as part of the materials for my teaching programme at the University of Portsmouth (Frosdick 1999b). This made a useful bridge between the two settings since I was able to present my students with the NSPIS case as a means of thinking about the application of Cultural Theory in a different context to their own work in PAFs. Alongside the ongoing NSPIS work, I developed a detailed service description covering the various tasks and activities which would form part of my Cultural Theory risk consultancy and thus the case study protocol and coding frame for my research data collection and analysis (see Appendix A). I formed an association between my company and Redfern Consultancy, who were happy to support the marketing of my service to the police business (see Redfern Consultancy 1997). This association ended in January 2000 when my company began marketing under its own brand. Up until April 2004 I completed some 80 consultancy assignments, 41 of which were directly related to my research question and thus provided the data set for this stage of the research.

The 41 cases analysed in Chapters Six and Seven are derived from a total of over 500 days – over two working years – research effort in the field. The cases fall into four broad categories. First are the 15 cases which were management of risk exercises undertaken in support of the initiation of a police information technology project. For example, between 1996 and 1999 I worked with a police force on the risks associated with their development of a system for processing cases within the criminal justice system.

Second are the 12 cases which were management of risk exercises undertaken in support of a police business project. For example, between 1998 and 1999 I worked with a police force on the risks associated with taking over responsibility for policing part of another police force area.

Third are the eight cases which were management of risk exercises undertaken as projects in their own right. An example here would be my work in 1999 to facilitate an assessment of the business risks associated with a major national policing operation.

Fourth are the six computer security risk assignments which I undertook between 1997 and 1998. For example, in 1998 I worked with a police force to develop system security and disaster recovery recommendations for a new Command and Control computer system.

The investigation is very much grounded in the description and analysis of the cases. As Martin and Turner argue, 'An emerging grounded theory primarily justifies itself by providing a detailed and carefully crafted account of the area under investigation' (Martin and Turner 1986:143). The analysis has a particular focus on the participation (or non-participation) of stakeholders drawn from each of Cultural Theory's four social solidarities.

The consultancy nature of my work on managing risk in the police business has meant efforts to bring about organisational learning for my clients on Cultural Theory, risk theory and their practical application to police project management. This approach represents the type of 'action science' expounded by Argyris and Schon (see Lundberg 1996 and Hampden-Turner 1996), where

> 'subjects become clients who participate in defining jointly the research goals, methods, participation and research costs and rewards. For Argyris, research produces knowledge that enhances client competence first and change secondarily, as well as aiding the development of theory.' (Lundberg 1996:241)

My work also accords with the design and methods for case study research set out by Yin (1994), for whom the 'case study, like other research strategies, is a way of investigating an empirical topic by following a set of pre-specified procedures (Yin 1994:15).

Definition and design involves the development of theory, selection of cases and the design of a data collection protocol. I had my Cultural Theory research question, a non-probability sampling approach to case selection and the menu of tasks and activities in my service description – the case study protocol and coding frame (Appendix A) – which helped to ensure a standard approach to each case.

Data collection and analysis covers the conducting of each case study, followed by the preparation of each individual case study report. Some of my assignments had been long term, lasting three years or more, with various data collected, analysed and reported at intervals. These were assignments where the management of risk exercise had been followed by regular reviews to ensure the analysis was kept up to date, and here the individual case studies were built up over time. Other assignments had been shorter term with final reports completed and delivered to the clients as I had gone along. Each case has been undertaken following the relevant activities within the case study protocol, which also constitutes the coding frame for the analysis. The case data has been entered into a Microsoft Access® database comprising a single table derived from the coding frame. Each of the 41 cases forms an individual record in the database from which the 41 samples of records outlined in Chapters Six and Seven represent the first set of files needed for a grounded theory analysis (see Turner 1983).

Final analysis and conclusion refers to the drawing of cross-case conclusions, the writing of the cross-case report, the modification of theory and the development of policy implications. The first two of these areas are addressed in the comparative discussion of the cases set out in Chapter Eight. This cross-case analysis provides the second set of data required for the grounded theory approach. Theory and policy are also dealt with in Chapter Eight, which proposes a Cultural Theory-based approach to managing risk.

Quality and Usefulness

The more qualitative approaches to research are inevitably open to charges that the findings lack validity and reliability. Hibberd (1990) identifies five criteria by which the general quality and usefulness of research can be assessed, namely: reliability, objectivity, openness, validity and acceptance of limitations. Strauss and Corbin (1990) offer four specific criteria for assessing the quality and usefulness of a grounded theory. First, it should be rooted in data which reflect the everyday reality of the phenomenon. Second, it should make sense to the people who have been studied and to others who work in the same field. Third, it should be capable of being used for generalisation. Fourth, it should provide a basis for action in the area.

Strauss and Corbin's criteria are all encompassed within Hibberd's five criteria, which therefore provide a useful checklist against which to consider the methods used in conducting this grounded theory research.

Evidence may be said to be reliable if it is found to be consistent over two dimensions. The first is inter-observer reliability. Would an independent observer deduce the same evidence from an analysis of the same phenomenon? This is closely linked with the question of objectivity. How far, in other words, are the findings and conclusions based on evidence, the meaning of which would be agreed by two or more independent people?

Inter-observer reliability and objectivity are difficult tests for qualitative research. Okely notes that

'After fieldwork, the material found in notebooks, in transcripts and even in contemporary written sources is only a guide and trigger. The anthropologist writer draws also on the totality of the experience, parts of which may not, cannot be cerebrally written down at the time. It is recorded in memory, body and all the senses'. Okely (1994:21)

Both my participant observation and case studies have been total experiences, inextricably linked with my professional career. I alone have undertaken the research, gathering a unique base of data from a social world in a particular state at particular points in time. It would be quite impossible for an independent observer to replicate the study. Inevitably, the findings draw on my own judgement and experience and I cannot contend that the work, although reflexive, has been entirely objective. One of the reasons, however, that I have published as I have gone along is to allow independent observers, whether academic referees or practitioners, to reflect on my various analyses and to determine whether or not they make sense to them.

The second reliability dimension is one of time. This refers to whether the results of an investigation would be replicated in an identical study carried out at a later time. In the case of risk in PAFs, my general findings have so far withstood the test of time. My Cultural Theory ideas first argued in 1996 (Frosdick 1996a) are still being accepted as part of an academic course in 2006.

For case studies, Yin (1994:36) notes that 'the emphasis [for reliability testing] is on doing the *same* case over again, not on 'replicating' the results of one case by doing another case study' (notwithstanding that the latter serves as evidence of validity). This is difficult in any management of risk context. Effective risk management serves over time to reduce identified risks, whilst changes in the external environment mean that new risks arise, some of which could not have previously been foreseen. Doing the same case over again is simply impracticable. I have, however, sought in all my cases to followed my risk consultancy service description. Yin (1994:63) suggests that the use of such a case study protocol is 'a major tactic in increasing the reliability of case study research'.

Yin also advocates the use of a formal case study database to enhance reliability. This is also a feature of openness in research. The base of data collected during the research should, subject to the appropriate safeguards, be open for inspection by the critical reader and for secondary data analysis by other researchers. Similarly, the methods chosen should be openly set out for examination by the reader. I have set out in some detail the methods adopted for this research. I have the explained the rationale for the approach adopted, openly acknowledging the difficulties encountered and even the partial failure experienced with access. A great deal of the data and findings are already in the public domain, having been published as the research has progressed. Other data and analysis have been included in reports to clients.

My computer has a separate folder for each case, and each folder was backed up onto disk. The relevant data from each case is gathered together into a Microsoft Access® database. The base of data thus exists in electronic formats in my office, although I do not underestimate the difficulties another researcher would have had in trawling through it all. All paper records were shredded as confidential waste subsequent to the award of my doctorate.

For the research evidence to be valid, it should properly represent what it is intended to represent. Research validity may be tested in three separate ways: namely construct validity, internal validity and external validity. Construct validity considers whether the correct operational measures have been selected for the concepts being studied. Lack of demonstrable objectivity means that this is problematic for qualitative research. Yin (1994) however suggests that construct validity in case study research may be enhanced by drawing on multiple sources of evidence, by seeking to build a chain of evidence and by having the draft findings reviewed by key informants.

I have sought to apply these three tactics to both my main areas of study. My data and method triangulation in risk in PAFs and multiple case study approach in the police business both qualify as multiple sources of evidence. My use of ongoing and incremental dissemination of the research and multiple replication logic (for case studies) equates with the building of a chain of evidence. The use of key informants for review purposes is apparent in my exposure of ideas in conference papers, in the validation of my academic course and in my experience of Quality Review as part of the PRINCE2 (Projects Run in a Controlled Environment) project management method (CCTA 1998; OGC 2002a) in use throughout my consultancy business.

Internal validity, i.e. the tracing of causal connections between events, is not relevant for a qualitative pre-experimental research design such as mine and I cannot claim any evidence of such validity. The question of external validity, i.e. establishing to what extent my findings can be generalised, is addressed in Chapter Eight.

Denzin and Lincoln suggest the concept of triangulation as 'an alternative to validation' (2000: 5). There are different types of triangulation. Hammersley and Atkinson (1995) refer to data sources, researchers and techniques. Denzin (1978) goes further, noting that triangulation can involve multiple data sources, multiple methods, multiple observers, multiple theoretical perspectives, or, in the case of 'multiple triangulation' – 'the most refined goal any investigation can achieve' (Denzin 1978:304) – various combinations of data sources, methods, observers or theories. This research draws on theories of risk and risk perception, on Cultural Theory and on grounded theory. It has used multiple data sources from two research settings. It has used multiple methods – participant observation, interviews, documentary analysis and case studies. It has even used multiple observers[8]. The construct validity of this research is therefore additionally supported by this use of multiple triangulation.

Finally, then, it should be accepted that any research has its limitations. These arise for two main reasons. First, there may be perfectly sound reasons for policy makers to be guided by political or economic considerations rather than research findings. I have to, indeed have had to, accept that not all my clients will be persuaded of the need to involve all four social solidarities in a risk analysis. For example, in 1999 I undertook a risk assessment for a police client who chose, for political reasons and against my own recommendation, not to involve the Police Federation and trade unions in the work. But these 'missing' stakeholders provide valuable evidence for the discussion of the cases.

Second, and perhaps more fundamentally, almost all research is open to criticisms regarding its methods and thus the validity and reliability of its results. No theory can cover everything and no book, however comprehensive, can provide more than a partial view of its research setting(s). Nobody can either know or find out everything. Nor can anyone hope to be proved right. Research can be shown to be wrong or not wrong. But you can never be sure you are actually right. Something can always come along to surprise you at a later stage. Whatever addition to knowledge my research is able to make, it is humbling to reflect that the best I can hope for is to be 'not wrong' for a while.

SIGNIFICANCE OF THE RESEARCH

The grounded theory and consequent Cultural Theory based approach to risk assessment and risk management are presented through two new methodologies in Chapter Eight. The first is a refined management consultancy approach to undertaking risk assessment and risk management. The approach is generic and, it is suggested, lends itself to widespread practical application both within and beyond my two research settings. The

---

[8] Through the use of associates for data collection.

second is the consultancy-led development of a project risk training course which I was contracted (after winning a competitive tender) to develop and deliver for a major UK public sector organisation.

There are two main reasons why these outputs from the research make a significant and original contribution to the body of knowledge. First, they meet the requirements for originality. Second, they work and thus offer new evidence-based practice.

The claim to originality may be assessed using the six-point framework proposed by Hart (2000:24). The work has been produced using my own facilities. I have carried out the vast majority of the empirical research myself and acknowledged any secondary data analysis. The research is authentic i.e. my own work and of undisputed origin. The findings are the result of thought, i.e. the grounded theory set out in Chapter Eight. The work has not been done before, is without imitation and is therefore new. This assertion may be substantiated with reference to three trawls of the relevant literature.

First, there are no references to either of my research settings in the sources which contain extensive references to previous applications of Cultural Theory (see Thompson *et al.* 1990, Thompson *et al.* 1999, GG-CT 1999, Mamadouh 1999, Hoppe 2002 and Ney 2003). Second, there are no known references to Cultural Theory in any of the risk in sports grounds literature (other than those which I have published). Third, there are no references to Cultural Theory in the key sources for the wider body of project risk knowledge. These are a classified bibliography of project risk research (Williams 1995); the risk references (for example Chapman and Ward 1997) within the project management body of knowledge (Dixon 2000); and the risk-related publications produced by OGC (CCTA 1994a, 1995a, 1995b, OGC 2002c, 2004).

I have not sought to 'prove' that Cultural Theory 'works' through orthodox 'experimentalism'. Rather my ambition is to have shown that, on realist evaluation i.e. on plausible reflection, applied Cultural Theory has worked in the two settings for the research. Thus, as a theory of the middle-range, Cultural Theory ought to work in some other settings too. It is helpful supporting evidence to know that some academic colleagues and client organisations are also convinced of this. They have variously peer reviewed my work, invited me to present papers, commissioned repeat consultancy business, learned how to apply the method themselves and even awarded a competitive training contract, all on the basis that applied Cultural Theory is good evidence-based practice.

CHAPTER THREE: REFLEXIVE HISTORY

SUMMARY

This Chapter presents a 'natural history' of the research process leading up to the submission of this book. The chapter opens with a discussion of 'reflexivity'. It then sets out the author's personal biography and shows how this links into the evolution of the research. It concludes by briefly explaining how the author does his work as a consultant.

REFLEXIVITY

Chapter Two discussed the qualitative 'grounded theory' approach adopted for this investigation over the course of a personal journey which began in October 1992 and which reaches its destination with the publication of this book. Following Whyte (1961), the discussion showed my complete immersion in the two research settings and how the emerging theory grew out of an iterative process of immersion, reflection and development.

Hammersley and Atkinson (1995) call this approach 'reflexivity', which they define as representing,

> A rejection of the idea that social research is, or can be, carried out in some autonomous realm that is insulated from the wider society and from the particular biography of the researcher, in such a way that its findings can be unaffected by social processes and personal characteristics (1995:16).

Hammersley and Atkinson note that there is no conflict between reflexivity and realism. Social research is no different from our everyday activities in the sense that,

> We can work with what 'knowledge' we have, while recognizing that it may be erroneous and engaging in systematic inquiry where doubt seems justified; and in doing so we can still make the reasonable assumption that we are trying to describe phenomena as they are, and not merely how we perceive them or how we would like them to be (*ibid.* p.18).

They conclude that, 'we are part of the social world we study, and that there is no escape from reliance on common-sense knowledge and methods of investigation' (*ibid.* p.21).

Reflexivity is an approach which has commanded growing interest in social research, particularly by researchers who include personal biographies or 'natural histories' of their research within the research report. Hammersley and Atkinson (1995:22) confirm the emergence of this tradition by citing 20 examples of such 'natural histories'. Thus who I am and how my intellectual journey has brought me to this point is significant to the interpretation of the data and analysis presented in the remaining Chapters of this book. The research has been highly personalised. It has involved extensive participant observation, 'action science' case studies and the consequent discovery of grounded theory. Since I am integral to the research, a personal biography is the appropriate first step in presenting the data and analysis for this book. The biography will demonstrate how my personal journey is inextricably linked with the research process.

PERSONAL BIOGRAPHY[9]

My father first took me to Griffin Park on 18 March 1967. Along with 6339 other people, I saw Brentford beat Rochdale by four goals to nil. I was nine years old and fascinated by the spectacle: the stadium, the sense of belonging to the crowd, the colour, noise and smells, the excitement of the play, the whole atmosphere of the place. So began a lifelong interest in football, crowds and sports grounds. I continued to visit Brentford regularly throughout my youth and, later on, in my bachelor years having joined the police service in London.

From the early 1980s, I became involved in the policing of large crowds. Whilst on duty at a rally on 11 May 1985, I stood outside a television showroom and watched in horror as over fifty people burned to death in a grandstand in Bradford. I was deeply touched by what I saw. My feelings were compounded by the stadium disaster at Heysel in Belgium later that month and by the Hillsborough stadium disaster in Sheffield in April 1989. Later that year, I returned to Brentford as a police inspector and saw at first hand the policy responses to that disaster. I thus developed a passion for safety and security in PAFs which is deep-rooted in my love of football and my horror of stadium disasters.

In the summer of 1992, I met Gerald Mars as part of the admissions process to study for a Masters degree at the Cranfield University School of Management. From October 1992 to October 1993, I looked in detail at how sporting events were managed. I wanted to understand more about disasters and how they might be better prevented. My dissertation (Frosdick 1993a) sought to show how Cultural Theory could be used to inform a holistic approach to public safety risk management in stadia and sporting venues. At

---

[9] The personal biography is partly derived from the preface to Frosdick and Walley (1997).

that time, I had no notion of continuing the research, although I retained all my data sources as a matter of good practice. This was a fortunate decision since it allowed for the data to be revisited and further analysed later on.

With several fellow students, I dabbled with the idea that Cultural Theory could be used as the underpinning for a consultancy business. Although I did not realise it at that time, this was the origin of the research question for this book. We held a couple of meetings, but matters never progressed and I returned to the police service in November 1993. Again, at this stage, I had no intentions of continuing my research, but worked in a variety of research and consultancy roles for the National Criminal Intelligence Service, the Police Foundation (see Irving, Faulkner, Frosdick and Topping 1996) and the Metropolitan Police Service.

In 1995, I finally had the chance to put my nascent Cultural Theory ideas into practice, albeit in a quite different setting from PAFs. Whilst still a serving police officer I became the risk adviser on a project to develop a computer software application for the police service. This led to programme and project risk work with the National Strategy for Police Information Systems (NSPIS), where I first sought to apply Cultural Theory as a practical consultancy tool (see Frosdick and Odell 1996). This was thus the source of the development of the second research setting and this work, which continued for several years until July 1999, forms part of the analysis presented in Chapter Six. In 1995, however, I still had no clear idea that I had restarted the personal journey which would lead to this book.

In parallel, during 1995 I became involved with the church and became a Christian. This was a significant and life-changing event since I could not reconcile my previous harsh and arbitrary style of policing with the more Christ-like behaviours I now wished to adopt. After careful and prayerful reflection, I decided to leave the police to earn my living as a writer, researcher and consultant in risk. In June 1995 I formed a business[10], left the police service and took up a contracting position with the Centre for Public Services Management and Research (CPSMR) at Staffordshire University. In addition to the change of lifestyle and career, this decision was also to lead to the formal start of my doctoral studies, to the continuation of the research in the first setting and to the development of the research in the second setting.

At CPSMR, I enrolled as a doctoral student. My work in this role had its main focus on the completion of a taught course in social research methods. However my research in the first setting now also began to re-remerge

---

[10] IWI Associates Ltd – 'IWI' stands for 'independence with integrity'.

through my establishment of the CPSMR Safety in Sports and Leisure Programme. This was intended to involve both academic research and management consultancy in a climate of risk as blame and accountability (Frosdick 1996c; 1996d; 1997b; 1998a). The consultancy aspect, which I had envisaged as a source of research data for my doctorate, did not develop as I had hoped. Although I did manage to win and complete an assignment to prepare a Training Package for Stewarding at Football Grounds (Frosdick 1996e; 1996f; Frosdick and Sidney 1996b), it quickly became apparent that there was no interest in the sports grounds market for my Cultural Theory consultancy services. I almost managed to negotiate access to one Premier League club but the effort foundered when, after negotiations spread over several months, my contact changed jobs. As Chapter Two explained earlier, this would require some compromise in my research design.

However the research aspect continued. It involved a secondary analysis of the data collected for my Masters degree, additional fieldwork, further analysis and quite extensive publication of the results. The secondary analysis was first published in refereed journals (Frosdick 1995a; 1995b) and the ideas were then further developed through conference papers (for example Frosdick 1996b; 1996c) and journalism (for example Frosdick 1996h). Finally, the research was refined for publication in an academic book (Frosdick and Walley 1997).

Since my status at CPSMR was that of a fees-for-services contractor, it was necessary for me to bring in my agreed share of fee income. Thus I brought the NSPIS work under the CPSMR contractual banner. I further developed my work on applying Cultural Theory in the second research setting and also completed five of the consultancy assignments included in the case studies analysed in Chapters Six to Eight.

Thus my 18 months at CPSMR brought three early benefits to my research: they provided me with training in social research methods; they re-started my research in the first research setting of PAFs and they initiated my research in the second research setting of police programmes and projects. My research question was thus beginning to become clearer.

In late 1996, it was planned that I would leave CPSMR because the Centre was not breaking even and needed to reduce its costs. I was a fees-for-services contractor not a permanent employee and so my contract was to be allowed to lapse. I needed to take the research elsewhere and met up again with Gerald Mars, who was then affiliated to the University of Bradford Management Centre.

I was also appointed as an Honorary Fellow at Bradford, where the fieldwork, analysis and publication work in the PAFs setting continued (for example see Frosdick 1997l; 1998c). This provided the source material both for the analysis presented in Chapters Four and Five and for a new Certificate of Higher Education in Stadia and Arena Safety. I tried to develop this at Bradford but without success. Accordingly, I took the idea to other colleagues at the University of Portsmouth, where I developed that programme as an associate during 1998 (see Frosdick 1999a).

My departure from CPSMR had little impact on either my business or my clients since I simply took my clients under another umbrella. My company thus joined Redfern Consultancy as an associate contractor. My research question having now become clear, I developed a range of risk consultancy services, theoretically underpinned by Cultural Theory, and set about marketing these in the British police service (see Redfern Consultancy 1997 and Appendix A). Between January 1997 and November 1999, I completed three-quarters of the assignments analysed in Chapters Six to Eight. The services were refined as I learned what I was doing and this evolutionary process is reflected in the case study vignettes presented in Chapter Seven.

In autumn 1999, the consultancy market began to go slack. Anecdotal evidence from my clients suggested that organisations were not engaging in new work until the Millennium date change was out of the way. At the same time, Redfern Consultancy was taken over. The business development director with whom I worked was made redundant and so I ended my relationship with Redfern. This hiatus in the market and change of circumstances brought my data collection to a temporary halt. It also meant that my company was no longer earning any fee income. Given my associate relationship with the Institute of Criminal Justice Studies at the University of Portsmouth, I applied and was selected for an academic vacancy, taking up the post from 1 January 2000.

In April 2000, I was invited to follow Gerald Mars from Bradford to the University of North London – now London Metropolitan. The transfer process took several months and was finally approved in December 2000, backdated to 1 January 1997. However I had restarted the data collection from April 2000 onwards with additional case studies from new business won under its own brand by my company, which I continued to run in parallel with my academic post. Up until 2004 I continued the case study data collection, coding and analysis process and developed the case study database.

I then moved on to the analysis of the police case study material presented in Chapters Seven and Eight. This required careful application of the reflexivity approach and was a drawn out and time-consuming process. In July 2004, I submitted a draft doctoral thesis to my Director of Studies and, as an academic, had the advantage of being able to ask five friends and colleagues who already had Doctorates to also read and comment on the draft. I collated the various feedback during the remainder of 2004, rewrote various sections and chapters as I had been advised and thereafter prepared the thesis for examination. I was awarded my doctorate in September 2005 and subsequently converted the thesis into this book.

DOING CONSULTANCY WORK

This book is about me as a specific, historical social agent and so my personal biography is an integral part of the research. However much of this book, particularly Chapters Six to Eight, is also about how I operate doing personal, proprietary, original and idiosyncratic management consultancy work. Thus a brief explanation of how I do my work as a consultant is also important in understanding the data and analysis for this book.

Margerison (1995) has identified three stages and twelve steps in the consulting process. The three main stages are appraisal, assessment and application. There are four steps within the appraisal stage, namely: contact, preparation, contracting and contract negotiation. The assessment stage comprises the four steps of data collection, analysis diagnosis, data feedback and data discussion. The four steps in the application stage are proposals, decision, implementation and review. These stages and steps provide a useful framework within which I can set out how I do my consultancy work.

The Appraisal Stage

This stage equates to the task '100 – Organise the Project' and its sub-activities set out in my case study protocol and coding frame (see Appendix A).

Step 1 – Contact

This step involves the initial approach made by one side or the other and any initial discussion about the problem the client faces and the opportunity this presents for the consultant.

I have rarely done any active marketing of my services. Only in a handful of cases have new leads been provided by an 'umbrella' business such as CPSMR or Redfern Consultancy. The vast majority of my clients have been repeat or referral business. Thus the initial approach has tended to be a telephone call or email with the offer of a new opportunity, either from an existing client or from someone known to an existing client. A few of my clients have come from the PAFs industry but the majority have come from the police service.

In the case of an existing client, I will jump straight to step 2. In the case of a new client, I will sometimes go and see them to have an initial discussion to simply get to know them before arranging a subsequent meeting to move to step 2. I will let new client have copies of my service descriptions and a copy of my Curriculum Vitae.

Step 2 – Preparation

This step goes beyond the initial contact and involves a more detailed scoping of the problem.

There have been a few cases where an existing client and I know each other well and their telephone call inviting some repeat business results in me adapting and sending a proposal. Following contact, however, I will almost always go and see the client face to face to scope the work and gather the necessary information for a proposal. In the case of the risk-related cases in this book, this has involved the use of my protocol and coding frame (see Appendix A), which represents a more detailed menu of the tasks and activities set out at a high level in the service descriptions.

When scoping work with clients, I always work backwards from desired outcomes, through the outputs needed to achieve those outcomes, to the throughputs needed to deliver those outcomes, to the inputs needed to process the throughputs.

Some cases have involved a formal presentation to the client team, others a more informal discussion around a table and the majority of cases a one-to-one meeting. In a number of cases, this step has involved explaining Cultural Theory and its use for stakeholder analysis to the client. These aspects are covered in more detail in Chapter Six[11] and Chapter Eight[12].

I specialise in single tender work below a public sector organisation's ceiling for competitive tendering and so am rarely required to wait for the client to issue a specification and formal invitation to tender. Having scoped the work, my style is to always sketch out with the client the number of days consultancy involved in the work and to explain my requirements for fees and expenses. I am thus able to give the client a very good idea of the costs

---

[11] See the sections on 'Explaining Cultural Theory' and 'Stakeholder Analyses'.

[12] See the Cross-Case Report.

before I leave the room. I also always negotiate with the client the required timescales for the work.

Step 3 – Contracting

This is the formal submission of an outline proposal.

Having met with the client and agreed the specific tasks and activities required from within the protocol (Appendix A), the next step is to prepare a proposal. In most cases, this has been a simple letter setting out the desired outcomes, outputs, throughputs and inputs, together with a cost and time schedule.

Step 4 – Contract Negotiation

This is where the proposal is negotiated and the formal contract agreed.

Because the work has been almost all been single-tender, this step is simply the client's acceptance of the proposal. This may be by email, letter or the issue of a purchase order. Sometimes the latter takes time, so I am usually quite happy to start the work before the procurement has been resolved. This is particularly the case with an existing client. But even with a new client, I have never done work for which I have not subsequently been paid.

The Assessment Stage

This stage equates to tasks 200 to 700 inclusive and their sub-activities set out in my case study protocol and coding frame (see Appendix A).

Step 5 – Data Collection

Data are now gathered using an appropriate methodological approach.

Absolutely key within this step is the application of Cultural Theory's requisite variety condition at a stakeholder analysis session with the client[13]. As was explained in Chapter Two and as we shall see in Chapters Six to Eight, I am deploying Cultural Theory as organisation theory. Where, I will ask, are Cultural Theory's four forms of social solidarity to be found in my client's particular organisational context?

This focus on group relations places my consultancy work very much in the tradition of the Tavistock Institute of Human Relations. Even today 'the Tavistock' has its own consultancy focus on matters of 'inter-organisational relationships' and 'problems of organisation' (see Tavistock Insitute 2002).

---

[13] For a detailed explanation, see the sections on 'Explaining Cultural Theory' and 'Stakeholder Analyses' in Chapter Six.

In the post war years, however, 'the Tavistock' developed methods of 'action research' which were precursors to the consultancy industry. They developed the theory of socio-technical systems – one legendary study being of the Yorkshire coal industry (Trist and Bamforth 1951). The essential notion of socio-technical systems theory is that you cannot *maximise* new technology without destabilising the social system and so causing productivity to actually fall. The management task, then, is to *optimise*.

This notion has underpinned many modern participative management developments. My own consultancy efforts to construct what Mary Douglas (1986) would call 'clumsy institutions' follow clearly in the footsteps of this tradition. I use Cultural Theory to disaggregate an organisational context to identify participants to participate in risk assessment and risk management processes around programmes and projects to develop new police systems.

I have used one of two main methods in my data collection for the risk identification and risk estimation processes. The first main method has been a set of structured interviews with identified representatives of the stakeholder groups and the second main method a workshop attended by those stakeholder representatives.

The interview method has had the advantage of simultaneously providing a full data set for subsequent analysis, however it has the disadvantage of not yielding any ethnographic data on the interactions between the different stakeholder groups.

The workshop method is the flip side of the coin. It has the benefit of providing some ethnographic data, but contemporaneous field notes have been impossible because of course I have been facilitating the meeting and not observing it. Thus I have had to rely on later recollection of particularly memorable comments or interactions.

Step 6 – Analysis Diagnosis

This is where the consultant analyses the data and plans how to feed the analysis back to the client.

In the case of the workshop approach to data collection, I have often written the risk analysis up 'live' by typing straight into a template document in my laptop computer whilst I am facilitating. I type the perceived threat in as it is raised in the plenary discussion and then type in the estimates of probability and consequences as they are decided through processes of individual voting, discussions of differences in perceptions and aggregation. My laptop computer is connected to a video projector and screen thus the workshop participants physically see the analysis emerging at the same time as the data is being collected. Without being immodest, this is a process which requires considerable skill on my part.

In the case of the interview approach, the analysis will involve taking the individual threats perceived by the interviewees and coding them into categories. In cases where I have employed associates to assist with the work[14], this process has been undertaken with the relevant associate colleague, because they understand the meaning behind the data. In other cases where I alone collected the data, I have done the analysis alone. The coding process stops when I am satisfied that the categories are mutually exclusive. The next steps will establish whether they are also as jointly exhaustive as is possible in risk-related work.

Step 7 – Data Feedback

This is where the data and analysis are presented to the client. The presentation may be oral or in writing.

I will always prepare a written report, usually in the form of a draft risk log, which sets out the risk analysis without the risk management (which comes later on). I am keen on respondent validation and find that interviewees and workshop participants usually want to see the results of the work. So I always ask the client for permission to circulate the analysis to them. This may happen either at this feedback stage, where I ask them to comment on the analysis; at the very end of the work, when I provide a copy of the report for their information; or indeed at both stages.

During this respondent/participant validation process, I always deal with the 'jointly exhaustive' issue by asking people to comment on whether they think all the reasonably foreseeable risks have been captured.

I will always email the client a copy of the report. The findings can sometimes be a bit bruising for the client and I want to make sure they understand what people are saying before we go on to discuss their response. So I will usually also take the report to a meeting with the client and take them through the research process and findings line by line.

Step 8 – Data Discussion

This is where the client reflects on the implications of the data and analysis.

---

[14] Cases where associates were involved in the data collection are clearly identified in Chapter Seven.

In the case of a risk analysis, I am not asking a client whether they agree with it – I am telling them what people's perceptions have been[15]. My experience has been that, having been educated about theories of risk perception, clients will accept the analysis presented to them. Again, I am looking for confirmation from the client that, from their own perceptions of the risks, the coding appears to meet the 'mutually exclusive' and 'jointly exhaustive' requirements of classification.

It is during this step that I will facilitate the client through a decision-making process to make the risk evaluation decision (see tasks 800 to 900 in Appendix A). This will determine which risks will require management action and which can be tolerated. Typically, the decision rules will be that high risks must be managed, medium risks may be managed and that low risks will be tolerated.

The Application Stage

Step 9 – Proposals

This step is closely linked with the 'data discussion' and is where any options or proposals for taking the work forward are discussed.

I frequently make the point to clients that I do not 'do' risk assessments. Similarly, I do not 'tell' clients what they ought to do about the risks. My role is to provide theoretically underpinned process, supported by research, analysis, facilitation and drafting skills, to draw out stakeholder perceptions and help negotiate solutions.

Accordingly, this step represents tasks 1000 to 1300 in Appendix A, whereby proposals for risk management controls and contingency plans are devised at facilitated sessions. These sometimes involve the client alone, sometimes a larger group of stakeholders but typically three to six key players. I always try to get the client to involve stakeholders from Cultural Theory's three active constituencies. An important part of facilitating these proposals is to get the session to identify a named individual who is the appropriate person to take responsibility for implementation.

Subsequently, the complete risk log will be put through some form of assurance process, either informally by circulation for comments or using a formal quality review process.

---

[15] For a detailed example, see the discussion of the risk evaluation process in the NSPIS case study in Chapter Six.

Step 10 – Decision

This step is where the client decides what is to happen next.

Having got to the point where the client is satisfied with the risk analysis and with the proposals for risk management, I always ask the client to formally 'sign off' the report. This means that they are formally sanctioning the implementation of the agreed risk management plans by the persons identified as being responsible for implementation.

Step 11 – Implementation

This is where the agreed proposals are implemented.

In cases where the client has an in-house risk manager or programme/project support office staff who will take responsibility for overseeing the implementation, my role may end at this point. In other cases, the client will commission me to communicate the risks and controls to the responsible persons and negotiate with them an implementation plan[16]. This represents task 1400 – 'Undertake Risk Monitoring' – in Appendix A.

Step 12 – Review

This final step takes place after the work has ended so that both sides can reflect on how the work has gone.

I do not use formal processes for determining the extent of client satisfaction with my consultancy work (although I do use evaluation methods for my training work). I informally solicit feedback on the work from the client and maintain personal contact over time. For me, repeat business, referral and willingness to be a reference site is the best evidence that a client has been content with my work.

Because risks change as a result of being managed and because new risks come along over time, my consultancy work also includes within the concept of 'review' the risk review processes outlined under tasks 1500 to 1800 in Appendix A. These essentially involve re-running Margerison's assessment and application stages but with the original report as the starting point rather than a blank canvas.

---

[16] For a detailed example, see the discussion of the initial and subsequent risk monitoring processes in the NSPIS case study in Chapter Six.

CONCLUSION

Having now fully set the scene with a review of theories of risk, a detailed exposition of applied theory and methods for this research, a personal biography and an explanation of how I do my work as a consultant, this book will now move on to the main data and analysis chapters. Chapters Four and Five deal with the first research setting of PAFs and Chapters Six to Eight with the second research setting of police programmes and projects.

CHAPTER FOUR: PUBLIC ASSEMBLY FACILITIES RISK – PART I

SUMMARY

This Chapter sets out the first part of a Cultural Theory analysis of the British risk in Public Assembly Facilities (PAFs) industry. The analysis is presented in three main sections and begins by introducing the research setting. The research covers the period between the nadir of the Hillsborough disaster in 1989 and the present and it is emphasised from the outset that this research is not another discourse about football hooliganism. PAFs are defined and the particular focus of risk as danger and blame is explained. The history of PAFs disasters and the regulatory responses are detailed and the significance of the setting justified as a subject for research. Finally in the first section, the impact which the research has had on the setting is discussed.

The second section summarises the data sources for the research. The third section notes that the history of 'regulation by crisis' in the British PAFs industry has failed to prevent successive disasters and continued near misses. To reduce the risks, there is a need to better understand why the mistakes and misunderstandings leading to such incidents actually occur. Such understanding can be informed by applying Cultural Theory. This section uses Cultural Theory to analyse ethnography from and literature relating to risk in British PAFs. The analysis reveals the conflicting risk perceptions of individualist clubs, hierarchical regulators, long suffering fatalist spectators and their more egalitarian colleagues in supporter and local resident pressure groups.

THE RESEARCH SETTING

Public Assembly Facilities: Beyond Football Hooliganism[17]

PAFs are venues of extremes. On the one hand, they are the setting for some of the most exciting, enjoyable and often profitable events in the world. On the other, they have been the scene of many terrible disasters. Managing PAFs is a highly complex problem. It includes questions of architectural and engineering design, operational management, technological sophistication, health and safety, public order, customer care and an understanding of how people behave in crowds. The central theme of these subjects is one of management of risk. Designing, planning and managing a facility is

---

[17] This section is derived from Frosdick (1997a).

fundamentally all about identifying the things that could go operationally wrong, working out which things matter the most and putting in place control measures to design or manage them out before they happen.

As we saw in the conclusion to Chapter Two, there is a particular focus in this setting on risk as danger and on blame. PAF managers have a moral and legal duty of care towards participants, performers, spectators and staff alike. They have a statutory duty to deal with risks to the health and safety of people who might be affected by the operation of their facility. Official guidance documents make it clear that that responsibility for safety lies at all times with PAFs management (see Department of National Heritage and Scottish Office 1997; Football League *et al.* 1998; Health and Safety Executive 2000). Following a number of high profile legal cases, there is growing awareness of the civil and even criminal liability of PAFs management in the event of a disaster precipitated by negligent preparations. Dealing with safety hazards and the risks to which they give rise is thus an integral part of PAFs management.

Because it is football, specifically British football, which has suffered the disasters and had to learn the resultant lessons (see Elliott and Smith 1993; Elliott, Frosdick and Smith 1997), it is unsurprising that the research focuses on the experience of football and British football grounds. But the wider setting for the research is in an international world of stadia, arenas and sports grounds in general. These may be collectively referred to as 'public assembly facilities', which, according to Wootton and Stevens,

> 'have a number of characteristic features which require special consideration in their planning, design, management and operation. They ...
> - provide amenities for spectator viewing of sporting and non-sporting events;
> - must be accessible, comfortable and safe for a range of users and participants;
> - attract large number of spectators attending events of relatively short duration;
> - are managed to ensure the safe movement of people in a smooth, unimpeded, fashion in the time before, during and after the event;
> - provide pleasurable experiences in an enjoyable and safe way;
> - provide a range of ancillary services and amenities to meet the needs and demands of spectators, participants and promoters;
> - provide environments to encourage the highest standards for sporting participants within the criteria required by the regulations of that sport;

- may be open to the elements, or may be covered or enclosed into total or in part;
- involve an ensemble of features creating a sense of place and identity;
- contribute to the wider community, through economic, social and cultural benefits;
- adopt a responsible approach towards community aspirations and concerns;
- have the potential to be used for a range of sporting and non-sporting events on single or multiple use basis.' (Wootton and Stevens 1995:6)

Toft and Reynolds (1997) have shown that, since disasters within any single industry (even football) are low frequency events, thus each industry needs to look beyond itself to find the lessons which will enable it to learn the active foresight necessary for improved management. Thus the experience of British football should be a source of useful learning for both for PAFs management in general and for other management of risk settings.

As Inglis points out, 'It cannot be emphasised enough, if emphasis were needed, that the death of 96 Liverpool fans at Hillsborough on 15 April 1989 was an absolute turning point' (Inglis 1996:7). Thus the research has as its starting point the nadir of Hillsborough in 1989 as the catalyst for change and subsequent improvement.

Some seven years later, the 1996 European Football Championships were successfully staged in England in a way that nobody could have envisaged even a few years previously. For their (failed) bid to stage the World Cup in 2006, the Football Association (1999) were able to boast that English stadia were the finest in the world. Thus the research has as its end point where the management of risk in PAFs had got to from 1996 and onwards through to 2004.

Having thus established what this research setting is about, I want to emphasise what it is not about. This is not more research about football hooliganism.

When I originally entered this research setting, I quickly discovered that 'it has become almost impossible to research into the regulation of football without being seen to be an integral part of the discourses about 'football hooliganism'' (Redhead 1991). The risk in sports grounds debate has been dominated by football hooliganism, the treatment of which bears all the hallmarks of the type of moral panic described by Cohen (1987). This moral panic has arisen for a combination of amplification factors, including over-reporting by the media (see Murphy, Williams and Dunning 1990:96-128), police over-emphasis (see Bale 1993:28-29; Frosdick 1997a:5-6) and excessive academic research.

> 'It is generally agreed that British football hooliganism has probably been over-researched. Despite a general decline in violence at British football matches, the phenomenon still attracts a disproportionate amount of research activity' (Carnibella *et al.* 1996:6).

The various discourses have been extensively reviewed elsewhere (see Dunning, Murphy and Williams 1988:18-31; Canter, Comber and Uzzell 1989:107-118; Hobbs and Robins 1991; Williams 1991; Giulianotti 1994; Carnibella *et al.* 1996). I have also published on the subject (see Frosdick 1997a; 2002c; 2002f; 2002g), including a co-authored monograph (Frosdick and Marsh 2005). I do not propose to cover the same ground in this book.

The Significance of the Setting for Research[18]

Football Ground Disasters

Throughout the twentieth century, considerable numbers of people have been killed or injured in sports and leisure disasters of all kinds. British stadia however, and particularly British football grounds, have been strongly represented in the history of such disasters. Evidence of at least forty four British-related incidents involving deaths and multiple injuries up until 1989, the watershed of Lord Justice Taylor's reports into the Hillsborough disaster (Home Office 1989; 1990a), have been gathered together from several sources (FSADC 1991a:153-157; Wyllie 1992; Elliott 1996; McGibbon 1996; Inglis 1996:9; FLA 1996). This catalogue of British football disasters is shown in Table 4.1.

Table 4.1: Disasters and Incidents Involving British Stadia or Supporters
(Source: Elliott, Frosdick and Smith 1997:13-14)

Venue	Year	Fatalities/Injuries	Disaster/Incident Type
Valley Parade (Bradford) #	1888	1 dead, 3 injured	Railings Collapse
Blackburn	1896	5 injured	Stand Collapse
Ibrox (Glasgow)	1902	26 dead, 550 injured	Collapsed Temporary Stand

---

[18] This section is derived from Frosdick (1995a), Frosdick (1998a) and Elliott, Frosdick and Smith 1997.

Brentford	1907	multiple injuries	Fence Collapse
Leicester	1907	multiple injuries	Barrier Collapse
Hillsborough (Sheffield)	1914	70-80 injured	Wall Collapse
Charlton	1923	24 injured	Crowd Crush
Wembley	1923	1000+ injured	Crowd Crush
Burnley	1924	1 dead	Crowd Crush
Manchester (City)	1926	unknown injuries	Crowd Crush
Huddersfield	1932	100 injured	Crowd Crush
Huddersfield	1937	4 injured	Crowd Crush
Watford	1937	unknown injuries	Crowd Crush
Fulham	1938	unknown injuries	Crowd Crush
Rochdale#	1939	1 dead, 17 injured	Roof Collapse
Burnden Park (Bolton)	1946	33 dead, 400 injured	Crowd Crush
Shawfield (Clyde)	1957	1 dead, 50 injured	Barrier Collapse
Ibrox (Glasgow)	1961	2 dead, 50 injured	Crowd Crush Stairway 13
Oldham	1962	15 injured	Barrier Collapse
Arsenal	1963	100 injured	Crushing
Port Vale	1964	1 dead, 2 injured	Fall/Crushing
Roker Park (Sunderland)	1964	80+ injured	Crowd Crush
Anfield (Liverpool)	1966	31 injured	Crowd Crush
Leeds	1967	32 injured	Crowd Crush
Ibrox (Glasgow)	1967	8 injured	Crowd Crush Stairway 13
Dunfermline	1968	1 dead, 49 injured	Crowd Crush
Ibrox (Glasgow)	1969	24 injured	Crowd Crush Stairway 13
Ibrox (Glasgow)	1971	66 dead, 145 injured	Crowd Crush Stairway 13
Carlisle	1971	5 injured	Barrier Collapse
Oxford	1971	25 injured	Wall Collapse
Stoke	1971	46 injured	Crowd Crush
Wolverhampton	1972	80 injured	Barrier Collapse
Arsenal	1972	42 injured	Crowd Crush
Lincoln	1975	4 injured	Wall Collapse
Leyton Orient	1978	30 injured	Barrier/Wall Collapse
Middlesborough	1980	2 dead	Gate Collapse
Hillsborough (Sheffield)	1981	38 injured	Crowd Crush
Walsall	1984	20 injured	Wall Collapse
Bradford	1985	54 dead	Fire
Birmingham	1985	1 dead, 20 injured	Disorder/Wall Collapse
Heysel (Brussels)	1985	38 dead, 400+ injured	Disorder/Wall Collapse
Easter Road (Edinburgh)	1987	150 injured	Crowd Crush
Hillsborough (Sheffield)	1989	95 dead, 400+ injured	Crowd Crush
Middlesborough	1989	19 injured	Crowd Crush

Note that two of the disasters (marked #) occurred in rugby league grounds, whilst one, involving supporters of Liverpool football club, was at Heysel in Belgium. The remainder took place in British football grounds.

Evidence of at least twenty six football disasters outside Britain up until 1996, derived from the same sources, is set out in Table 4.2. With the exception of the tragedies at Heysel and at Bastia in Corsica in 1992, all occurred in what might be described as developing countries.

Table 4.2: Disasters in Football Grounds Outside Britain

(Source: Elliott, Frosdick and Smith 1997:15)

Venue	Year	Fatalities	Disaster Type
Ibague (Colombia)	1961	11 dead, 15 injured	Stand Collapse
Santiago (Chile)	1961	5 dead, 300 injured	Crowd Crush
Lima (Peru)	1964	318 dead, 1000+ injured	Riot
Istanbul (Turkey)	1964	70 injured	Fire
Kayseri (Turkey)	1967	34 dead	Riot
Buenos Aires (Argentina)	1968	74 dead, 150 injured	Disorder/Stampede
Cairo (Egypt)	1974	49 dead, 50 injured	Crowd Crush
Port-au-Prince (Haiti)	1976	6 dead	Disorder/Police Shooting
Piraeus (Greece)	1981	21 dead, 54 injured	Crush/Stampede
San Luis (Brazil)	1982	3 dead, 25 injured	Riot/Police Shooting
Cali (Colombia)	1982	24 dead, 250 injured	Crushing/Stampede
Algiers (Algeria)	1982	10 dead, 500 injured	Roof Collapse
Moscow Spartak (Soviet Union)	1982	69+ dead, 100+ injured	Crowd Crush
Heysel (Belgium)	1985	38 dead, 400 injured	Disorder/Wall Collapse
Mexico City (Mexico)	1985	10 dead, 100+ injured	Crowd Crush
Tripoli (Libya)	1987	20 dead	Unknown
Katmandu (Nepal)	1988	100+ dead, 500 injured	Hailstorm/Stampede
Lagos (Nigeria)	1989	5 dead	Crowd Crush
Mogadishu (Somalia)	1989	7 dead, 18 injured	Riot
Orkney (South Africa)	1991	42 dead, 50 injured	Riot/Stampede
Nairobi (Kenya)	1991	1 dead, 24 injured	Stampede
Rio de Janeiro (Brazil)	1992	50 injured	Fence Collapse

Bastia (Corsica)	1992	17 dead	Temporary Stand Collapse
Free Town (Sierra Leone)	1995	40 injured	Gate Collapse
Lusaka (Zambia)	1996	9 dead, 52 injured	Crowd Crush
Guatemala	1996	80 dead, 150 injured	Crowd Crush

This all suggests that British football up until 1990 had a unique history of disaster and disorder. This prominence has arisen for a variety of historical, economic and social reasons. These include the overall popularity of football as a symbolic form and focus of collective identification (Dunning 1989; Critcher 1991), dilapidated grounds, hooliganism, and poor leadership (Home Office 1989; 1990a), and general neglect of supporters safety and comfort (Taylor I. 1991:12). Crowd pressure, either direct or leading to structural collapses, was the immediate cause of all except the Bradford and Birmingham tragedies. Accumulated refuse caught fire at Bradford, whilst the disorder commonly associated with football was the immediate cause of only the Birmingham disaster.

Ten official reports have been commissioned into safety and order at British football grounds. An analysis of these reports and some subsequent incidents demonstrates the ineffectiveness of the 'legislation by crisis' response to crowd related disasters.

The Shortt Report (Home Office 1924) followed the near disaster at Wembley in 1923 and included recommendations about responsibility, licensing, stewarding and fire safety. Inattention to the two latter were contributory factors at Bradford in 1985. The Moelwyn Hughes Report (Home Office 1946) arose from the Bolton overcrowding disaster. Recommendations about calculating maximum capacities and coordinated counting of numbers admitted were not pursued. Had they been so, the Hillsborough disaster may have been avoided.

The growth of football hooliganism prompted the Chester Report (Department of Education and Science 1968), Harrington (1968) Report and Lang Report (Ministry of Housing and Local Government 1969). Harrington reviewed previous reports and noted that their helpful suggestions had often been ignored. He went on to comment on the lack of legislation covering standards of safety and amenity at grounds. Lang included references to the benefits of closed circuit television (CCTV) and the impact of alcohol on behaviour. The Wheatley Report (Home Office 1972) was prompted by the 1971 Ibrox disaster in Scotland and resulted in legislation requiring safety certificates at designated grounds. The first edition of the 'Green Guide' to

Safety at Sports Grounds was also published. It had been fifty years since Shortt first recommended such action.

The McElhorne Report (Scottish Education Department 1977) was concerned with spectator misbehaviour in Scotland. Recommendations included legislation to control alcohol, spectator segregation, perimeter fencing, CCTV, improved amenities, stewarding, club membership and club community involvement. Set up following disorder at England matches abroad, the Department of the Environment (1984) Working Group repeated similar recommendations for English clubs.

The Popplewell Reports (Home Office 1985; 1986) dealt with the Bradford and Birmingham disasters and the Heysel tragedy in Belgium. Many recommendations echoed the 1977 and 1984 reports. The Football Trust funded the installation of CCTV, the Green Guide was revised and there was considerable legislative activity. The range of grounds and stands requiring safety certification was increased. Exclusion and Restriction Orders were introduced to keep convicted hooligans both away from British grounds and unable to travel to matches abroad. A national membership scheme for fans and the establishment of a National Inspectorate and Review Body were both provided for.

Following the fatal crushing of 95 Liverpool supporters at Hillsborough Stadium on 15 April 1989, the Taylor Reports (Home Office 1989; 1990a) proved to be the catalyst for radical change. There was swift implementation of changes in planning, responsibilities, testing and improving the fabric of stadia, involving considerable energy and expense for clubs, local authorities, police and others. Other key areas of change included the revision of the 'Green Guide' (Home Office 1990b), the scrapping of the proposed national membership scheme and the establishment of the Football Licensing Authority (FLA) and Football Stadia Advisory Design Council. New criminal offences of pitch invasion, racist chanting and missile throwing were also created. The police role shifted to concentrate on crime, disorder and major emergencies, (Wilmot 1993) whilst the clubs appointed safety officers and began to improve the quality of their stewarding schemes (Football League *et al*. 1995). The most notable change involved the elimination of standing accommodation at all Premier and Football League stadia, although the all-seater requirement was subsequently relaxed for the lower division clubs. There are only 115 designated sports grounds in England and Wales, yet the Taylor Report, the implementation costs of which will exceed £600 million (Inglis 1996:13), gave rise to the overnight appearance of a thriving industry offering a diverse range of services and products.

The improvements in structures and management subsequent to the Taylor Reports have undoubtedly had significant impact. An explanatory note to a Safety at Sports Grounds Bill being introduced in the House of Lords during 2001 suggested that, 'Football stadia are much safer places for spectators than they were, with only one significant safety incident recorded since 1990' (House of Lords 2000). The incident referred to was the death of a supporter struck by a flare during a football match at the former Welsh National Stadium in Cardiff.

Yet notwithstanding the post-Hillsborough changes and the claim of just one significant incident, there is continued good evidence of potential disasters in and around British football grounds since 1989. A comprehensive analysis of club accident records, inspections, police match reports, media reports, anecdote and my own experiences as a researcher in the field would reveal many examples of such near-misses.

For example, I was present in the control room at a North-East derby match when away supporters experienced crushing both whilst queuing at the turnstiles before the match and on leaving the ground afterwards. In fact they burst a huge gate open to get out of the ground. Following an FA Cup Final at Wembley Stadium, I was one of many people crushed in the crowds making their way off the concourse to the underground station. On the following Monday, the Daily Telegraph expressed its concerns in a story headed, 'A Disturbing Crush Down Wembley Way'.

The early rounds of the FA Cup saw intense crowd pressure cause structural failure in the pitch perimeter walls at two non-league grounds in 1993-1994 and another in 1994-1995. The ongoing problems associated with fans standing up in areas designed for sitting down were described by one key official as 'an accident waiting to happen' (see Winter 2000). Not to mention any of the risks to public safety posed by the hostile pitch invasions and/or disorderly behaviour seen throughout the 1990s and 2000s, for example at grounds such as Celtic Park in Glasgow (see McCarra 1999), Ninian Park in Cardiff (see Moore 2002) and Millwall in London (see Scott 2004).

Looking at this chronology of disasters, reports and continued near misses, we can see that the whole approach had come from the unitary perspective of a world organised by rules. Each report had been commissioned to serve the political purpose of being seen to have done something in response to the disaster. This had been achieved by each post-disaster report proposing further rules and prescriptions, ostensibly to prevent future disaster. There are problems with this 'disaster ... inquiry ... legislation' approach. It is centrally oriented, remote from the ground, ignores the more frequent near misses from which learning could take place and results in piecemeal, generalised and short term panic measures. As Canter *et al.* have argued,

> 'it has all the quality of closing the stable door after the horse has bolted. An accretion of legislation adds in a piecemeal fashion to previous controls. As a consequence there is never any possibility of examining the system of legislation as a whole.' (Canter *et al.* 1989:92)

Critically, the disasters and near misses continued to occur. A Channel Four television documentary on 12 October 1994 also claimed that British football grounds remained 'An Accident Waiting to Happen'. Much of that documentary was mischievous, but the underlying point was, at that time, still true of a number of stadia.

Other Public Safety Scenarios

Whilst football grounds are most prominently represented in the history of British sports and leisure disasters, there have also been fatalities in at least three other British leisure contexts (not including transportation disasters such as Zeebrugge and the Marchioness). In 1973, fifty people died in a fire at the Summerland Leisure Complex on the Isle of Man. In 1988, two people died in a crowding incident during a rock concert in Castle Donington. Subsequently, in 1993, four teenagers drowned in a canoeing accident at an activity centre in Dorset. And an examination of media reports of other incidents reveals plenty of examples of near misses too. Three examples illustrate the point.

The Pavarotti Concert in Hyde Park in 1991 was expected to attract 250,000 people. Sir John Wheeler, MP, wrote to 'The Times' on 21 August 1991 to report the absence of proper safety and stewarding arrangements and to suggest that '... the Government may well have been saved from a Hillsborough disaster by the wet weather which deterred so many people from attending.' In the world of motor racing, a near disaster resulted from the mass celebratory circuit invasion after Nigel Mansell's victory in the 1992 British Grand Prix at Silverstone. In 1995, the injuries to spectators caused by a motorcycle leaving the circuit during the TT races on the Isle of Man, were widely reported.

Beyond the United Kingdom, media monitoring would again reveal numerous examples of disasters and potential disasters. In December 1999, five girls and young women died in a crush in the Bergisel ski jumping and snowboarding stadium in Innsbruck, Austria. And the Crowd Management Strategies (2004) website maintains a chronological news log of fatal and other serious incidents, particularly at pop concerts. Thus the problems of disaster and continued near misses are not confined to the football industry. Managing risk in sports grounds, particularly public safety risk, is an important issue for the whole of the sports and leisure industry.

The Impact of the Research on the Setting

The research setting has quite considerably evolved over the prolonged period since I entered the field in 1992. And through my own involvement as agent and academic I have had a small part to play in the changes.

During 1995 and 1996, the Football Licensing Authority (FLA) were able to examine the whole system of guidance and controls with a major revision of the 'Green Guide. The FLA Chief Executive noted that,

> '[previous] revisions had always been disaster or crisis driven and produced under acute time pressure. For the first time it was now possible to re-examine the Guide in detail. It quickly became apparent that much of it had stood the test of time. However, there were many areas that required updating or clarification.' (De Quidt 1997)

The revised guide (Department of National Heritage 1997) quickly became established as a world-wide benchmark and, in the absence of other guidance, was used for example as the standard to which Stadium Australia was built for the 2000 Olympic Games in Sydney. Also during 1995 and 1996, I was involved in helping to bring about the vision of higher profile stewarding and safety management supported by lower profile policing (House of Commons Home Affairs Committee 1991a:xxv). I worked with the Football Safety Officers' Association and the football authorities to produce the national Training Package for Stewarding at Football Grounds (Frosdick 1996e; Frosdick and Sidney 1997). This was adopted as the training standard for the 1998 World Cup in France (see Frosdick 1996f) and later updated in the UK to reflect various changes and introduce new material (see Frosdick 2003d).

In my own book with Lynne Walley (Frosdick and Walley 1997) I argued that 'the FLA role should be extended to include responsibility for all public assembly facilities which require safety certification' (Frosdick 1997f:259). This will eventually happen. The Cultural and Recreation Bill (Part One – Safety at Sports Grounds), introduced in Parliament during 2001, included a provision which 'reconstitutes the FLA as the Sports Grounds Safety Authority so that it can share its expertise with sports other than football' (Department of Culture, Media and Sport 2000). That bill ran out of time. The Government remain committed to introducing primary legislation to bring this change about, although at the time of writing they had made no progress with this.

DATA SOURCES

The participant observation, analysis and publications methodology adopted
for this research setting is set out in Chapter Three. The data sources for the
analysis in this Chapter and in Chapter Five are summarised in Table 4.3.

Table 4.3: Data Sources for the PAFs Risk Research Setting

UK Football - Match Day Visits	UK Football - Non-Match Day Visits
Arsenal	Arsenal
Blackburn Rovers	Aston Villa
Blackpool	Birmingham City
Bolton Wanderers	Blackburn Rovers
Bournemouth	Brentford
Brentford	Chelsea
Cambridge United	Colchester
Charlton Athletic	Coventry City
Crystal Palace	Derby County
Derby County	Ipswich Town
Everton	Leeds United
Glasgow Rangers	Leicester City
Huddersfield Town	Leyton Orient
Leeds United	Liverpool
Liverpool	Millenium Stadium (Cardiff)
Luton Town	Millwall
Manchester City	Norwich City
Manchester United	Nottingham Forest
Millwall	Notts County
Newcastle United	Portsmouth
Norwich City	Reading
Nottingham Forest	Sheffield United
Notts County	Sheffield Wednesday
Portsmouth	Southampton
Queens Park Rangers	Stoke City
Sheffield Wednesday	Sunderland
Shrewsbury Town	Tottenham Hotspur
Southampton	Walsall
Tottenham Hotspur	Watford
Tranmere Rovers	West Bromwich Albion
Watford	West Ham United
Wembley Stadium	Wolverhampton Wanderers
West Ham United	Wycombe Wanderers

Other Events and Venues	**Overseas – Non-Match Day Visits**
CCTV Rugby Broadcast, Richmond	Nou Camp Stadium (Barcelona, Spain)
Cricket Test Match, Lords	Olympic Stadium (Barcelona, Spain)

Emergency Exercise, Silverstone
British Grand Prix, Silverstone
Ideal Home Exhibition, Earls Court
London Arena
Bank One Ballpark (Phoenix, USA)
America West Arena (Phoenix, USA)
Atlantico Pavilion (Lisbon, Portugal)
Overseas – Match Day Vists
Olympic Stadium (Munich, Germany)
Stadium 'De Goffert' (Nijmegen, Holland)

Stade Charlety (Paris, France)
Stade La Meinau (Strasbourg, France)
Stade De L'Aube (Troyes, France)
Stade De L'Abbé Deschamps (Auxerre, France)
Gelredome (Arnhem, Holland)
Stade De Genève (Geneva, Switzerland)
Olympic Stadium (Munich, Germany)
San Siro Stadium (Milan, Italy)
Anjalay Stadium (Mauritius)
George V Stadium (Mauritius)

ANALYSIS: THE BRITISH STADIA SAFETY INDUSTRY[19]

Introduction

We have seen how the disaster-inquiry-legislation approach has failed to prevent a succession of disasters, major accidents and near misses in British stadia, particularly British football grounds. According to Turner, 'disaster equals energy plus misinformation' (Turner 1978:189). Whilst Toft concludes that, 'the evidence also suggests that accidents are not the product of divine caprice, nor of a set of random chance events which are not likely to recur, but that they are incidents, created by people' (Toft 1992).

Similarly, Cox and Tait argue that, 'the majority of accidents are, in some measure, attributable to human as well as procedural and technological failure' (Cox and Tait 1991:93). There is therefore a multi-causality of failures. Like other disasters, stadia disasters arise from people's mistakes and misjudgements. The analysis presented here uses Cultural Theory to argue that these may arise from clashes in the value systems and attitudes to risk to be found between the different cultural constituencies in the stadia safety industry.

The organisational structure of the British stadia safety industry is extraordinarily complex. It incorporates all those people and organisations who have variously been involved in the design and building of stadia and spectator stands; ownership and operation of stadium facilities; safety regulation of stadium operations; performing in, or spectating at, stadium events; and representing views on stadia safety related issues. In 1997, the industry included at least all the separate bodies listed in Table 4.4.

---

[19] This section is derived from Frosdick (1995a) and Frosdick (1997c).

Table 4.4: Organisations Involved in the British Stadia Safety Industry
(Source: Frosdick 1997c:117-118)

Fédération Internationale de Football Association (FIFA)
Union of European Football Associations (UEFA)
The Football Association (FA)
Scottish Football Association (SFA)
Welsh Football Association (WFA)
FA Premier League Ltd
The Football League Ltd
Scottish Football League
BBC, ITV, BSkyB and other Television Companies
Association of Premier and Football League Referees and Linesmen (APFLRL)
Football Licensing Authority (FLA)
The Football Foundation (formerly the Football Trust)
Football Stadia Advisory Design Council (FSADC) (defunct)
Football Stadia Development Committee (FSDC)
Building Research Establishment
Architects, Engineers and Construction Companies
Football Pools Companies
Parliamentary Bodies
        House of Commons Home Affairs Committee
        House of Commons All-Party Football Committee
Government Bodies
        Department of the Environment
        Department of Culture, Media and Sport
        Home Office
Local Authority Organisations:
        Fire Brigade
        Building Control Departments
        Planning Departments
        Environmental Health Departments
Medical Organisations
        Local Health Authority Ambulance Services
        Voluntary Ambulance Services (St Johns, Red Cross)
Police Services:
        Football Sub-Committee of the Association of Chief Police Officers
(ACPO)
        National Criminal Intelligence Service Football Unit
        Police Forces
        Local Police Command Units
Football Safety Officers Association (FSOA)
Contracted-Out Stewarding Companies
British Security Industry Association (BSIA)
International Professional Security Association (IPSA)
Public Safety Consultants

Professional Footballers Association (PFA)
Institute of Football Management and Administration (IFMAA)
National Federation of Football Supporters Clubs (NFFSC)
Football Supporters Association (FSA)
Fanzines and Fanzine Editors
Federation of Stadium Communities (FSC)
Footballs Family Forum
Football Joint Executive

Attempting to chart the relationships between these organisations produces an overloaded picture such as Figure 4.1.

To try and bring some order to the chaos, Cultural Theory can be applied at the macro level to analyse the various organisations, categorising them under the four archetypal headings of hierarchy, individualism, egalitarianism and fatalism. This macro level analysis will draw out aspects of 'grid' and 'group' and reveal the differences in attitudes to risk and disaster.

Figure 4.1: The British Stadia Safety Industry
(Sources: Frosdick 1997c:118; 2001e)

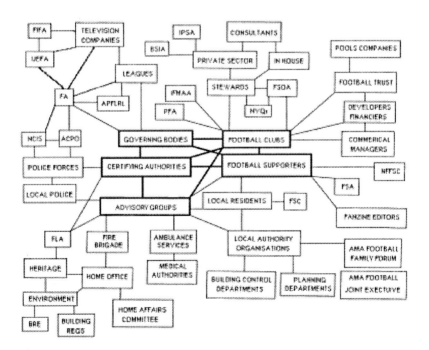

Hierarchy

Let me begin by seeking to demonstrate that the industry has been dominated by high grid high group regulatory organisations for who safety means compliance with rules. The individual rules imposed by one organisation have conflicted with those of another.

Football Organisations

Football is governed by international (FIFA), European (UEFA), and national football associations, together with the various leagues operating under their jurisdiction. Whilst the English Football Association and English national leagues have been streamlining and modernising their structures since about 1998 (see for example Frosdick 1998d), it remains the case that these governing bodies conduct their business through unwieldy management structures comprising large councils with numerous committees and subcommittees. Each body issues its own wide ranging criteria and technical requirements for stadia features and crowd management. These rules vary enormously and a summary once produced by the Football Stadia Advisory Design Council (FSADC) occupied 92 pages (FSADC 1992).

Match Officials

The laws of football provide that the referee is the sole judge of whether conditions are safe for the game to take place. Where there is to be a crowd however, the situation is more complicated. The referee's primary concern is with the playing surface. The pitch may be fit but the safety certificate holder may report for example that the terraces are too icy and dangerous to admit spectators. Conversely, the police may fear disorder if the game were to be called off after the crowd had been admitted. This conflict in rules is illustrated by a Newcastle United versus Sunderland match I attended. It had rained solidly all morning and the pitch was badly flooded. But this was the traditionally volatile derby match and it was inconceivable that it might be called off. As the police commander put it in his briefing, 'I don't care if the waves are eight feet high out there, this game is on'. I am in no doubt the referee was put under pressure to play the game.

Television Companies

The circumstances in which football is played are increasingly high grid and prescribed by television. As 'When Saturday Comes' magazine argued in their November 1994 editorial,

> 'Some teams now find themselves having to play three times in less than one week in order to fulfil the demands of television contracts.... Television now determines the names of old competitions - it's the

audience reach that pulls in the sponsor. It determines the format of new competitions - the Champions League, for instance. It determines what day they are played, forcing the people who actually go to games to adjust to Monday night and Sunday teatime kick-offs.'

More recently, the demands of television have resulted in televised football matches being offered seven days a week. Even Thursday nights are now used for UEFA Cup matches.

The Football Licensing Authority

The Football Licensing Authority (FLA) is a regulatory body. As De Quidt (1997) has shown, it has historically had four main roles – licensing grounds, advising Government on all-seater accommodation, ensuring the safety of any remaining terracing, and reviewing certifying authorities' performance. The FLA have published eight guidance documents of their own, from safety certification (FLA 1992) through to accessible stadia (FLA 2003), and contributed to various other guidance, for example on safe terracing (FSADC 1993) and on safety management (Football League *et al* 1998). Forthcoming legislation will see their licensing role subsumed within the safety certification process and their advisory remit extended to other sports (see House of Lords 2000).

The Certifying Authorities

Certification and annual inspection of designated sports grounds and designated stands is carried out by the appropriate London Borough, Metropolitan District, County Council or Unitary Authority. These responsibilities have been variously delegated to the Fire Service, Trading Standards, Legal Services and other departments such as Building Control. All certifying authorities are advised by safety advisory groups of varying nomenclature and membership. And no two stadia are identical. As Inglis describes it, 'so many different approaches, so many different shapes and sizes' (Inglis 1987:7). Given these wide ranging structural differences in both organisation and design, the safety requirements of the certifying authorities are, unsurprisingly, locally different.

The Government

At government level, there is a messy sharing of responsibility. Building regulations for new stadia are the province of the Department of the Environment, who are advised by the Building Research Establishment (BRE). Fire safety and policing fall under the Home Office, whilst safety certification legislation, guidance and the FLA are the responsibility of the Department of Culture Media and Sport.

The Police

National policy comes from an Association of Chief Police Officers (ACPO) Sub-Committee. Individual police forces have their own policy guidelines on such matters as Sunday kick-offs, all-ticket matches, match categorisation etc. At operational level, local police divisions liaise with clubs and other agencies both directly and through the safety advisory groups. Intelligence on hooligans is provided through a national network of local football intelligence officers, co-ordinated by the Football Unit of the National Criminal Intelligence Service.

Safety officers and stewards

Like night-club doormen or swimming pool attendants, stewards enforce venue regulations and implement management policies for safety and order. Operationally, stewards are commanded by stadium safety officers, who are represented nationally by the Football Safety Officers' Association (FSOA). Some clubs operate in house stewarding schemes, whilst others have contracted out to private security companies. These may be members of a trade body such as the British Security Industry Association (BSIA), who have published their own guidelines on stewarding (Frosdick 1993b).

Stadium designers

Much post-Hillsborough stadium design has been constrained by the inflexible application of quantified (although largely unsubstantiated) technical rules (see Elliott *et al.* 1997; Frosdick 1997e). However, 'the engineering simplicity of these calculations does not bear psychological examination' (Canter *et al.* 1989:96). As Cox points out, 'some of the assumptions concerning human movement, ingress and egress and escape times need to be revised on the basis of existing research findings as well as refined through further research' (Cox 1992:98). The lessons from such research have been widely ignored because untidiness is 'anathema to an engineer' (Canter *et al.* 1989:95).

Reports by other agencies

Following in Lord Justice Taylor's wake and subsequently, several other agencies commissioned their own reports into managing public safety and order both at football grounds and in the wider context. These include the Institution of Structural Engineers (ISE 1991), the Home Affairs Committee of the House of Commons (1991a; 1991b), the local authority associations (Joint Working Party on Ground Safety and Public Order 1991), the Health and Safety Commission (1993), the Sound and Communications Industries Federation (SCIF 1992) and the Health and Safety Executive (Au *et al.* 1993). All these well intentioned reports contained a host of recommendations for rules, some complementary, some contradictory, and much lost in the deluge of proposed regulation replacing past laxity and neglect. As we have seen, the FLA subsequently revised the 'Green Guide', the 1997 edition of which rationalised and incorporated much of this ad hoc guidance.

Applying Cultural Theory: The Hierarchical Risk Perspective

What we have here is a morass of rules, regulations and guidelines emanating from a large number of individual professions, regulatory bodies and their national umbrella organisations. In terms of Cultural Theory, this is all very high grid. All these high grid organisations have strong corporate identities and structures to enable members to meet frequently and do business face to face. Each is therefore also high group. Since these organisations are in the majority, we can see that the industry is dominated by hierarchical organisations. These, in turn, are dominated by hierarchical perceptions of risk and disaster.

Since the hierarch would blame disaster on deviance and rule breaking, hierarchical risk perception is informed by an emphasis on rules, history, tradition and deference to authority. There are problems with potential risk blindness here. In the first place, the hierarch's ethnocentricity inhibits awareness of the equally valid risk perceptions of the other cultural categories. Secondly, since information in hierarchies does not flow up anywhere near as well as down, senior managers make their plans without asking the advice of the more junior staff who actually know what the problems are. Thirdly, a reliance on local historical experience generates only a limited risk awareness, informed by hindsight and the parochialism of individual hierarchies. Thus the police are preoccupied with public order risks, the ambulance service with illness or injury, the fire service with fire risks and the engineers with structural and mechanical failure risks.

As we saw in Chapter Two, the failures of hindsight have been well reviewed by Toft (1992; Toft and Reynolds 1997). Organisations fail to turn passive learning from near misses into the active learning needed to prevent repetitions. Since any learning is confined to similar system types, the opportunities for isomorphic learning are lost. Moreover, hindsight cannot predict the new risks that have never happened before.

Individualism

The analysis will now move on to draw out the weak grid weak group cultural bias, diametrically opposed to hierarchy, of those involved in owning football clubs, developing stadia and playing the game itself.

Players and Managers

These are represented by the Professional Footballers' Association (PFA) and the Institute of Football Management and Administration (IFMA). Although the former Millwall player, Eamon Dunphy, has argued that, 'I've never believed that terrace violence has anything to do with what happens on the field' (Dunphy 1986:55), the evidence suggests that spectator safety is affected by the behaviour of players and managers (see Frosdick 1997m). Murphy *et al.* point out that, even before 1915, the largest category of spectator disorder, 'resulted from anger at the decisions of the referee or the attitudes of opposing players' (Murphy *et al.* 1990:42). The historical causal link was further was confirmed by Johnes (2000), whose research covers South Wales during the period 1906 to 1939. Since the late 1990s players who inflame the crowd, for example through excessive goal celebrations, have been punished with a yellow card.

Football is a team game, yet there is 'no true club ethos in pro football' (Dunphy 1986:20). Players are maximising income from a very short career. The newspapers carry daily stories of players unsettled because they 'can't agree terms' with their club. Contracts are individually negotiated. Poor performance means the sack for the manager and the transfer list for the player. Scandals abound about tax evasion, massive cash payments and corrupt transfer dealings involving illegal use of players' agents (see Bower 2003).

Football Clubs and Stadium Owners

Many European stadia were built and are owned by the municipalities. For many years however, British stadia were privately owned and run by local benefactors. As Walvin points out, 'until the 1980s, it was virtually impossible to break into the local team's boardroom simply by financial clout' (Walvin 1986:28). Since the 1980s, whilst a handful of clubs, for example Manchester United, have become hugely successful public companies, the majority of football has found itself in a deep financial crisis (see Walvin 1986:17-30; Murphy *et al.* 1990: 216-217). The clubs financial incompetence was compounded by the slump, the cost demands of the Taylor report, and the escalating wages paid to players. Deliotte and Touche (the accountants) publish an 'Annual Review of Football Finance' and reported in 2000 that, 'Seven out of every ten Premier League clubs made operating profits whilst more than nine out of every ten Football League clubs made operating losses' (Deliotte and Touche 2000).

Furthermore, the increasing gulf between the few rich clubs and the impoverished remainder in a climate of media led globalisation has been well

documented (Arnold 1991; Goldberg and Wagg 1991). In Murphy *et al.*'s
succinct summary,

> 'these concentrations have been facilitated by a series of processes,
> among them the abolition of the maximum wage, freedom of contract
> for players, retention of all the gate money for League matches by the
> home club and the increasingly skewed distribution of TV money'.
> (Murphy *et al.* 1990:216).

Benefaction has had to give way to making the business pay. This has led to
an enormous growth in marketing and commercial sponsorship of sporting
events. Clubs are in commercial as well as sporting competition with each
other.

Stadia Design and Redevelopment

Improvement grants are made by the Football Foundation (formerly the
Football Trust), which is funded from a levy on football pool betting duty, as
a National Lottery 'good cause' and from contributions from the football
authorities. The 'bottom line' philosophy has had a major impact on
approaches to stadia design and redevelopment. The FSADC was disbanded
in March 1993 after the football authorities declined to fund the £30,000 –
less than one star player's weekly wages – it needed for 1992 to 1993. Why
should this be? According to Robert Chase, former chairman of Norwich City
and of an FA Premiership committee on safety and standards, the Football
Stadia Advisory Design Council (FSADC),

> 'threw the Green Guide out of the window and simply said, how can
> we design a nice new stand? ... Anyone can do that. What we wanted
> from them was to say, here's the ground rules, I'm going to show
> you how to achieve the best possible value for money within those
> ground rules' (transcript of an interview tape recorded on 15 April
> 1993).

This issue of design and cost is illustrated by British envy towards the
'stirring contexts and breathtaking design' (Luder 1990:1) of the Italian
stadia built for the 1990 World Cup. Indeed, an entire television documentary
was devoted to contrasting the Italian stadia with our own (Channel 4,
Without Walls – Et in Stadia Ego, 10 November 1992). Simon Inglis (1990)
exhorted designers to make a stylish and locality enhancing architectural
statement. Yet harsh financial realities led to new grounds at Scunthorpe and
Walsall being described as 'more resembling edge-of-town industrial units
than cathedrals of football' (Brewster 1992). There have been appalling
examples – such as the dreadful away end at Luton Town – of good terraces
becoming poor seating where spectators have to stand up to get a view,

because 'the conversion of football grounds ... is being undertaken with cost rather than quality as the overriding imperative' (Pettipher 1992). The exceptions – such as the splendid new stands built at Arsenal and Liverpool – have tended to be confined to the super-rich clubs.

Policing Costs

Policing costs are a further factor affecting the bottom line. Clubs had traditionally been part charged only for the police resources deployed inside the ground. Following pressure from the Audit Commission (see Home Office 1991), police forces increasingly sought to recover the full costs of all their services to football clubs. This trend was accompanied by a change in philosophy about responsibility for safety (see Frosdick and Sidney 1997). Clubs were required by certifying authorities to appoint ground safety officers and the House of Commons Home Affairs Committee (1991a) expounded the principle of higher profile stewarding, supported by lower profile policing. Thus questions of principle and increased police charges encouraged clubs improve their own stewarding schemes or else to look at the cost effective alternatives offered by the private sector (see Ford 1994).

Applying Cultural Theory: The Individualist Risk Perspective

As Murphy *et al.* point out,

> 'professional soccer in England and Wales is loosely organised. Notwithstanding the existence of a central administration, the predominant forces are centrifugal ones ... The League consists of ninety-two self-governing entities: the clubs.' (Murphy *et al.* 1990:214)

These forces – taken with a bottom line philosophy, commercial competitiveness, individual contracts, frequent staff changes, lack of club ethos and public blame shuttling through the daily washing of football club dirty linen in the pages of the tabloids – all point clearly to a weak grid and weak group macro football club culture of individualist, competitive, entrepreneuriality.

Since nature is regarded as benign, rule breaking is considered fine if short term advantage results. Disaster is seen as caused by random chance events or treachery. Perceptions of risk are more commercial than safety related. Responsibility for safety can be discharged through provision of the cheapest functional security permitted by the minimum necessary insurance cover. Management of risk is otherwise all about revenue protection. This point is particularly well illustrated by the security arrangements adopted by Silverstone Circuit for a British Grand Prix. The external perimeter fence was heavily patrolled and access points well controlled to ensure only those who had paid got into the circuit. Grandstand attendants duties were more concerned with ticket control than manning fire exit gates, some of which were locked. Private security patrols were bought in for cash handling and to seize pirate merchandise and touted tickets. Although excellent arrangements had been made to prevent spectators getting onto the circuit, the crowded terraces and viewing slopes were virtually unsupervised and blocked with deck chairs, cool boxes and even smouldering barbecues! There were no gangways for emergency access, few railings to stop people toppling backwards off the slopes and constant unexpected changes in levels underfoot.

Egalitarianism and Fatalism

Having dealt with the individualist to hierarchical axis within Cultural Theory, the analysis will now show how the egalitarian to fatalist axis is occupied by stadium communities and football supporters. These two constituencies have differing views of risk both from each other and from the two already examined. Thus the full complexity of conflicts in risk perception will be revealed.

Stadium Communities

The Federation of Stadium Communities (FSC 2001) aims to improve relationships between clubs and their local communities. As Bale (1990) has shown, football grounds can be landscapes of topophobia – fear and nuisance – for those who live around them. In general, there is passive acceptance of the nuisance, which in many cases, given the age of most grounds, the residents knew was there before they moved in. However, there is evidence of successful activism by ad hoc local resident pressure groups against extensions of activities at grounds (see Bale 1990; Mason and Robins 1991). 'The most opposition appears to come from the threat of potential football grounds coming to the backyards of residents' (Bale 1993:132). For example, throughout the late 1990s, Arsenal have been seeking to increase their ground capacity and have been compelled to seek a new brownfield site for relocation because 'the idea of buying 39 neighbouring houses and increasing the size of the historic West Stand is fiercely opposed by residents' (Bond 1999).

Supporter Groups

There were previously two main national supporter groups. Traditional supporters clubs were represented by the National Federation of Football Supporters Clubs (NFFSC). These were more hierarchical and deferential to authority. As their deputy chair put it, 'I've been rather worried about the anti-police attitude from some sections of supporters' (Football into the

1990s 1989:118). The Football Supporters Association (FSA), was acknowledged in its early days to be unrepresentative of the general characteristics of football crowds and '... best understood as a tenacious, committed and highly vocal pressure group which is growing in influence, rather than as a mass movement' (Williams et al. 1989b:6). The essential difference between the National Federation and the FSA was explained by the latter's chair in evidence to the House of Commons Home Affairs Committee (1991b:134). The FSA, 'provides a structure for policy making and consultation ... We are primarily a campaigning organisation seeking to achieve certain objectives. Now the Federation of Supporters Clubs is just that [a federation]' (*ibid.*). The two organisations merged to form the Football Supporters Federation (FSF) in August 2002. The FSF website notes that,

> 'We are a democratic fan-led organisation with an elected national
> council that seeks to campaign and influence by lobbying
> government and meeting with the FA, Premier League, Football
> League and other football authorities. We also comment and
> contribute on all major issues that affect fans, supporting and
> articulating fans' views' (FSF 2004).

Campaigning against proposed bond schemes to finance stadium reconstruction led to the formation of Independent Supporters Associations at West Ham and Arsenal. These and other groups came together to form Independent Fans United. In the typical egalitarian style of organisational fission, 'the IFU found it difficult to create a national network of their own, however, probably because in many places independent supporter organisations were inextricably linked to local FSA branches, in fact in some places there were virtually the same group of people. In response to their initiative, the FSA has reconstituted itself' (Brewin 1992). Further campaining supporters groups have emerged at a good number of clubs, again often as a result of single issues. For example, Crick (2000) describes how Manchester United fans opposed to the proposed take-over of the club by BSkyB joined together with the Independent Manchester United Supporters Association to form 'Shareholders United Against Murdoch' – and to successfully campaign for the bid to be blocked.

The literature purporting to represent supporter perspectives betrays a distinctly egalitarian bias. Change is opposed unless there is extensive consultation with supporters and everyone agrees. One prominent writer, Rogan Taylor (1991; 1992), is himself a former chair of the FSA. The emergence and growth of the alternative popular culture 'fanzine' movement represents a similar growth in egalitarian perspectives (Haynes 1995). The 'fanzine' publisher, Martin Lacey described them as follows,

'fanzines instantly struck a chord. Fans wanted coverage of their
team that was intelligent and knowledgeable but also biased,
committed, outspoken and irreverent. It reflected themselves. The
pioneers ... had a lot in common. They were loosely left in outlook,
campaigned vigorously and had a firm idea of the line between
making fun of other clubs and pointless abuse' (Lacey 1992).

The Fatalist Majority

But most supporters do not belong to any organisation. Notwithstanding poor
facilities, the threat of hooliganism or crushing and the increasingly high grid
territorialisation of football, these low group individual supporters come to
football because of what Bale (1991; 1993), referring to Tuan (1974),
describes as 'topophilia' – the coupling of positive feelings with a sense of
place. The stadium represents a focus of local pride and collective
identification, a sacred place, 'home', an attractive scenic space and a source
of local heritage.

Unsurprisingly, the fatalist perspective is not well represented in the
literature, although there are some popular accounts of personal obsession
with a team, such as Hornby (1992) with Arsenal. The available evidence,
however, does supports the analysis of the majority of football supporters as
passive fatalists. Football hooliganism is the preserve of young males from
the rough working class (Dunning *et al.* 1988). Moral panic can lead to an
assumption that the football crowd as a whole is dominated by young
working class males. Yet a longitudinal review of football spectator
demographics by Malcolm, Jones and Waddington (2000) suggests that little
has changed; females have consistently constituted between 10% and 13% of
spectators and all age groups and social classes remain well represented.
However, notwithstanding the profusion of black players and the composition
of the communities in which clubs are set, very few football spectators are
drawn from visible minority ethnic groups (*ibid*). Racial abuse has been a key
feature here (see Holland 1993) and has led to the formation of campaigns to
'Kick Racism out of Football'.

Thus whilst the football crowd is not a complete cross-section of the
community, since visible minority ethnic groups and women are under-
represented, the range of age groups and percentage of female fans does
refute the assumption of a predominantly young male crowd. There has been
less clarity about the proportion of upper class and upper middle class fans,
however, these are likely to dominate the executive and hospitality boxes
whose glass frontages segregate them from the rest of the crowd. The
majority of entrepreneurial club directors are also likely to be drawn from
their ranks. This all still supports Dunning's enduring analysis that the

majority of football spectators seem likely to be drawn from the respectable working class and lower middle class. These may be termed the 'fatalist majority' because as Dunning succinctly summarises their position,

> 'The section of the population from which the majority of soccer supporters come tend on the one hand to be the relatively passive recipients of decisions taken by people above them in the social scale, people whose expertise lies primarily in some area of business rather than in football per se. ... On the other hand, the 'respectable majority' suffer both from the actions of the football hooligans who come below them on the social scale and from the effects of decisions taken in an attempt to rid the game of the 'hooligan scourge'.' (Dunning 1989)

Thus, supporters and stadium communities occupy the fatalist to egalitarian axis. In the interests of a specific cause or campaign, fatalist supporters or local residents are ripe for recruiting to more egalitarian pressure groups.

The Egalitarian and Fatalist Risk Perspectives

Since nature is ephemeral, the egalitarian is forever conscious of the need for precautions against disasters, which are blamed on 'the system', on the intrusion of the authorities beyond the group's own boundaries. Risk perception is dominated by environmental considerations. For the disaffected local resident, this means the impact of noise, litter, traffic, vandalism and disorder on the quality of their lives. For the supporter, aware of the risks, it means being left alone to choose whether and where to stand or sit and to watch the match without being commercially exploited or having one's enjoyment intruded upon by bureaucratic regulation.

For the long suffering spectator or passive local resident, disasters are acts of God. As far as risk is concerned, the 'topophilia' outweighs the 'topophobia', and there is thus a resigned acceptance of whatever indignities or annoyances are to be endured. The terrace chant, 'Que sera sera, whatever will be, will be', typifies the fatalist position.

Having thus used Cultural Theory to present a macro level analysis of the British risk in sports grounds industry, let us now develop the analysis at the more meso level of the individual PAF. Because of the particular emphasis in this research setting on risk as danger and blame, the focus of the analysis in the next Chapter will be on ways of organising for safety – the 'safety culture'.

CHAPTER FIVE: PUBLIC ASSEMBLY FACILITIES RISK – PART II

SUMMARY

This Chapter is the second part of the Cultural Theory analysis of the British PAFs industry. The analysis is presented is four main sections. The first section opens by discussing the concept of 'safety culture'. Cultural Theory is then used at the meso level of analysis to propose the indicators for a fourfold categorisation of 'safety cultures'. The analysis reveals the four contrasting, viable and archetypal models of organising the cross-organisational collaboration required for managing risk in sports grounds. The section concludes by drawing out some implications for the crowd.

The next section looks at PAFs as systems broken down into five zones: the event area, viewing accommodation, inside concourses, outside concourses and the neighbourhood beyond the venue. It draws out the different types of hazards perceived in each zone by each of four different groups of stakeholders. Owners and operators are concerned with threats to their revenue streams. Spectators wish to view and enjoy events staged in comfortable surroundings. Regulatory agencies seek to enforce safety and security rules and the community want their environment disrupted as little as possible.

The third section uses a worked example to suggest a practical management approach which acknowledges the validity of these different perceptions and thus allows for greater richness, diversity and consensus in the analysis. The final section draws conclusions from the analysis and makes the link to the second research setting of programme and project risk in police management.

ANALYSIS: 'SAFETY CULTURE' IN BRITISH PAFs[20]

'Safety Culture'

Pidgeon, Turner, Toft and Blockley (1991) note that the expression 'safety culture' was first seen in the technical literature following the 1986 nuclear disaster at Chernobyl. In the UK, Inquiries into disasters such as the Kings Cross station fire have adopted the term and emphasised the need for organisations to develop a 'safety culture' to work to prevent future disasters. But what is meant by 'safety culture'? According to Turner, the term is

---

[20] This section is derived from Frosdick (1995b) and Frosdick (1997d).

'narrower and more specialised [than 'culture']. 'Safety culture' is
the specific set of norms, beliefs, roles, attitudes and practices within
an organisation which is concerned with minimising exposure of
employees, managers, customers, suppliers and members of the
general public to conditions considered to be dangerous or injurious'
(Turner 1991).

Given its origins in heavy industry, general understanding of 'safety culture'
seems based on an engineering and hierarchical view of the world. It implies
rigid compliance with rules and regulations; in control systems or arising
from Inquiry recommendations. It implies a bureaucratic structure of
meetings and inspections to ensure co-operation, consultation and control
across the various agencies involved.

In the PAFs context, 'safety culture' seems to comprise the collective effort
and interactions between venue management, contractors, regulatory bodies
and the police, fire and ambulance services. But is there just one hierarchical
model for such 'safety cultures', or are there other viable and different ways
of organising the cross organisational collaboration required?

Canter *et al.* (1989) have linked the football phenomenon with crowd
psychology and a sense of 'place'. Bale (1993) develops the 'place' concept,
drawing together perspectives on the stadium as a source of both pleasure and
nuisance. Sense of 'place' is created by a combination of the atmosphere,
which is generated by both design features and by the crowd, and of the
organisation and style of management employed. 'Place' is therefore
synonymous with 'culture'. Each venue has a unique sense of place and thus
a unique culture. The agencies involved have a unique 'safety culture'.

In the discussion of Cultural Theory as organisation theory in Chapter Two, it
was argued that Johnson and Scholes (1999) 'Cultural Web' (see Figure 2.3)
was descriptive rather than analytical. Cultural Theory offers a model for
more disaggregated analysis. Cultural Theory applied at the meso level can
offer a new way of explaining how individual organisations provide the
subcultures which interact to create the overall 'safety culture' at a particular
venue.

Factors for 'Safety Culture' Analysis

The organisations shown in Table 5.1 are most closely involved in
constituting a local safety management system. Each of these component
organisations and their representatives may have different internal structures
and cultural biases. But the focus for this analysis is the way they all interact
with each other as constituent parts of the safety management organisation
for a particular stadium or sporting venue.

Table 5.1: Organisations Typically Comprising a PAFs 'Safety Culture'

(Source: Frosdick 1997d:139)

Football club stewards and other personnel
Agency stewards from the private security industry
The police service
Ambulance services and medical staff
The fire brigade
Local authority officers
Representatives from governing bodies
Representatives from regulatory inspectorates

Cox and Tait (1991) have emphasised the growing trend towards a more integrated approach towards health and safety, bringing together engineering systems ('hardware'), management systems ('software') and a practical understanding of people ('liveware'). Table 5.2 sets out the indicators of how this interaction takes place, across the three dimensions of 'hardware', 'software' and 'liveware'.

Table 5.2: Indicators of Cross Organisational Collaboration

(Source: Frosdick 1997d:140)

'Hardware'
Coordination and control of technological life safety systems for:
Access control
Surveillance and monitoring
Communications
Emergency warnings
Means of escape
'Software'
Management structures
Safety certificates and licenses
Statements of intent
General procedures and operating instructions
Handbooks, manuals and instruction cards
Police operation orders and deployment schedules
Contingency and emergency plans
Briefings and debriefings
Training programmes and emergency exercises
'Liveware'
Safety group membership/nomenclature/operation
Individual attitudes of personnel
Individual behaviours of personnel

Human error
Ergonomics
Information rejection
Deviance and rule breaking
Disagreement and blame

These three dimensions of 'safety culture' may now be analysed using the
Cultural Theory framework shown in Figure 5.1, which is derived from the
published work (Mars 1994) and unpublished research (Mars and Mars 1996)
of Gerald Mars.

Figure 5.1: Framework For Cultural Theory Analysis

(Source: Frosdick 1997d:141)

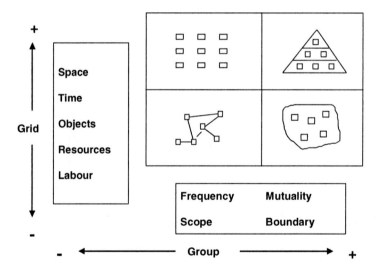

The relative strength of the grid aspect is determined from analysing the data
sources in terms of use of space, time, objects, resources and labour; whilst
aspects of group within the data sources are considered under the headings of
frequency, mutuality, scope and boundary.

These key indicators of the relative strengths of grid and group are set out in
Tables 5.3 and 5.4.

Table 5.3: Aspects Concerned With the 'Grid' Dimension
(Source: Frosdick 1997d:143-143)

Space
territorialisation of viewing areas
- all-ticket matches?
- tickets for designated seats?
- unrestricted seating/standing?
- segregation of different viewing areas?
means of segregation from the playing area
- high or low fences/walls?
- permanent or contingency perimeter track cordons?
policies for dealing with pitch incursions/invasions
attitudes to breaking rules about space
- infiltration of segregated areas?
- admission of nonticket holders?
sectorisation for operational command purposes
control room
- extent of restrictions on access?
- 'police' or 'ground' control room?
- open plan or designated pods/booths?
Time
ritual or 'as it happens' opening of the venue
time rituals
- the '10 minute walk'
- 'three-quarters time'
- 'phase one'
enforcement of liquor licensing laws
procedures for opening the exit gates
departure of 'away' supporters
Objects
separate, conflicting or joint contingency plans?
extent of reliance on technology
access to/control of technological and life safety systems
use of separate radio command channel
issue of handbooks and instruction cards
insignia of rank/grade
Resources
prescribed emergency roles or broad framework?
control of all resources by one lead agency?
Or, competition for resource control/decision making?
staff to spectator ratios
post specific or general instructions?
posting staff to functions or to areas?
division of responsibilities in statement of intent
posting requirements in safety certificate

detailed identification of specific postings
mechanism for 'crisis coordinating committee'?
Labour
'personality' leaders
ranks/grades involved in planning and debriefings
level of radio traffic
freedom to act without reference to control room
number of supervisory layers in command structure
distinct functional separation at operational level

Table 5.4: Aspects Concerned With the 'Group' Dimension

(Source: Frosdick 1997d:143)

Frequency
of safety advisory group meetings
repeated or irregular events at the same venue
continuity of personnel in key posts
Mutuality
attendance at safety advisory group meetings
sense of collective responsibility/accountability
consultation on key operational decisions
attendance at/input to other agency briefings
interdisciplinary teams of staff
isolation or co-operation in front line operations
separate control rooms for each agency?
Scope
range of different event types held at venue
extent of joint training and exercising
all agencies inputting to training programmes
Boundary
blame absorption at safety group meetings?
overt blaming/bickering at safety group meetings?
safety group decisions by consensus or voting?
prevent meetings between agencies
post-event debriefings between agencies
control room nomenclature
open plan or separate control rooms?
joint contingency plans
'crisis co-ordinating committee'
difficult access for visitors
visitor access through one agency
control room as focal point of activity

Examples of Factors For 'Safety Culture' Analysis

Introduction

These brief illustrations are not strictly ethnographic in the sense that there is no systemisation in their selection and presentation. However they are ethnographic in the sense that they have been reflexively sampled from empirical data. Their purpose at this stage in the book is to do no more than exemplify the analytical frameworks (set out in Tables 5.3 and 5.4) from which the subsequent fourfold typology of 'safety cultures' is derived.

Space

On my match visits to several grounds, spectators in one end area have been allowed to occupy whichever seats they wished. Thus areas behind the goal quickly fill up whilst seats on the wings are last to be taken. This low grid has been reflected in the fans' exuberant behaviour and the laissez-faire approach of the police and stewards. At other grounds, each spectator has had to occupy their designated seat. Stewards check tickets and direct fans to seats. This high grid is further reinforced by ticket office databases knowing the name and address of each seat occupant.

Time

At one ground, the stewards carried out a synchronised walk up and down the gangways of all four stands precisely every ten minutes. This was a visually impressive display of high grid. The police Match Commander commented to me that 'If I were here as a spectator and saw that, I would feel confident that somebody was in control'. At another ground, I watched from the control room as 'three quarters time' was announced over the radio system. Immediately, the console operator solemnly threw the switch to release the electro-magnets of the exit gates. This ritual happened every match.

Objects

At one ground, the chief steward, his deputy and the stand supervisors all wore white geltex jackets to distinguish them from the other stewards. Thus rank was clearly visible, which is high grid. At another ground, lower grid was evident since all stewards wore an orange coat with their function – supervisor, safety steward, etc. – printed on the back. All grounds have a stewards radio system, but only some of these provide a separate radio channel for senior staff. This is an indicator of high grid.

Resources

A useful indicator is to establish who is in charge? At one venue I participated in an emergency exercise which became largely a low grid competition for supremacy between the different agencies involved. At other venues the 'statement of intent' – a protocol agreed between the police and the club – sets out who is in charge of what, when and where. This is high grid. The protocol also details the formal mechanisms by which command change takes place, for example if serious public disorder breaks out and the safety officer 'hands over the keys' to the police match commander.

Labour

At several grounds, the safety officer and police match commander have been very strong personalities and very clearly in command of their staff, who have not felt free to act without reference to their leader. This is high grid. At other grounds, the style has been hands-off and facilitative, which is low grid. Strong grid is evident where division of labour is prescribed and visible. Here different types of stewards wear different coloured jackets – for example orange for safety, blue for security, red for fire and green for first aid. The allocation of teams of identically clad stewards to take responsibility for all functions within an area implies lower grid.

Frequency

Some safety officers work regularly with the same police match commander and the same representatives from other agencies. This continuity in personal contact breeds a high group familiarity. At other grounds the police match commander role is rotated through a cadre. The larger the cadre, the lower the group dimension. One ground I visited was home to two football clubs and so hosted five or six rather than two or three games a month. This frequency contributed to high group. Another venue I visited held only one major event a year and the group dimension was inevitably lower.

Mutuality

The extent of consultation on key operational decisions provides a strong indicator. In several control rooms, I have observed the safety officer and police match commander sitting together, discussing with each other how they will jointly respond to an incident. On occasions, quite frank exchanges have taken place before a collective agreement is made. This suggests strong group. At other grounds, lower group has been evident when the police commander makes operational deployments inside the ground without reference to the safety officer.

Scope

One ground I have visited is home to both a football and a rugby club. Thus scope and frequency of events are increased, which suggests strong group. The delivery of stewards training is also a key indicator. Some safety officers commission a single external provider to deliver all or most of the training, implying low group. Others have visiting speakers from the various agencies identified in Table 5.1. This collective involvement in training suggests high group.

Boundary

The negotiation of my own access provides a good indicator. In the earlier days of my research, when I was still a police officer, my access was usually obtained by negotiating an invitation from a police football liaison officer. The key question was then the extent to which that individual had to seek permission from others to confirm my attendance. At one ground, a police sergeant felt able to invite me without further ado. He obtained an 'access all areas' pass for me and casually introduced me to various parties as I followed him around on match day. Thus one junior gate-keeper had authority to admit me, implying strong group within the boundary. At another ground, my telephone enquiry had to be followed up with a formal letter asking for access. My host then sought formal authority from the club for me to attend. Thus in this case the boundaries were around the individual agencies, implying low collective group.

Following Cultural Theory, these indicators provide the framework for hypothesising four archetypes of 'safety culture'.

A Fourfold Typology of 'Safety Cultures'

The Competitive Low Interaction Model

This is the weak grid and weak group way of organising corresponding to the individualist way of life within Cultural Theory. The model is most likely to be found where individual organisations come together for one-off or irregular events at a venue.

Attitudes towards space are relaxed. Within broad limits, spectators are likely to be allowed to sit or stand where they like. The selling of tickets for specific seats and the designation of events as all- ticket will be confined only to those events that are absolutely certain to be sold out. Segregation is likely to be minimal. The timing of occurrences such as the opening of the turnstiles or of the exit gates at the end of the event will be by default – 'The ground always opens at 1.30pm' – unless one agency sees a reason to ask for a delay. Since the emphasis is on functionality with lowest possible cost, there may be a low emphasis on collective technological aids, although the individual agencies may use gadgets to compete with each other in the fashion stakes.

Stewards are more likely to be provided with a tabard or arm band than an expensive high visibility jacket. There will probably be no stewards' dress code. Instructions to staff will be couched in general rather than specific terms. Staff to spectator ratios will be low and staff will be posted to a general area rather than to a specific post. The ratio of supervisors to staff will also be low. Each agency may have its own control room and its own contingency plans, which may compete and conflict with those of other agencies. Collective emergency planning may be more about establishing who is in charge than rather than planning any actual activity. There is unlikely to be continuity in key personnel from event to event. Functional separation is likely to be strict and staff are unlikely to interact or actively co-operate at front-line levels. When things go wrong, each agency is likely to perceive the fault as lying with others. Blaming and bickering may be overt.

Risk perception is likely to be biased towards commercial risks which pose a threat to revenue. The emphasis may therefore be on access and ticketing control, pirate merchandise and protecting the interests of accredited sponsors.

The 'Barons and Fiefdoms' or 'Silo Management' Model

This is the strong grid and weak group way of organising corresponding to the fatalist way of life within Cultural Theory. The model is most likely to be found at venues where the range of events is limited and the lead agency does not have confidence in the venue management's ability to properly manage its responsibilities for safety. There are two key features in this model. First is the presence of a 'personality' leader – the baron – at the head of each agency – the fiefdom. Second is the absence of significant forward planning, based on a fire-fighting approach to risk and problem solving.

One agency, almost certainly the police, will clearly perceive itself and be perceived by others to be in charge of events. This perception may be driven by a strong sense of responsibility and accountability. Leaders may be particularly charismatic, and the majority of inter-agency interaction will take place at their level, or involving inadequately briefed deputies of senior rank. Lower grade staff may operate in 'silos', with strict functional separation and low interaction on the ground. The main control room may be called the 'Police Control Room' and those of the subservient agencies may be separate from it, yet perceive the need to refer the most minor matters to it. What limited planning has taken place, particularly in respect of spatial and timing issues, may often have been at short notice and even then may be thwarted in practice.

Emerging risks and problems will take everybody by surprise, be blamed by each agency on the poor performance of others and be responded to with higher grid solutions, for example, increasing territorialisation or staff to spectator ratios. Thus safety strategies will evolve incrementally in response to crises. Contingency plans will have been separately prepared without consultation. Where contradictions exist, the need to reconcile the differences may not be perceived until after a problem has arisen. The safety certificate may be highly prescriptive about the locations to which stewards are to be posted and in what numbers.

The Bureaucratic High Interaction Model

This is the strong grid and strong group way of organising corresponding to the hierarchical way of life within Cultural Theory. The model is most likely to be found at venues where a variety of events are regularly held and where there is continuity in the personnel occupying the key posts.

The nomenclature of the control facility, for example the 'Ground Safety Management Centre', reflects a strong sense of collective responsibility. The control room may be large and open plan, allowing everybody access to all the equipment. The room may be a focal point where staff drop by and visitors gather. Joint briefings may be held, particularly for police and stewards. Alternatively, each agency may send a representative to give an input at other agency briefings. Risk perception will be heavily influenced by historical experience at the venue at the views of the senior personnel. Briefings will be very full and every perceived eventuality covered by rules.

Bureaucracy is evident in mechanistic planning. Police operation orders and steward handbooks will be full and procedures set out in some detail. The safety certificate may prescribe the precise posts to be occupied. For each of these, the club and police may have prepared detailed post-specific instruction cards prescribing the postholders duties in both normal and emergency operating conditions. Joint exercising and training may be regularly undertaken. Rank is important in this model. Each agency may have several internal supervisory grades. The most senior may each have their own 'command' radio channels. Collectively, one agency is always 'in charge' in any given scenario. For example, the club may control all routine activity, the ambulance services all medical emergencies, and the police any outbreaks of serious disorder. There may be competition to be 'in charge' overall, but this is a game played within the rules laid down by the safety certificate and statements of intent.

When staff encounter incidents for which they have not been briefed or which are not covered by their instruction cards, they are likely to initiate a process of reporting up the line to the control room, where a decision will be taken by the appropriate 'in charge' agency and eventually communicated back down the line. Territorialisation for spectators is likely to be high, with supporters occupying designated seats, well segregated both from each other and from the pitch. Time rituals are important. For example, stewards may walk up and down the gangways every ten minutes on the dot and exit gates may always be opened at three-quarters time.

The 'Middle Out' Consensus Driven Model

This is the weak grid and strong group way of organising corresponding to the egalitarian way of life within Cultural Theory. The model is most likely to be found at venues which have experienced a serious incident, from which all the agencies involved perceived a need for increased communication and co-operation to avoid a recurrence. The key feature of this model is the strong desire for management through consensus, arising from a sense of collective responsibility and, more importantly, a sense of collective accountability if disaster strikes. Safety advisory group meetings may also be consensus driven, with change being approved only if everybody agrees.

Management structures are likely to be relatively flat, with fewer grades and wider spans of command than in hierarchy. Since delay may be perceived as a cause of potential disaster, all staff will be encouraged to intervene in situations on their own initiative, without seeking approval from control. There is likely to be continuity in staff at all levels, certainly in key posts, and staff may operate in interdisciplinary teams deployed to geographical areas rather than to function specific posts. An open plan multi-agency control room is likely. Since staff are familiar with the venue and acting on their own initiative, radio traffic may be light. Where control room intervention in operational decision making is needed, this may be preceded by consultation between agency representatives. For serious emergencies, there may be plans for a multi-agency 'Crisis Co-ordinating Committee' to assemble to manage the consequences.

The egalitarian view of nature as ephemeral may create a fear of impending doom if the most careful precautions are not followed. This suggests a wide awareness of possible risks and extensive collective contingency planning. However, this is likely to be in broad rather than detailed mechanistic terms. In order to be ready for any eventuality, considerable resources may be available and staff to spectator ratios may therefore be high. However, these resources may be more held in reserve than deployed since the need for territorialisation of spectators may not be so keenly felt. Important timing issues such as the opening of the ground may happen only after consultation has determined that everybody is ready.

Ethnographic Examples of 'Safety Cultures'

My fieldwork has provided examples of various different safety cultures. Whilst none of them conform exactly to one of the four hypothetical types I have proposed, my argument is that each of them has a specific bias towards one of the four models and thus a bias towards one of four different ways of perceiving and managing risk. Like all organisations, all my examples have been dynamic; adapting and evolving themselves. As a result, some may now be substantially different, even in cultural bias, from when I studied them. This does not detract from their value as ethnographic examples. The four vignettes which follow most closely exemplify the key features of the four hypothetical models.

Silverstone Circuits

Overall weak group was reflected in poor communications, separate agency control rooms and competition for primacy between the racing authorities and the emergency services. The management of the whole venue was compartmentalised. In emergency exercises, all the agencies turned up and gave individual situation reports on individual radio systems to individual control rooms. In exercise debriefings, blame for things not going well was overtly expressed rather than absorbed. The Unified Emergency Action Plan contained no plans at all but was a political document establishing a co-ordinating framework in the event of a disaster. There were no contingency plans. There was a view that plans cannot cover every contingency and therefore there was no point being prescriptive about what to do if emergency happened. Security personnel were deployed to tackle revenue protection risks and, although there had been some increase in territorialisation of spectators, the majority of spectator activity was unregulated. Motor racing is about danger and excitement and spectators shared in this by abnormal risk taking behaviour. This indicated that grid was also weak.

Goodison Park – Everton FC

The police, under the command of a highly charismatic leader, were very clearly in charge of the event and their operation was highly planned and resourced, almost to the point of rendering the club's involvement superfluous. This was strong grid. Since the various agencies involved did not communicate with each other very well, and interaction at lower levels was low, overall group was weak. This lack of communication between the different agencies gave rise to a variety of surprises, for example the blocking of an access route by a temporary structure, which could only be addressed through last minute crisis management. When several medical and public order emergencies occurred together, the safety management system was unable to cope. In the police debriefing, the system failure was largely blamed on the stewards.

Selhurst Park Stadium – Crystal Palace and Wimbledon FCs

The police and stewarding operations were individually and collectively highly planned and organised. The police were clearly in charge, although they were preparing to hand over and let the club take command. Planned territorialisation of spectators was high. This was all strong grid. The control room was shared by several agencies. There was continuity in key posts and front line co-operation between staff was evident. Relations between all parties within the Safety Advisory Group were good. Selhurst Park stadium was shared by Crystal Palace FC and their tenants Wimbledon FC. The staging of twice as many matches as at most other stadia reinforced the frequency element of group, which was also strong.

The Sheffield Clubs – Wednesday and United

The shadow of the Hillsborough disaster hung heavy over the police and other agencies involved in managing safety in South Yorkshire. There was collective risk aversion and a strong sense of collective responsibility and accountability among all parties here. The Safety Advisory Group had supervised the evolution of higher profile stewarding and lower profile policing at Sheffield United FC through a cautious, incremental and consensual approach to change. At Sheffield Wednesday, the police spoke warmly of the good relations between them and the club and pre-event consultation was evident. This indicated a bias towards strong group. The delegation to individuals at low levels of the authority to take action on their own initiative and the remarkably low level of radio communication between individuals and the control room suggested that grid was relatively weak.

Implications of the Analysis

Each of the four archetypes has both strengths and weaknesses. Awareness for policy makers will be more enhanced by discussion of weaknesses than a more comfortable focus on strengths. The weaknesses have already begun to be indicated in the models set out above. What I want to do here is emphasise the main points and suggest the possible implications of these pathologies for the crowd.

The Competitive Low Interaction Model

Weak group and competition suggests the likelihood of poor communication between the various agencies and duplication of effort. What communication there is may not be trusted. Each agency may send its own representative to every incident to find out what is 'really' going on and whether there is 'anything for us' at the scene. Weak 'grid' suggests that overall control and coordination in routine situations may be poor. A view of nature as benign and emphasis on commercial risks may lead to blindness to potential safety risks. Liability for safety may in any event be discharged through insurance cover rather than the deployment of adequate resources.

This 'safety culture' may create a laissez faire environment which encourages risk taking behaviour by spectators. Minor accidents may be more frequent, yet go unreported because spectators will shrug them off as part of the experience.

The 'Barons And Fiefdoms' or 'Silo Management' Model

One agency may have taken all the burden of organisation and responsibility on its shoulders. Whilst this may be fine in routine situations, the agency may find itself unable to cope in crises where rapid communication with and assistance from others is required. Inter-agency communication is likely to be restricted to the 'barons' at the head of each agency. These may keep important information to themselves, leaving their 'fiefdoms' to operate in isolated ignorance. Frequent minor mistakes in safety management may result. A lack of effective forward planning may leave this 'safety culture' constantly surprised by events, which have to be addressed through last minute fire-fighting responses.

This 'safety culture' may create a constrained and confusing environment for spectators, whose general passive acceptance of apparent poor organisation may occasionally boil over into frustrated protest.

The Bureaucratic High Interaction Model

Since information flows down better than it does up, and rank and status is afforded more weight than knowledge and experience, plans may be made in ignorance of the operating problems and potential solutions to them known to those actually doing the work. Although such mechanistic planning ensures that routine operating scenarios work smoothly, with most minor problems referred to and resolved by a central control, this stifles innovation and can result in ineffectual individual performance at operational level. In emergency situations, the command structure is too cumbersome to respond with sufficient speed and flexibility to provide the support required. The reports of lower grade staff may not be trusted and higher ranks deployed to 'assess the situation' before any response is made. Bureaucratic regulation and delay in responding to emergencies are inherent features of this model.

This can create an environment where spectator enjoyment is spoiled by the unthinking enforcement of petty regulation. When serious problems do occur, the inability to respond quickly may result in disastrous delay.

The 'Middle Out' Consensus Driven Model

The strong awareness of delay leading to potential disaster may encourage ad hoc low level interventions which are not informed by a strategic awareness of the whole picture. Overall co-ordination and control in routine scenarios may prove difficult to achieve. A 'just in case' philosophy may lead to excessive staffing and unnecessary costs for the organisers. Many staff may lack a meaningful role in the operation. The need for consensus in policy issues may require resource intensive and costly debating and consultative procedures. There may be a tendency to concentrate on minor matters on which agreement is easily achieved, deferring the more difficult and contentious decisions.

This may create an environment where the approach to spectator regulation is compliance rather than enforcement oriented, seeking spectator agreement and co-operation with consensually agreed measures. Thus considerable tolerance may be shown towards misbehaviour, with strenuous efforts made to encourage compliance and ejections or arrests being regarded as a last resort.

ANALYSIS: RISK PERCEPTION IN PAFs[21]

Cultural Conflict

Chapter One showed that, whilst Cultural Theory posits four different ways of life, they cannot exist independently of each other. And we have seen that all four social solidarities are clearly present within the risk in sports grounds industry. Regulatory (hierarchical) perceptions of risk as breaking safety rules are predominant, and a multitude of agencies are involved in safety and security management. PAFs owners and operators are more entrepreneurial (i.e. individualist) and give priority to commercial risks such as access control, pirate merchandise, ticket touting, cash handling and ambush marketing. Spectator and local residents pressure groups (i.e. the egalitarians) are more concerned with quality and environmental risks. The vociferous minority of spectators demand the right to sit (or stand) where they choose to watch the event as they please without being commercially exploited or having their enjoyment intruded upon by petty-minded officialdom. Local residents voice concerns about the impact of noise, litter, traffic, vandalism and parking. The majority of spectators tend to shrug their shoulders with a

---

[21] This section is derived from Frosdick (1996c), Frosdick (1997g), Frosdick (1998a), Frosdick (1998b) and Frosdick (1998c).

fatalist acceptance of the various hazards they endure as a result of the commercial, regulatory, and behavioural excesses of all the others.

The management of risk forms an essential and integral part of PAFs management. For reasons of danger and blame, the emphasis is on public safety hazards. Whilst these are paramount, it can be shown that looking at them in isolation can create operational difficulties. These problems arise from cultural conflicts between hierarchy, individualism and the fatalist/egalitarian axis.

Two examples drawn from my own experience show how financial considerations can create a conflict between the commercial priorities of the marketing industry and the safety priorities of the regulators. At Newcastle United versus Sunderland in April 1993, disorder broke out as a result of stewards and the police attempting to remove a Sunderland banner draped over a sponsor's advertising hoarding. The commercial manager had deployed the stewards without asking the safety officer and the police got involved to support the stewards. Two officers snatched the banner and a fight broke out. I was watching from the control room with the safety officer. He was furious.

A second example comes from 1995 from a football ground in the north-west of England. Part-way through briefing the senior stewards, the safety officer was called away to speak urgently to the commercial manager. The latter told him there was a fire in a hospitality suite and requested his immediate attendance. The commercial manager was teasing – 'I thought that would get you here quick'. In fact he wanted the pitch covers to be moved from where they had been folded up because they were preventing the advertising hoardings being seen. He had thought nothing of disrupting the essential briefing for the senior stewards, which had to be curtailed. What would any subsequent inquiry into a real fire have made of the disruption and the irresponsible lie?

The conflict between safety and commerce can even result in the cancellation of planned events. In a wider public events setting, the Mayor of London cancelled the 2001 New Year's celebrations with only six weeks to go. 'The major obstacle was a clash between the management of crowd safety and the commercial viability of the event' (O'Neill 2000).

The case of whether or not to ban alcohol in stadiums illustrates the conflict between regulation, commerce, enjoyment and disruption (see Frosdick 1998g; 1998h). For the commercial manager, a ban on alcohol sales creates a risk to revenue. The fans will not buy cola instead. They will drink outside and come in late, reducing what is known in the trade as 'ancillary spend per head'. For many spectators, a ban on alcohol quite simply reduces their enjoyment of the event, and where it has been needlessly imposed from outside, may create feelings of resentment. Thus local residents and businesses have to put up with more noise and disorder around the ground than might otherwise be the case. From a safety point of view, there are compelling arguments that a total ban results in late arrivals and a last minute rush to get in at the turnstiles.

This issues are well illustrated by the case of Stoke City football club, who moved to a new ground in August 1997. At their old ground in the town centre, all the catering outlets had at least a small view over the pitch and so it was not possible for the club to get permission to sell any alcohol in the ground. According to the stadium manager, many of the fans remained in the local pubs until 2.55 pm, arriving very late and causing long queues at the turnstiles. The police often asked for the kick-off to be delayed because large numbers of fans were still queuing to get in. On one occasion, a public address announcement was made at 2.55 pm that the kick-off would be delayed until 3.15 pm. The fans waiting outside promptly turned round and went back to the pubs until 3.10 pm! The new Britannia Stadium is built on the site of an old coal mine about 20 minutes walk from the town. Parking is difficult and the only public transport is a bus service. Having a new ground meant the club were now able to get a liquor licence. Alcohol is sold up until kick-off, from 15 minutes before until 15 minutes after half-time and then again after the match. The fans now tend to arrive early to enjoy a drink before the game, at half-time and even after the match, although this tends to be only when their team have won. There have been no arrests for drunkenness and no matches when the sale of alcohol is prohibited. Sales were even permitted for the last game of the 1997 to 1998 season, against Manchester City, when very serious disorder was anticipated and indeed did break out. In fact more than 20 people were hurt, 300 ejected from the ground and 15 arrested. But the stadium management felt that a ban on alcohol at the ground would have caused very serious problems in the town. It was better to get the fans in and control them at the stadium.

A Strategic and Systems Approach to Risk Analysis

We saw briefly in the discussion of risk management in Chapter One how the essential problem for PAFs management is the need to take account of four competing demands. Commercial pressures require them to optimise the commercial viability of the venue and its events. This is Cultural Theory's individualist perspective. Regulatory and other requirements for safety and security must also be met and this is Cultural Theory's hierarchical perspective. Spectator demands for excitement and enjoyment require credible events staged in comfortable surroundings, whilst any negative effects which the venue and event may have on the outside world must be kept to a minimum. These two latter demands reflect the egalitarian end of Cultural Theory's fatalist/egalitarian axis.

To expand the analysis, I want to look again at PAFs as a system, broken down into zones, such as we saw in Figure 1.2 in Chapter One. My site visits and analysis of briefing documents, contingency plans and training material has enabled me to catalogue, probably not exhaustively, the variety of hazards which have been perceived by each of the four constituencies in each part of the system. So let me begin by looking at the most commonly perceived hazards in the area where the event is held (the pitch, track, or court, etc.) and the perimeter between it and the viewing zone.

The Event Area and Perimeter

The Commercial Perspective

Threats to the interests of advertisers and sponsors form the principal sources of event area hazards perceived from a commercial perspective. It is important to ensure that perimeter advertising is clearly visible to the television camera and conflicts can arise between commercialism and safety when supporters drape their banners over the hoardings. Since accredited sponsors will have paid substantial fees to be associated with the event, there is also a perceived need to prevent 'ambush marketing' by other brands. At the Portugal versus Turkey match in Nottingham during the Euro '96 recent European football Championships, several banners advertising Portuguese products were brought into the stadium and displayed whenever play and thus the cameras went in their direction. Stewards had to be more active dealing with these banners than they did with the well behaved crowd! Television companies also pay handsomely for their access and are inevitably anxious to minimise the risks of high installation costs and poor broadcast quality in their choice of camera positions and cable runs around the event area perimeter. Conflicts arise when these choices create trip hazards or obstruct spectator sightlines.

The Spectator Perspective

Since their main purpose is to watch the event, any deficiencies in sightlines, in the physical event area, in lighting and in the event itself provide sources of hazard to the enjoyment of the spectators. Restricted views arise from old PAFs designs, with roof props and even floodlight pylons around the perimeter of the event area. Unusually high perimeter hoardings, cage-type fences, inappropriately sited television cameras or excessive deployments of police and/or stewards around the perimeter represent further sources of hazards to sightlines.

Sports events may either become a farce or else be unplayable if surfaces, particularly grass, become too wet. The high jump section of the women's pentathlon competition at the1996 Atlanta Olympics, where standing water was not properly cleared from the runway, adversely affecting the athletes' performances, provides an example. The heavy rains which turned the car parks at Silverstone into a quagmire resulted in the April 2000 British Grand Prix being branded a 'farce' and a 'shambles' (see Pook and Eden 2000).

Enjoyment may also be threatened by a lack of credibility in the event itself. In boxing, a number of 'big fights' have ended in the first round because of the mismatching of opponents. The early dismissal of a star player, even if justified, denies spectators the chance of enjoying that player's skills and may lead to their team adopting boring defensive tactics for the remainder of the match.

The External Disruption Perspective

Whilst it is clearly the zone beyond the venue which provides most hazards perceived by the outside world, nevertheless the event area itself provides two main sources. First is the noise created by the participants or performers. This is a particular issue with music events staged in stadia, where the sound travels beyond the stadium through the open air. Second is the threat of articles from the event area being projected beyond the facility. Cricket balls 'hit for six' or parachutists trying to land on the event area as part of a display can cause damage to property or injury to passers-by outside the ground. Pyrotechnics set off on the event area provide a further source of hazard. During an early satellite television broadcast from a Premiership football ground in South London, some of the pre-match fireworks landed, still burning, on the forecourt of a petrol station down the street!

The Safety and Security Perspective

The principal sources of hazards from this perspective involve perimeter obstructions and the potential for adverse interaction between spectators and participants in the event. Television cables, perimeter hoardings, fences and gates all provide tripping or obstruction hazards which may delay spectator egress onto the event area in emergency evacuations. The 1989 Hillsborough stadium disaster in which 95 football fans were crushed to death against a perimeter fence provides an extreme example. Incursions onto the event area, by people or objects, are a principal concern. The perceived hazards range from attacks on officials or players, for example the on-court stabbing of tennis star Monica Seles in Germany, through the throwing of missiles, to damage to the event area, such as at Wembley Stadium after a notorious England versus Scotland football match in the 1980s. Conversely, participants or objects leaving the event area cause similar concerns. Players who run into the crowd to celebrate goals or points scored frequently cause the crowd to surge towards them. Players may even attack the crowd! Who could forget the pictures of Manchester United's Eric Cantona leaping into a stand to karate kick a spectator?

Team benches provide a source of similar hazards, either because spectators misbehave towards them or vice versa. Spectators can be hurt or killed by things leaving the event area. For example, several spectators have been injured by footballs kicked into the crowd during the pre-match 'warm-up'. And two track marshals were killed by crash debris over the course of five Formula One motor races in 2000/2001. Finally, we have the health and safety hazards which the event, the event area or the perimeter pose to the participants themselves. For safety reasons, the English football team nearly refused to play on a poor surface in China in summer 1996. More extremely, several boxers have died in the ring.

Thus from the event area alone, it can be seen that strategic risk assessment requires a broader focus than safety and security alone. Let us continue by looking at the next two zones, taken together. These are the viewing accommodation and inside concourse zones, including the various technological systems used to support their management.

Viewing Accommodation and Inside Concourses

The Commercial Perspective

Design and fitting out are very much shaped by commercial risk concerns. Developers will want to recover as high a percentage of their capital costs as possible through advance sales of executive boxes and term tickets for premium seats. Operators will want to maximise the revenue streams from ordinary ticket sales by fitting as many seats into the facility as the various constraints will allow. Funding for many redevelopments has also been underpinned by the idea of diversifying the uses made of the facility, through conferences and banqueting, on days when there are no spectators in to view an event.

Factors which interfere with the opportunity for spectators to gain access to the event represent a further source of risk. Venues want to sell as many tickets as they can, yet police insistence on 'all-ticket' matches or their refusal to allow sales on the day have adversely affected attendances at some British football grounds. Access to the event – yes – but free admission – no. Revenue protection means that entry to the inside concourses needs to be strictly controlled. This ensures that only those who have either paid or else been properly accredited are permitted to enter the facility. Having got the audience in, merchandising seeks to address the risk that ancillary spend per head will not be optimised. More and better retail outlets, together with branded confectionery and catering items, increasingly seem to provide the answer here.

Risk may also arise from anything which increases costs or which prevents the maximisation of promotional opportunities. As we have seen, there are frequent tensions here between commerce and safety/security. Commercial managers will want the level of security personnel employed to be no more than is necessary to deal with the numbers and type of crowd expected, whilst regulatory agencies will be tempted to up the staffing levels 'just in case'. Commercial managers will want to earn revenue by allowing access to promotions, yet the promotional activity may itself compromise safety. At an old London football ground, a local publisher was allowed to place a free copy of his newspaper on every seat in the main stand, which happened to be made of wood. Finally, there are concerns not to offend the occupants of executive boxes and damage repeat business by over-controlling their behaviour. Thus normal security personnel may be replaced by 'lounge stewards' who are encouraged to show more tolerance and tact than would be the case with the ordinary public.

The Spectator Perspective

The main areas of spectator perceived risk concern the ease with which they can purchase the right to a seat/space and the quality of their enjoyment of the event. Ticketing systems have become ever more sophisticated. Theatre box-offices are used to allowing the customer to choose exactly which seat they wish to purchase, but this has been a rarity in British sports. There are still venues where even credit card sales over the telephone are not provided for and the prospective customer has to attend the venue in person to purchase the ticket.

Once they have gained access, spectators worry about whether they will be able to see the event. In addition to the viewing obstructions around the perimeter, the view quality is affected by three factors: preferred viewing location, viewing distance and sightline (see FSADC 1991b; John and Campbell 1993). The preferred viewing location for athletics is the side where the finishing line is. Rugby fans prefer the sides whereas younger football fans prefer the ends. For most team events, optimum viewing distance is a radius of 90 metres whilst the accepted maximum is 150 metres. Yet in several famous stadia, most spectators are beyond the optimum and far too many are beyond the maximum. Sightlines are assessed using riser heights, tread depths and angles of rake. Ideally, the spectator should be able to see over the head of the person in front, but this has often not been achieved. Given a decent view, the spectator is then concerned with enjoyment. Risks here arise from failures in maintenance – such as dirty or broken seats, from poor amenities and, above all, from being prevented from having a good time.

Spectator amenities will mainly be sited in the inside concourse areas. Here the fans are looking for both ready access and a choice of quality in catering and souvenirs, as well as for sufficient clean and decent toilet provision. All too often, they face the risk of their loyalty to the sport or team being unscrupulously exploited. Long queues, foul latrines and over-priced insipid fare are still the norm in too many venues. Enjoying the event is clearly key, and it is here that spectators may unwittingly come into conflict with the regulators. For some sports fans, being forced to sit in a designated seat rather than to choose where or even whether to sit, is an infringement of the right to enjoy themselves. The same is true of regulatory restrictions on the banners, flags, air-horns, drums and instruments which go towards creating the carnivalesque atmosphere which so contributes to the enjoyment of the live event. Risk for spectators also arises when security personnel respond to their passionate partisan support and letting off steam as though it was hooligan behaviour.

The Safety and Security Perspective

A considerable proportion of the perceived risks arise and are addressed in the preparations for the event. Periodic inspections will be carried out on the structural integrity of the viewing accommodation, for example to check loadings, and extensive pre-event checks will take place to ensure that risk is reduced. There is a whole range of technological life safety systems – turnstile counting, crowd pressure sensors, lighting, closed circuit television, fire safety, communications and public address – which need to be working correctly to fully support the operational management of the event. Furthermore, managers will want to be satisfied that the venue is clear of hazards and that all personnel are on post before they open the venue to the public. An England under 21 international football match at Wolverhampton was delayed for nearly three hours after a suspect object was found during a pre-match search of the viewing zone. Several stadium events have also been called off due to toilets or fire equipment having frozen.

In addition to its importance for revenue protection, access control is both a security and safety issue. Many venues are designed so that inside concourses and viewing accommodation together form self-contained areas, perhaps one for each side of the venue. Allowing too many people into an area creates a serious risk of overcrowding and possible disaster. Allowing unauthorised persons in compromises safety – if lots of people are involved – and security – if the person's intentions are sinister. At one London ground, a person walked through the players entrance dressed in a tracksuit and 'warmed up' with the teams until somebody realised he was an intruder.

Security risks arise from members of the crowd arguing over seat occupancy, committing criminal offences such as abusive chanting, throwing missiles, being drunk, fighting or reacting to the event with language or behaviour which is regarded as unacceptable by the authorities. Major crimes such as rioting, wounding or even unlawful killing are well known to have occurred in various sports. PAFs handle considerable sums of cash and several have been the victims of robberies. Safety risks arise from areas of the viewing accommodation approaching capacity and from any factor which necessitates either a partial or total evacuation of the venue. These range from equipment failures – for example floodlighting – to fires, floods, gas leaks, explosions, bomb scares, structural collapses or serious public disorder. Within the inside concourses, locked exit gates represent a particular safety hazard, since they prevent crowd egress in an emergency. Over fifty people burned to death in Bradford in 1985 and British football has learned this lesson. However the same cannot be said of all other sports or countries. I went to a cricket test match where I found the exit gates to a wooden stand locked. I was horrified to be told that the steward who held the keys was taking tea in the pavilion several hundred yards away. I also visited a French football ground where all the exit gates were kept padlocked yet unstaffed throughout the match.

The External Disruption Perspective

Since it is the viewing accommodation and inside concourses which form the bulk of the PAFs structure, thus it is the impact of the built form itself which provides the main source of risk to the world beyond the facility. This is less of an issue where PAFs are constructed on greenfield or redundant industrial sites. However many PAFs are sited in cramped inner city locations and any redevelopment has to take account of the environmental impact on local residents. For example, the huge new stand at Dublin's Croke Park (the home of Gaelic football) was designed so that houses in the area would not lose sunlight either in the morning or the evening. Research carried out by Helen Rahilly has shown how, to meet the considerable objections of local residents, the final design of Arsenal Football Club's North Stand was 'lower, lighter and far less bulky than the original plans had suggested' (Rahilly 1996).

Noise and light pollution are further sources of risk. Light pollution occurs when the glare from floodlighting spills over onto surrounding properties, whilst noise pollution refers both to the noise of the crowd, which is perhaps unavoidable, and to the transmission of music and messages over public address systems which carry beyond the venue. Let us now look at the principal hazards perceived in the final two zones – the outside concourses and the neighbourhood.

The Outside Concourses and Neighbourhood

The Commercial Perspective

Since merchandising makes a valuable contribution to revenue, thus pirate merchandise represents a serious commercial threat for PAFs managers. Not only will no license fee have been paid but the merchandise itself may be very poor, damaging customer perceptions of quality and thus reducing official sales. Within the UK, brands are protected by copyright legislation and a number of venues have employed security personnel to patrol the environs to seize any pirate merchandise. This is sometimes undertaken in conjunction with Trading Standards officers who have the power to prosecute offenders. Similarly, as PAFs look to earn more revenue from sponsorship and licensing arrangements, so ambush marketing becomes an important commercial hazard. Curl (1993) has described how ambushers can be 'locked-out' through the complete control of images in and around the venue. The use of brand images in the venue environs can be controlled by local government permit whilst the outside concourses can be strictly patrolled to enforce restrictions on banners, signs and even clothing. For UEFA Champions League matches, the host club is required to present a stadium 'clean' of all commercial images so as to protect the exclusivity of the official sponsors.

The Spectator Perspective

Spectators are rather less likely to perceive the wearing of a branded sweatshirt as a hazard. Outside the venue, their concerns centre around the ease with which they can gain access to the event and then how quickly they can get away afterwards. Perceived hazards arise from inadequate public transport, poor road capacities and difficulties in parking near the venue. Quite perversely, the same people who see their convenience threatened by parking restrictions before the event, will bemoan the absence of action against the parked cars which hinder the progress of traffic leaving after the event. Within the outside concourses, spectators wish to be guided effortlessly towards the right entrances and then gain admission without having to queue for more than a couple of minutes. Clear information on tickets, the best of signage and sufficient turnstiles or access points are essential if spectator frustrations are to be avoided. The needs of disabled patrons must also be met.

The Safety and Security Perspective

The principal hazards are perceived as disorder and overcrowding arising during the periods before and after the event. Particularly within football, there are public order concerns around spectators travelling to the match or gathering in public houses near the ground. Police have sophisticated intelligence systems which may cause them to believe there will be disorder and thus wish to make careful arrangements to provide supervised or even segregated routes to and from the stadium for the supporters of different teams.

The cramped inner city locations of many facilities create real risks of overcrowding in the surrounding streets, particularly as the start of the event approaches and many people are still outside waiting to gain admission. It is for this reason that the kick-off times of football matches are sometimes put back by 15 minutes and public address announcements made outside the ground to reassure fans they will not miss the match. Similar crowding risks arise where the venue is sold out and there are substantial numbers of people locked out of the event. Equally, at the end of the event, the exits onto the outside concourses will be opened in plenty of time and traffic stopped to ensure the crowds can disperse as freely as possible.

Within the outside concourses, supervised access control is perceived as essential to screen out drunken persons and minimise the risks of people taking dangerous articles such as flares, missiles or weapons inside the venue. For all-ticket capacity events, cordons may be placed at the boundary to the outside concourses, or even in the surrounding streets, to reduce crowding by restricting access to ticket holders only.

The External Disruption Perspective

As far as local residents are concerned, the principal hazards arise from the nuisances created on the days when the venue is open for mass spectator events. These include the noise of the approaching crowd, the litter which the crowd leaves in its wake, minor disorder or vandalism, people urinating in the street or in front gardens, traffic congestion and the impossibility of finding a parking place near one's own house. Whilst these quality of life issues may be less keenly felt where venues are sited out of town or on derelict industrial land away from the main conurbation, nevertheless studies by geographers have shown how negative effects are experienced over quite some distance around a facility (Bale 1991; Mason and Robins 1991). Such widespread effects go some way towards explaining the 'not in my back yard' campaigns so often mounted against PAFs developers seeking a site for a new facility.

MANAGING RISK IN THE PAFs INDUSTRY

Building Cross-Cultural Consensus

Having established that all four social solidarities are present in the risk in sports grounds industry, and that there is good evidence of problems arising from their conflicting risk perspectives, it is worth reminding ourselves of Thompson and Rayner's point that,

> 'the risk terrain is contested, and that progress lies not in our choosing one position on that terrain and rejecting those that are in contention with it, but in recognising and understanding all these positions and then finding ways of negotiating constructively between them.' (Thompson and Rayner 1998:144)

And during the course of my time in this research setting, during which I have expounded the need for negotiated cross-cultural consensus, evidence has begun to emerge of initiatives where such constructive negotiation has taken place. This is not to say that I claim any causal connection between the ongoing dissemination of my research findings in this setting and the emergence of the initiatives, but it has been most interesting to see.

'Supporters Direct' is a government policy initiative which grew out of the Football Task Force (1999) report on 'Investing in the Community'. Operational from the start of the 2000 to 2001 season, 'Supporters Direct' is 'a dedicated unit that will provide legal and practical advice to help supporters form supporter trusts and gain a say in running their clubs' (Hamil *et al.* 2000:4). What is key here is the coming together of all four social solidarities. 'Supporters Direct' was initiated by government. It is supported in clubs where a supporters trust representative has been elected onto the board of directors, as at Northampton Town (see Lomax 2000). It seeks to give a voice to the ordinary fans. And to qualify for support, the supporters trusts will have to be based on the principles of democracy, mutualism and not for profit (see Jacquiss 2000).

Anti-racism campaigns such as 'Kick it' represent a further example of such coming together. Originally a single issue lobbying initiative from 1993, 'Kick It' became nationally institutionalised within the industry during the late 1990s. There have also been several more local club initiatives such as the Charlton Athletic Race Equality partnership. Within these campaigns we find all the stakeholders – including supporters organisations, the police, safety officers, the football authorities. local authorities, race equality organisations and football clubs – working together to eliminate racist chanting from football (and with some success too). Moran (2000) has described his own dreadful experiences as a black professional footballer and highlighted the continued racist incidents in football during the 1990s. Smith, for example, reports how, following the murder of a Leeds fan in Turkey, a Leicester player 'was taunted with abuse and cut-throat gestures by a section of the visiting supporters for the crime of being the only player of Turkish descent in English football' (Smith 2000). Nevertheless, noting the various initiatives being undertaken, Moran concludes that 'there is reason to be optimistic about the levels of racism within football' (Moran 2000:198).

Looking to Europe, the Royal Dutch Football Association (KNVB) COTASS project, used database and networking technology to encourage Dutch football clubs to introduce an integrated approach to safety/security, commercial opportunity and fans enjoyment, through access control, club cards, ticketing and marketing (see Frosdick 1997o). From the outset, it was appreciated that for COTASS to address its security objective, it had to deliver commercial benefits to clubs and service benefits to fans. As the project manager told me, 'If you ratchet up security, you have to ratchet up service at the same time to take the fans with you'. Fans were required to be holders of club cards, which enabled them to purchase tickets through national lottery outlets for the 'home' areas of their club's home matches, the 'away' areas only of their clubs away matches and the 'neutral' areas of matches not involving their club. Club cards and tickets were scanned at access points to the stadiums, which helped support segregation policies. The cards allowed clubs to build databases for direct marketing to their supporter base, but also had benefits for fans, in the form of loyalty points, special offers and discounts.

A New Approach to the Management of Risk

The analysis has highlighted some of the principal areas of risk arising from each of the four perspectives. We have seen the operational conflicts which can arise and also some evidence of negotiated consensus. Of course the analysis is skewed towards my own research in British football grounds and other researchers elsewhere could undoubtedly be able to add considerably to what I have outlined. But having now looked in overview at the macro level of the industry, the meso level of the 'safety culture' and the zones in the PAFs system, the full complexity of the risk balancing act is becoming ever clearer.

So what I want to do now, using a simple worked example, is to suggest a practical management approach which acknowledges the validity of different perceptions and thus allows for greater richness, diversity and consensus in the analysis. Using the management of risk framework set out in Figure 5.2, the approach involves identifying, estimating, evaluating, managing and monitoring risks.

Figure 5.2: Management of Risk Framework

(Frosdick 1997g: 274 – derived from Scarf et al. 1993:23)

MANAGEMENT OF RISK FRAMEWORK			
Risk Analysis		*Risk Management*	
Identification		Planning	
	Estimation		Resourcing
		Evaluation	Controlling
Risk Monitoring			

Hazard identification and risk estimation can both be carried out at a risk assessment workshop at which representatives of each of the four groups – commercial, regulatory, spectator and neighbourhood – can be invited to participate. The representatives should have a 'hands-on' knowledge of the issues and may therefore be relatively junior in status. Three representatives from each group would give a manageable workshop of twelve participants. Adapting the HAZOPS risk identification technique referred to in Chapter One, we can use the idea of the PAF as a system, with each zone broken down into a number of smaller areas. The group should thus be facilitated through the identification of any hazards which they perceive in each area. Participants should be assured that there are no right or wrong answers, that candour is welcomed and the validity of all views will be recognised. This facilitated process will result in a comprehensive list of perceived hazards.

For our worked example, I want to go back to the playing area zone in a football stadium, and look particularly at the away team bench, which is one area within that zone. To keep things simple, we will assume that the hazard identification process has resulted in just four hazards. The first is that a missile will be thrown at the away team personnel on the bench. The second is that the substitute players will obstruct the front of an advertising hoarding while they are warming up. Third is that a spectator will shout verbal abuse at the away team personnel on the bench. Fourth is that the away team personnel will shout abuse at the referee or linesmen. So we have our list of hazards. Now we need to get an estimation of their probability and consequences.

Each hazard should now be considered by the whole group and a collective judgement made about its probability of occurrence. A second collective judgement should then be made about the potential adverse consequences if the hazard did occur. I would suggest that there are at least four types of adverse consequences to consider: for the profitability of the business (including its exposure to liability); for the enjoyment of the spectators or participants; for public safety and order; and for the community and environment in the outside world. All four types of consequences may be tackled in one exercise, or there may be a focus on just one type. These judgements about probability and consequences should be made using an appropriate scale upon which everyone in the group can agree. My preference is for a five point scale where 0 = None, 1 = Low, 2 = Low/Medium, 3 = Medium/High and 4 = High.

Going back to our example, let us imagine that the risk estimation process has come out with a hazards register something like Figure 5.3. This shows how the different hazards can have different implications for the four different types of consequences.

Figure 5.3: Example of a Hazards Register
(Sources: Frosdick 1997g: 279; Frosdick1998a: 206)

Ref	Hazard	Prob	Safety Conseq	Profit Conseq	Enjm't Conseq	Cmmty Conseq
A	A missile will be thrown at the bench	3	4	2	2	0
B	The subs will warm up in front of an advertising hoarding	2	1	3	1	0
C	A spectator will shout abuse at the bench	4	2	0	2	0
D	The bench will shout abuse at the referee	3	0	0	1	0

Such a hazards register should provide a substantial reference document to support the operational management of the venue. But PAFs managers cannot reasonably be expected to tackle all the risks, nor will it be cost-effective to try to do so. So the risks will need to be evaluated by an appropriate forum, which may well be the board of directors of the company running the venue, or their public sector equivalents.

One way of evaluating the risks is to multiply the probability and consequence ratings to give an overall risk evaluation rating. Using the five point scale outlined above would give a rating somewhere between 0 (0x0) and 16 (4x4). Another method is to plot each risk in the hazards register on a cross impact matrix.

Whatever the chosen method, the general principle governing such evaluation is that risk should be reduced to a level which is 'as low as is reasonably practicable' (Health and Safety Executive 1996:16). Hazards which have been judged to be of lower probability and consequences will be designated as 'low risk' and will be accepted as tolerable. At the other end of the scale, hazards which have been estimated as higher probability and consequences will be designated as 'high risk' and therefore subject to remedial action, in some cases irrespective of cost, through the preparation of appropriate risk management plans.

Where the boundaries fall between these two categories will be a question of management judgement, and, once decided, will determine which hazards are designated 'medium risk'. These may require careful monitoring with action where something can be done at a cost less than the benefit of the risk reduction.

Figure 5.4: Example Risk Evaluation Matrix
(Sources: Frosdick 1997g:280; Frosdick1998a:207)

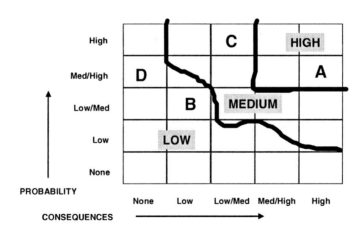

We shall use the cross impact matrix approach for our worked example. In the interests of simplicity and since the demand for risk assessment is often safety related, only the consequences for safety and order have been plotted in Figure 5.4 on the previous page. It can be seen that one of the hazards – the throwing of the missile – has been designated as high risk, whilst one – verbal abuse by a spectator – is medium and the other two are low risk.

The identification, estimation and evaluation processes should then be reported as a formal risk assessment. For each high risk or relevant medium risk, a second workshop should meet to consider what action can be taken to control the risk and reduce the probability and/or consequences to a tolerable level. Again, the workshop should comprise representatives of each of the four different groups, although it would now be appropriate for more senior people to be involved in the exercise. The countermeasures defined, the resources assigned and the responsibilities allocated should be recorded. The outcome of the process will be the risk management plan.

Taking the high risk in our worked example, we can ask ourselves what could be done to reduce the probability of a missile being thrown at the away bench. We might decide to sell the tickets in the surrounding area only to season-ticket holders or Family Club members. We would be able to vet applicants and would know who was in what seats in that area every game. Thinking about reducing the consequences for safety and order if a missile was thrown, we might decide to build a polycarbonate shelter around the bench and thus protect the occupants from harm.

Turning to the medium risk, the verbal abuse, we might decide that the same ticketing policy would reduce the probability a little. We might also decide to locate a steward adjacent to the bench. This would have a modest opportunity cost but would ensure that a member of staff was available to nip any problems in the bud and so reduce the consequences of the abuse escalating into potentially harmful disorder. Thus the implementation of the countermeasures identified should result both in increased protection for our guests and customers and reduced exposure to liability for ourselves.

But the management of risk process is not a 'single shot' to be forgotten after it is completed. Regular monitoring is important to ensure that the risk implications of any changes are considered and appropriately acted upon. A formal review of the hazards, their estimated probabilities and consequences, tolerability and any risk management measures proposed, should therefore be carried out at appropriate intervals, for example after major building work. The hazards register, risk assessment and risk management plan should be amended as appropriate and reissued accordingly.

This management of risk process thus documents which hazards have been identified as priorities, what is to be done about them and how and why those decisions have been made. So the process helps PAFs managers in discharging their accountability for profitable, safe, enjoyable and minimally disruptive facilities management. This approach can work not only for existing PAFs, but also for venues which are being renovated or even which have not yet been built. Engineering drawings can be used to determine the zones and areas in the proposed system and workshop representatives can be drawn from the groups who will eventually be involved in the facility. Carrying out a risk assessment should assist in early resolution of potential operating difficulties, thus allowing for the design to be changed to eliminate unnecessary operating costs, safety problems, external disruption and so on. For example, there may be a perceived hazard that personal radio communications will not work under a large stand because of the density of concrete. Identified at the design stage, this allows for leaky feeders to be built in during construction rather than as an expensive retro-fit.

CONCLUSION

The risk in sports grounds industry is organisationally complex. At the macro level, the application of Cultural Theory reveals the presence of four competing social solidarities; hierarchical regulators, individualist clubs, fatalist spectators and egalitarian pressure groups. At the micro level, Cultural Theory suggests that the various agencies working at a venue are likely to interact with each other in a way that is biased towards one of four archetypal models of 'safety culture'. No one model has the monopoly on good practice and there is, therefore, no 'one best way' of organising the cross organisational collaboration required. Cultural Theory analysis has also revealed the complex mix of risk perceptions found within a PAF, and the management difficulties involved in balancing the necessary management of risk. The practical application of Cultural Theory suggests a possible management of risk approach which takes account of different risk perceptions and seeks to negotiate between them.

The cultural and organisational complexity revealed in this analysis of the risk in sports grounds industry seems likely to be archetypal of the complicated structures to be found in other management of risk scenarios. Cultural Theory offers a toolkit for disaggregated analysis in these contexts. A cultural audit or stakeholder analysis of the organisational context – macro or micro – would seem to offer the opportunity for all parties to confront the existing culture and be aware of its implications for overall attitudes to risk. Such awareness should encourage an appreciation of the validity of alternative points of view and thus enable each party to manage the interactions between themselves and other agencies in a more constructive and enlightened way.

Looking to the wider context of project management and the strategic management of major organisational change, for example the installation of a major new technological system or relocation to a new building, the same kind of cultural audit would seem to be an important component of strategic analysis. Asking 'where are we now?' involves not only environmental scanning and a focus on the key internal competencies of the business, but also a clear understanding of the internal culture. The operationalisation of Cultural Theory suggests a method of adapting the existing models to undertake such cultural audits and assess and manage competing perceptions of risk in a new and revealing way.

From Risk in Sports Grounds to Police Project Risk

Having proposed a hypothetical new approach for assessing and managing risk in PAFs, the ideal research design for a grounded theory approach would now have gone on to undertake some case studies in a sample of PAFs, to analyse the individual cases and then to prepare a cross-case analysis from which the theory would emerge. But as we saw in Chapter Two, attempts to get the necessary access foundered. This was unfortunate, but a change of job within the police service presented the opportunity to take the research in a new direction. If I thought my proposed new approach might work in the PAFs industry, and if similar organisational complexity existed in other management of risk scenarios, then my approach might work in those scenarios too. And the change of job meant I now had good access to the world of police programme and project risk. When I described my hypothetical new approach to my employers they asked me to use it to facilitate the preparation of a risk assessment and risk management plan for a police project. That work was quickly followed by other projects and in a short space of time I had so much work that I was able to leave the police service and set up in business.

This change of research setting from risk in PAFs to police project risk was very much in line with Toft's ideas of isomorphic learning, i.e. learning from which 'the more universally applicable lessons can be drawn' (Toft 1992:52). Isomorphism suggests that the lessons from research into managing risk in PAFs ought to be applicable to the management of project risk. And here was a management of risk scenario with similar characteristics to the PAFs industry. The project management industry has a history of disastrous failures, for example in Information Technology (Collins 1997). It is organisationally complex. Different projects configure the relationships between their different players in different ways, thus 'project cultures differ' (Dingle 1997:250). And Chapman and Ward note that, just as we have seen in PAFs, 'a fundamental point is that different parties involved in a project frequently have different perceptions of project risk' (Chapman and Ward 1997:267).

So to take the analysis on to the next stages – the individual case studies, the cross-case report and thus the grounded theory, we will now move on into a new research setting. But before we move to the next stages, I want to press the pause button and seek to replicate, albeit much more briefly, the structure for the risk in PAFs analysis presented in this and the preceding Chapter. Thus Chapter Six opens with a short definition of the new research setting, followed by a briefer analysis of cultural complexity at both macro and micro levels. Chapter Six then closes with an extended case study. The other 40 individual case studies are presented in Chapter Seven, and the cross-case analysis follows in Chapter Eight.

CHAPTER SIX: POLICE PROJECTS RISK – PART I

SUMMARY

This Chapter sets out the first part of a Cultural Theory analysis of the management of risk within British police programmes and projects. The analysis is presented is five main sections. The first section explains the concepts of programme and project management and introduces the police research setting. The significance of the setting for research is justified and the impact which the research has had on the setting is discussed.

The second section gives an overview of the 41 case studies which form the data base for this setting. The next two sections then seek to replicate, albeit more briefly, the analytical structure of the PAFs risk setting. Section three shows how Cultural Theory has been applied in the case studies to disaggregate the stakeholders to be found in the police setting, whilst section four suggests how Cultural Theory might be deployed as organisation theory to support an analysis of project organisational cultures.

Taking the analysis in the police setting on beyond what was achieved in the PAFs setting, the final section gives an extended case study of the NSPIS, the one case which is in the public domain and the case on which about one-fifth of the research effort was expended.

THE RESEARCH SETTING

Police Programme and Project Management[22]

Programme and Project Management

As we saw in Chapter Four, managing PAFs is complicated and involves a wide range of disciplines. The same is true of projects. Managing projects is also highly complex and interdisciplinary. The UK Association for Project Management (APM) are the custodians of a body of knowledge (Dixon 2000), which is the source of a syllabus defining the topics which persons wishing to take the APM professional examination are expected to know (Hougham 2000).

The main headings in the APM body of knowledge (Table 6.1 on the next page) give us a good idea of the vast scope of the subject.

---

[22] This section is derived from Frosdick and Odell (1996), Frosdick (1999b), Frosdick (1999e) and Frosdick and Capon (2003).

Table 6.1: Association for Project Management Body of Knowledge
(Source: Dixon 2000)

1. General	45 Modelling and Testing
10 Project Management	46 Configuration Management
11 Programme Management	
12 Project Context	**5 Commercial**
	50 Business Case
2 Strategic	51 Marketing and Sales
20 Project Success Criteria	52 Financial Management
21 Strategy/Project Management Plan	53 Procurement
22 Value Management	54 Legal Awareness
23 Risk Management	
24 Quality Management	**6 Organisational**
25 Health, Safety and Environment	60 Life Cycle Design & Management
	61 Opportunity
3 Control	62 Design and Development
30 Work Content & Scope Management	63 Implementation
31 Time Scheduling/Phasing	64 Hand-Over
32 Resource Management	65 (Post) Project Evaluation Review
33 Budgeting and Cost Management	66 Organisation Structure
34 Change Control	67 Organisation Roles
35 Earned Value Management	
36 Information Management	**7 People**
	70 Communication
4 Technical	71 Teamwork
40 Design, Implementation & Hand-Over	72 Leadership
41 Requirements Management	73 Conflict Management
42 Estimating	74 Negotiation
43 Technology Management	75 Personnel Management
44 Value Engineering	

There would appear to be considerable overlap between project management and general management studies. So let us try and distinguish project management from other types of management.

Consider first the use of the word 'project'. People and organisations are very quick to use the word 'project' to describe things that are nothing of the kind. For example, let's imagine that a charitable organisation says it has a 'project' to feed starving people in the Third World. Or a local authority runs a youth centre where the youth leader is moving on, and so the authority advertises for a 'project' manager to take over.

In both these cases, the word 'project' is being used to describe running something which already exists. But the 'project' was about a unique change of some kind, i.e. to develop the food supply chain or to establish the youth centre. The 'projects' ended once they were handed over to the operational business or its equivalent.

The APM suggest that 'project management is widely regarded as the most efficient way of introducing unique change' (Dixon 2000:14). Projects thus have change management characteristics which distinguish them from maintenance matters (see Frosdick and Capon 2003).

Projects are daunting. The initial brief may be a short memo, or a few lines of committee meeting minutes, and it is for the project manager to turn this into something concrete. Projects have a temporary nature with a definite beginning and end. They have a particular purpose, which may be indicated by the name of project, for example 'privatisation of leisure services'. Projects are instruments of change – they have agreed end products and result in something being delivered. Projects are unique – no two projects are the same. The size may vary, for example from putting a person on the moon to organising a new office layout. The business sector may vary, for example from technology and construction to marketing, research and local government. Some projects may look like a previous one, but the objectives will be different, the circumstances changed and a new set of people involved. Finally, projects involve cross-functional coordination, drawing on a wide variety of resources and skills from different internal departments and outside organisations, for example consultancies.

So project management is not about maintenance through line management or operations management. It is more about innovation and complexity – and with these come uncertainty and risk.

The requirement for project management is determined less by the size of the change being planned and more by the complexity involved in integrating different sub-systems and reconciling competing demands. Take the example of the construction of a new building on a green-field site. Here the architect's aims (go for quality, time is no problem) are different from the builder's (cost is primary, elegance is of no concern) and also different from the environmental bodies (cost and time irrelevant, 'green' issues vital). The project manager has to bring all this together and find a way through.

Projects are also often part of a wider programme of change within an organisation. For example, let's imagine that an organisation has decided to replace all of its ageing stand-alone IT systems with the latest hardware and software. The future vision of a new IT infrastructure – with 'once-only' data entry using light pens onto new software packages all working seamlessly together across a network using the latest operating system sat on a brand new server – represents the blueprint for the future business operation. Delivering this vision requires more than one piece of unique change, and so more than one project. We need a project to procure the new server. We need a project to build the new network. We need projects to develop or procure the various software packages and to build the interfaces between them. We need one or more projects to procure the data entry devices.

All of this needs to be managed in a co-ordinated way, which is where 'programme' as opposed to 'project' management comes in.

> 'Programme management is a structured framework for defining and implementing change within an organisation. The framework covers organisation, processes, outputs and ways of thinking that focus on delivering new capabilities and realising benefits from these capabilities. The new capabilities may be services, service improvements, working practices or products that are developed and delivered by projects. The programme selects or commissions projects, providing the overall co-ordination, control and integration of the projects' delivery.' (OGC 1999:9)

Projects rarely exist in isolation. We have already seen that a project may well be part of a programme, which itself will be driven by the overall requirements of the business, which is itself part of and impacted by the wider world. So it is unlikely that the project can be divorced from its wider environment.

As an example, consider the case of one of my clients, a police organisation which initiated a programme of projects to redevelop its entire property estate. The strategy was to dispose of those assets which were poorly located and no longer fit for purpose in order to acquire better quality assets in improved locations. This was a massive change programme which inevitably carried a lot of risk. When asked to describe the consequences of things going wrong with the programme, the organisation produced the list of outcomes shown in Table 6.2.

Table 6.2: Adverse Outcomes for a Police Programme

The project will be stopped, abandoned or radically changed;
Timescales will over-run (i.e. the project will be delayed);
Costs will exceed the available budget;
The organisation will be exposed to ongoing financial liabilities;
The organisation will be exposed to legal liabilities;

The new building will not be delivered to the required specification;
The new building will not be fit for purpose;
The business benefits of the strategy will not be realised;
The quality of service to internal customers will suffer;
The quality of service to external customers will suffer;
The reputation/credibility of the organisation will be damaged;
The efficiency and/or effectiveness of the operational service will be undermined;
The performance targets in the annual plan will not be realised;
The morale of the workforce will be damaged;
Staff health and safety/security will be compromised;
Public health and safety/security will be compromised;
There will be public dissatisfaction/protest/public order issues;
The organisation's ability to function as a partner will be compromised;
There will be an adverse impact on staff retention; and
The organisation will be unable to respond fully to major incidents.

Clearly, this list goes beyond the adverse outcomes for the programme, to the organisation as a whole, and indeed beyond the organisation. This illustrates how a programme and its projects cannot be considered in isolation from their wider environment.

The Police Setting

As we have seen in Chapters Two and Three, my background as a police officer and my clients in police organisations meant it was in the police programme and project management setting that I had access to the field. Accordingly, although the disciplines of programme and project management may be found across the public and private sectors, it was in police organisations that the case study research was set.

The background to the case of the NSPIS programme and its projects clearly shows the richness of this police setting for research.

Policing in England and Wales is a highly complex activity. Its core businesses: crime prevention and detection; public order; community safety and partnership; traffic; and emergency response, involve a wide diversity of tasks. These are variously undertaken at national, regional, force and local levels. To be able to manage efficiently, effectively and economically, police managers require information from one or more levels about the demands they face and the resources available to them. Historically, this need had been dealt with only piecemeal. During the 1990s, however,

> 'there has been a growing recognition that a national strategy for police information systems and information technology was

necessary to enable information flows to be rationalised, information to be available where it is needed and analysis of this information to be more easily undertaken and more effectively used.' (NSPIS 1995a)

Furthermore, since police forces perform largely the same functions, it was recognised that, 'it does not make economic sense for each to develop separately its own IT systems to support these functions' (*ibid.*). For example, sixteen forces were found to be developing their own prisoner processing systems, yet custody procedures are derived from national legislation and codes of practice and are therefore largely the same in each force.

Thus on clear grounds of economy and effectiveness, the case for a national IS/IT strategy was recognised by both the Home Office and by the police service. Following a Scoping Study in 1992, the Association of Chief Police Officers, the Local Authority Associations and the Home Office decided to jointly sponsor a national police IS/IT strategy study. The results of that study (Home Office Police Department 1994) laid the foundations for the NSPIS. The overarching vision was

> 'to achieve the position where all the police forces of England and Wales (and where appropriate Scotland and the Royal Ulster Constabulary) and the Home Office are co-operatively developing a service-wide IS strategy. This comprises standard practices and procedures supported by common IT applications and infrastructure, from which a continuously improving service to the public is delivered.' (NSPIS 1995b)

The programme consisted of 38 applications representing opportunities for applying IS/IT to support the objectives, business processes and functions of the police service. Implementation of the first tranche of NSPIS was based on the principle that individual police forces would apply to lead on the specification and procurement of each IT application. The first tranche of applications to be developed by lead forces is shown in Table 6.3, together with two applications (marked #) which were already being centrally procured and implemented by pilot forces.

Table 6.3: NSPIS Local Applications

Case Preparation (Greater Manchester Police and Avon and Somerset Constabulary)
Custody (Avon and Somerset Constabulary and Greater Manchester Police)
Management Information (Metropolitan Police and Hertfordshire Constabulary)

Command and Control (Metropolitan Police)
Crime and Incident Reporting (West Yorkshire Police)
Legal Database/Force Reference Database (West Yorkshire Police)
Human Resources (Derbyshire Police)
#Vehicle Procedures and Fixed Penalty Offices
#HOLMES 2 (the replacement Home Office Large Major Enquiry System).

In addition to these application projects, the programme was responsible for technical architecture (TA) projects, the production of a common data model (CDM), Police National Computer (PNC) projects, the National Fingerprint Identification System (NAFIS), the Police National Network (PNN), the national trunked radio system (PSRCP, latterly branded as 'Airwave') as well as common services such as procurement and information security. The full complexity of the NSPIS programme is depicted in Figure 6.1

Figure 6.1: The NSPIS Programme and its Projects

(Source: Frosdick 1999e)

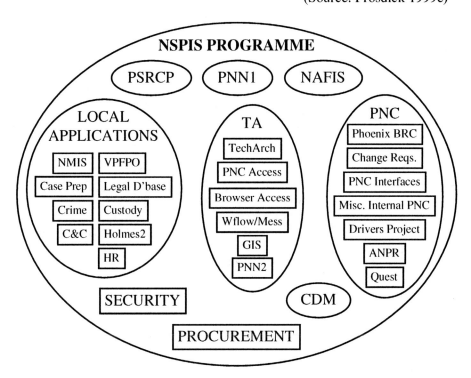

The effective co-ordination of such a massive undertaking required proper systems for management and control in accordance with the programme and project management methodologies produced and recommended by the Office for Government Commerce (see CCTA 1990; 1993; 1998; OGC 1999; 2002a; 2002b; 2004). These evolved during the course of the research. My case study work was thus set within a complex and evolving context, and thus a setting representative of other public and private sector programme and project contexts.

The Significance of the Setting for Research

We have seen that programmes and projects involve the management of considerable scope, change, innovation and complexity. There is thus considerable potential for costs to escalate, timescales to slip, quality to disappoint and reputations to suffer. Space precludes a detailed discussion of programme and project disasters along the lines of our discussion of football ground disasters in Chapter Four. But there is no doubt that management failures have resulted in many previous programmes and projects going seriously awry. A few examples must suffice to make the point that, like PAFs, programmes and projects are the settings for things going spectacularly wrong.

In his 1997 book entitled 'Crash', Collins details some of the most well-known computer disasters, including the infamous London Ambulance Service system, which went live on 26 October 1992, 'with disastrous results' (Collins 1997:160). Patients lives were quickly put at risk as the system failed to deploy ambulances to them. The system crashed on both 26 and 27 October and was switched off on 4 November after only a few days of unacceptable operation.

In 2001, the National Audit Office set out,

> 'Lessons from more than 25 cases in the United Kingdom in the 1990s where the implementation of IT systems has resulted in delay, confusion, inconvenience to the citizen and, in many cases, poor value for money for the taxpayer'. (National Audit Office 2001)

A subsequent report by the Royal Academy of Engineering and British Computer Society (2004) confirmed that the UK wasted billions of pounds every year on failed IT projects.

But such failures are not just an IT problem. The National Audit Office also publishes an annual report on major projects undertaken by the Ministry of Defence. An article headed, 'MoD bungles cost taxpayer £6bn in 10 years', reported that

'Analysis of the National Audit Office reports on the 25 largest equipment projects during the period, which cover defence expenditure of about £36 billion, shows that most of the new equipment for the Armed Forces will enter service at least three years late and cost at least seven per cent more than originally estimated.' (Hall and Almond 2000)

The 2003 report, whilst noting improvements, nevertheless found that four major projects had incurred cost overruns of a staggering £1541 million (National Audit Office 2003:1).

Such problems are not confined to the public sector. For example, in 2002, the engineering consultancy giant WS Atkins reported a major profits warning, partly as a result of being unable to bill its clients due to problems implementing a new internal computer system (see Osbourne 2002).

The 25 cases reported by the National Audit Office (2001) did not include any police programme or project failures, and it is fair to say that the police service has not yet seen anything on the same scale as some other parts of the other public sector. Nevertheless, police project cases do exist involving considerable cost and time over-runs, and in some cases the complete cancellation of a project and the loss of its development costs. Such cases are not in the public domain and I shall not therefore record them here in any detail. But for example, two of the police IT projects on which I have worked were initiated before 1996 and were only being implemented in Forces during 2003. Another police IT project on which I worked ran with a full-time staff for at least five years from 1995 to 2000 before being closed down.

Scarff, Carty and Charette point out that

'in post-mortems of IS-related programmes and projects that have gone badly wrong, it has become apparent that many of the difficulties could have been avoided if the manager involved had possessed the right information as well as sufficient time to deal with the situation. That is, to make an informed decision about, or exercise adequate control over, the situation.' (Scarff *et al.* 1993:1)

The current effects of past decisions frequently manifest themselves as operational problems for the programme or project manager. All too often, these difficulties could have been foreseen. Such foresight could be generated by thinking proactively about the potential future effects of current 'risky' decisions, that is decisions where there was a choice available and where the choice involved risk. Managers could increase their chances of delivering their products as quickly as possible, to the required quality, with the minimum of work and at the least cost by reducing the risks to which their programme or project was exposed.

Government have recognised the importance of effective management of risk within programmes and projects through a succession of publications (for example see Scarff *et al.* 1993, CCTA 1994b; 1995a; 1995b; ILGRA 1996; HM Treasury 2001; OGC 2002c, 2004). Within this evolving context, what has been most significant for my research has been the failure of these official publications to take adequate account of previous research findings on risk perception. For example, let us examine both the guidance which existed at the start of my research in 1995 and the best guidance available in 2004.

Throughout the four sets of the original CCTA guidelines (Scarff *et al.* 1993, CCTA 1994b; 1995a; 1995b), only one paragraph addresses the issue of risk perception. There is an acknowledgement that 'perception is heavily influenced by individual biases and experiences' (Scarff *et al.* 1993:10). However, the implications of this are dismissed with the argument that,

> 'It is important, when trying to manage risk, that risk is viewed in a consistent way throughout the organisation. This consistency requires that a common perception of risk should be created and communicated to everyone within the organisation." (*ibid.*)

This is a very narrow approach. The contrary view would argue that it was important to capture as rich and diverse a range of risk perspectives as possible in the management of risk exercise, which of course is where Cultural Theory comes in.

The OGC Successful Delivery Toolkit 'describes proven good practice for procurement, programmes, projects, risk and service management. The Toolkit brings together policy and best practice in a single point of reference' (OGC 2004). Browsing the workbook section on risk, we find an acknowledgement that 'it is important to determine the interests of all stakeholders, who may represent different customer groups, and to resolve conflicting requirements' (*ibid*). Further, in respect of risk identification, OGC state that the analyst should 'consider stakeholder viewpoints as their views on what poses a threat will vary' (*ibid*). This represents considerable progress over the CCTA guidelines. But the guidance does not say **how** to go about identifying stakeholders.

My experience throughout my work with clients in this setting since 1995 has been that, without an understanding of Cultural Theory, police organisations simply round up the usual hierarchical suspects. For example, police clients will list as stakeholders hierarchical organisations such as themselves, including the Home Office, Her Majesty's Inspectorate of Constabulary, the Association of Police Authorities, Association of Chief Police Officers, etc. Without my application of 'grid' and 'group' as a heuristic, what they forget to list are stakeholders from Cultural Theory's other forms of social solidarity, for example their more fatalist customers and workforce, their more commercial supply chain and the more egalitarian pressure groups who may oppose them.

I will develop this analysis further in the section on 'Police Risk Stakeholders' below. For the moment I will content myself with the assertion that, notwithstanding the passage of time, my research in this setting has not lost its originality.

The Impact of the Research on the Setting

As was the case with the safety at sports grounds setting, my own involvement as a consultant and academic in the police programme and project management setting since 1995 has had some impact on the setting. This is particularly the case in respect of two police organisations.

We have already seen that, from 1995 to 2001, I was extensively involved in the management of risk within the NSPIS programme and its projects. I began by advising on risk on one project. As a result of that work, I was invited to develop the management of risk strategy for the whole programme. The exposure from that work in turn led to invitations to advise on risk on various projects within the whole programme. In fact, 17 of the case studies in this research refer to the NSPIS programme, the development of its projects and their implementation in police organisations. I wrote the overall NSPIS management of risk strategy which provided as a matter of Home Office policy that,

> 'Managing risk is about managing perceptions of future hazards, probabilities and consequences. It is widely recognised that different individuals and groups of stakeholders can perceive risk in entirely different ways, thus it is considered important to ensure a broad range of perspectives are adequately represented in any management of risk activity.' (Frosdick 1997q)

Thus by means of the strategy I affirmed the general principle I had already adopted in my work with the programme and some of its projects, namely that risk was a question of plural perceptions and that different perceptions needed to be captured and managed. The strategy then provided the authority to continue with this approach with subsequent projects with which I became involved.

From 1997 onwards I was involved with the management of risk on eleven of the programmes and projects undertaken within another large police organisation. Again, my early work on one project led to invitations to work with other projects and programmes. Again, in the various risk documents I produced for the organisation, I made use of the policy statement that

> 'It is widely recognised that different people perceive risk in entirely different ways. Risk assessment and management is not an exact science but seeks to draw out shared perceptions of uncertainty. It is therefore important to ensure that a broad range of stakeholders is adequately represented in the process.'

Not that the whole thing has become circular, there is thus a sense in which I the consultant have been able to influence the extent to which I the researcher have been able to apply Cultural Theory to the cases in this research.

DATA SOURCES: THE CASE STUDIES

Having now set out, albeit more briefly than for safety at sports grounds, the research setting for the police programme and project case studies, I now want to introduce the 41 cases from which the subsequent analysis and conclusions in this book are derived. The case studies are briefly described in Table 6.4.

Table 6.4: Case Study Descriptions

1   Risk assessment, risk management, risk monitoring and risk review within the National Strategy for Police Information Systems, a programme of IT projects to develop standard software applications for the police service.

2   System security and disaster recovery analysis for a police IT project to procure a new command and control system.

3   Risk assessment and risk management for a police IT project to develop a reference database.

4   Risk assessment and risk management for a police business project, the details of which are confidential for security reasons.

5   Risk review for a police IT project to develop a prisoner processing system.

6   System security and disaster recovery analysis for a police IT project to develop a crime analysis system.

7   Risk assessment and risk management for a police IT project to develop a data model.

8   Assessment and management of the risks associated with policing the Millennium celebrations in all police forces.

9   Risk assessment, risk management and risk review for a programme of police business projects on diversity training.

10   Risk assessment, risk management, risk monitoring and risk review for a police business project to take over responsibility for policing part of another police force area.

11   Risk assessment, risk management, risk monitoring and risk review for a police IT project to develop a system for processing cases within the criminal justice system.

12   Risk assessment and risk management for a police business project to consider the outsourcing of support services.

13   System security and disaster recovery analysis for a police IT project to procure a new personnel system.

14   System security and disaster recovery analysis for a police IT project to develop a system for processing cases within the criminal justice system.

15   Risk assessment and risk management for a police IT programme of technical architecture projects.

16   Risk assessment, risk management and risk review for a police IT project to develop a crime recording system.

17   Risk assessment, risk management, risk monitoring and risk review for a police business project to develop a new communications (radio, telephony, etc.) environment.

18   Risk assessment of Health and Safety liabilities arising from decisions about the training of police officers and civilian support staff.

19   Risk assessment for a police business programme of projects to develop and implement a new human resources strategy.

20   Risk assessment and risk management for a programme of police business projects for organisational change into a non-governmental body.

21   Assessment and management of the risks associated with an education contract.

22   System security and disaster recovery analysis for a police IT project to develop a prisoner processing system.

23   Risk assessment and risk management for a police IT project to develop new systems for internal and external communication.

24   Assessment of the risks associated with the quality of crime investigation.

25   Risk assessment and risk management for a police IT project to develop and install a new IS/IT infrastructure.

26   Assessment and management of the risks associated with organising an
      international police conference.

27   Risk assessment and risk management for a police IT project to implement new
      systems for processing prisoners and for the administration of criminal justice
      cases.

28   Risk assessment, risk management and risk review for a police IT project to
      develop a management information system.

29   Risk assessment for a police business project to develop a new training
      programme for police officers.

30   System security and disaster recovery analysis for a police IT project to develop
      a crime recording system.

31   Assessment and management of the risks associated with policing the
      Millennium celebrations in one police force area.

32   Risk assessment and risk management for a police IT project to implement a
      new crime recording system.

33   Risk assessment and risk management for a police IT project to develop a web
      browser.

34   Risk assessment and risk management for a police business project to consider
      changes to police recruitment and training.

35   Risk assessment and risk management for a police business project to develop a
      specialist criminal intelligence analysis capability.

36   Risk assessment, risk management and risk review for a police business project
      to procure domestic services.

37   Risk assessment and risk management for a police IT project to develop and
      implement a property recording system.

38   Risk assessment, risk management, risk monitoring and risk review for a
      programme of police business projects to redevelop a property estate.

39   Risk assessment and risk management for a police IT project to implement a
      personnel system.

40   Assessment and management of the risks associated with organising a national
      police conference.

41   Assessment and management of the risks associated with organising a series of
      national police seminars.

Case One (the NSPIS programme) is identified because it is already in the public domain (see Frosdick and Odell 1996; Frosdick 1999b; 1999e). But it is ethically proper to seek to preserve the anonymity of the other police organisations involved and their informants and I have taken several measures to assist in achieving this. First, the numerical identifiers in Table 6.4 have been allocated at random. Thus Table 6.4 is not a chronology of cases in date order. Second, each case, including the NSPIS programme, has also been allocated a unique codename. Third, the link between the numerical identifiers and the codenames is found only in my database of cases.

ANALYSIS: POLICE RISK STAKEHOLDERS

Introduction

I argued in Chapter Four that sports grounds disasters arise from people's mistakes and misjudgements. These in turn may arise from clashes in the value systems and attitudes to risk to be found between the different cultural constituencies in the PAFs safety industry. I now want to argue the same point in respect of the programme and project management industry – in the police setting.

In his principles of organisational isomorphism, derived from general systems theory (see Bertalanffy 1973), Toft makes the point that,

> 'Any failure which occurs in one system will have a propensity to recur in another 'like' system for similar reasons. And ... although two particular systems may appear to be completely different, if they possess the same or similar component parts or procedures then they will both be open to a common mode of failure'. (Toft 1997:91)

In the conclusion to Chapter Five and in the opening sections of this Chapter we have seen that the programme and project management industry has common features with the PAFs safety industry: a history of disasters, organisational complexity, organisational cultural divergence and differences in risk perception. So what I want to do now is demonstrate how Cultural Theory may be applied to disaggregate the stakeholders to be found in the police setting.

The analysis will be laid out in three stages. First I want to introduce the heuristic by which I explain the application of Cultural Theory to my clients. Second, I want to examine a sample of the stakeholder analyses I have undertaken with my clients. Third, I want to draw out the commonalities in the analyses.

Explaining Cultural Theory

I have a standard lecture/presentation to my clients and students which includes the slides set out in Figures 1.5 in Chapter One and 2.1 in Chapter Two. These allow me to offer a basic explanation of Cultural Theory and of the four views of nature from which four different ways of perceiving risk are derived. I then go on to show the slide set out in Figures 6.2 below.

Figure 6.2: Explaining Cultural Theory

(Source: Frosdick unpublished)

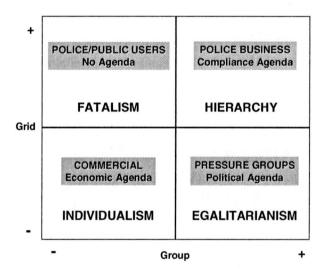

I explain that there are two groups of stakeholders within the hierarchical constituency – those who commissioned the work and those who are working on the project. They both see risk as deviance, in other words a failure to deliver on time, to budget and to specification. This deviance can lead to blame and accountability, with unpleasant consequences for those who failed to deliver. Accordingly, I describe this constituency as having a 'compliance agenda'.

As Douglas and Wildavsky (1982) show, hierarchy works in alliance with individualism, an alliance which Douglas and Wildavsky refer to as 'the center'. In this context the individualist constituency represents the supply chain for the programme or project. Within this supply chain we find commercial suppliers, consultants and other advisors, for whom risk is about denial of opportunities to make money out of the hierarchical constituency. I therefore describe this group as having a 'commercial agenda'.

Dealing next with the fatalists, I point out that the end users of the product have few concerns about timeliness, budget and specification. They may be aware of the programme or project but accept they have little say in what is being produced. They thus have no real agenda beyond wondering whether the thing will be any good. This is a fitness for purpose rather than specification compliance view of quality.

I then point out that there are organisations which purport to represent groups of users. These often have single interests in support of which they lobby vociferously. They are often pressure groups but it is sometimes more acceptable to refer to them as 'advisory groups'. They may see risk where the business and commercial constituencies see benefits, thus they may niggle at or even oppose what the programme or project is doing. This is the egalitarian constituency referred to as 'the border' by Douglas and Wildavsky (1982). Note their chapter titles that 'the border is alarmed' (chapter six) and 'the border fears for nature' (chapter seven). Accordingly, I describe this constituency as having a 'political agenda'.

I now want to demonstrate how this explanation of the application of cultural theory has assisted many of my clients in carrying out disaggregated stakeholder analysis.

Stakeholder Analyses

The case of the NSPIS Programme, which is set out in full below, includes a section showing how Cultural Theory was used to help select the participants in the risk assessment process. In addition to that case in the public domain, I have selected a sample of four other cases (two programmes and two projects) where my clients applied Cultural Theory to analyse their stakeholders. The analysis works in two stages. First, I ask the client to identify the names of organisations which fit the organisational structure and risk perception agenda of the constituency. Second, I ask the client to suggest the names of individual representatives of those organisations who might be approached and invited to participate in the management of risk process.

Case Study Ranger

This case identified stakeholders from Cultural Theory's four constituencies as shown in Table 6.5.

Table 6.5: Stakeholder Analysis for Case Study 'Ranger'

Hierarchy – Stakeholders from Police Governance
Association of Chief Police Officers Personnel and Training Committee
Relevant Home Office departments and units
Association of Police Authorities
Her Majesty's Inspectorate of Constabulary
Various named internal departments from within the organisation
Egalitarianism – Stakeholders from the Staff Associations
Police Federation
Superintendent's Association
UNISON (the trade union)
Fatalism – Stakeholders from the Police Force User Community
Crime training managers
Force training managers
Senior personnel and training managers
Members of practitioner groups
Individualism – Stakeholders from Other Education/Training Providers
University of [*Name 1*]
University of [*Name 2*]
[*Name of Company 1*]
[*Name of Company 2*]

Based on this analysis, a sample of twenty individual representatives was selected and interviewed to provide the source data for the risk assessment undertaken.

Case Study Bluegrass

This case identified stakeholders from Cultural Theory's four constituencies as shown in Table 6.6.

Table 6.6: Stakeholder Analysis for Case Study 'Bluegrass'

Fatalism – The User Community – Aware, But No Particular Agenda
A rank and file police user
A senior police user
A user from a community group
Hierarchy – The Police Business – Governance/Compliance Agenda
A Chief Police Officer
A Police Authority member
The head of an internal supplier department
Egalitarianism – Advisory/Pressure Groups – Concerned/Political Agenda
Black Police Association

Police Federation
UNISON
Individualism – Commercial Providers – Economic/Best Practice Agenda
A management consultant
A professional expert
An academic expert

This analysis yielded twelve interviewees who provided the source data for the risk assessment undertaken.

Case Study Orange

This case identified stakeholders from Cultural Theory's four constituencies and their predicted risk concerns as shown in Table 6.7.

Table 6.7: Stakeholder Analysis for Case Study 'Orange'

Individualism – Commercial Providers
Threats to fair procurement/competition
Threats to the profitable operation of the contract
A representative of the British Institute of [*name of function*]
An expert practitioner
Somebody who teaches the subject at an educational establishment
A representative from [*name of company 1*]
A representative from [*name of company 2*]
Fatalism – the User Community
Threats to the quality of services
Threats to the experience of attending sites
A senior police user
A probationer constable
A user who lives on site
Hierarchy – the Business
Threats to the successful letting of the contract (i.e. the completion of the project)
Threats to ongoing revenue liabilities
The Project Director
A senior supplier from an internal department
A procurement specialist
Egalitarianism – Staff Associations
Threats to terms and conditions of service
Threats to the morale of the workforce
A Trades Union side representative
A staff association representative from a supplier company
A representative from a social club

This analysis resulted in 15 individual representatives being invited to attend a risk assessment workshop.

Case Study Royal

This case identified stakeholders from Cultural Theory's four constituencies as shown in Table 6.8. This case involved the probation service rather than the police service.

Table 6.8: Stakeholder Analysis for Case Study 'Royal'

Governance – Compliance Agenda, e.g. on Time, to Budget, to Specification
National Probation Directorate
Association of Chief Probation Officers
Audit Commission
Customers/Users – No Particular Agenda, e.g. Fitness for Purpose, the Study 'Experience'
Current and future clients
Students (past, present and future)
Academic staff
Administrative support staff
Supplier – Commercial Agenda, e.g. Covering Costs, Sustainability, Reputation
The [Name of] University
The [Name of Faculty]
The [Name of Department]
Course Leaders
Representative – Political Agenda, e.g. Terms and Conditions, Workloads
National Association of Probation Officers (NAPO)
National Association of Teachers in Further and Higher Education (NATFHE)
National Union of Students (NUS)

This analysis provided the basis for a risk assessment workshop involving only six people, all drawn from the client organisation, but who were asked to think laterally and to consider the risk perceptions of each of the four groups.

Discussion: Cultural Theory Constituencies

The cases show that hierarchy refers to the police (or probation) business and governance community, who commission, pay for and have oversight of the work. The stakeholders mentioned include bureaucracies such as the Home Office, Police Authorities, the Audit Commission and Her Majesty's Inspectorate of Constabulary, together with senior managers from internal departments within the organisation. Predicted risk concerns are all about delivery within budget, on time and in compliance with specification.

The individualist solidarity is represented by the commercial world, from which consultants, potential tenderers and contracted suppliers are drawn. Stakeholders mentioned include representative trade bodies, named commercial companies, management consultants and academics who are willing to earn fees for providing expert advice. Predicted risk on this view is about fair competition in procurement and maximising profitability through return on current investment and preservation of reputation for future business.

Egalitarianism refers to pressure or 'advisory' groups. These include trade unions such as the Police Federation, UNISON and NATFHE, together with lobbying organisations such as the Black Police Association, Gay Police Association and British Association of Women Police. These 'border' groups are often at odds with the alliance of hierarchy and individualism (Douglas and Wildavsky's 'center') and can thus be predicted to see risk where the business and commercial constituencies see benefits.

The fatalists are the front line user community comprising both internal staff and the external public, all of whom have solutions imposed upon them by the hierarchical business and are open to exploitation by suppliers. Their predicted risk concerns are around implementation of change – will things be better or will they simply be different?

Having thus demonstrated that the police programme and project management industry may be disaggregated at the macro level, let us now continue to seek to replicate, albeit more briefly, the structure of the analysis laid out for the PAFs setting. We do this by turning to a brief consideration of the question of individual project cultures at the micro level.

ANALYSIS: PROJECT ORGANISATION CULTURES

Introduction

Projects are organisations, thus this section will seek to build on the discussion of Cultural Theory as organisation theory in Chapter Two. The limitations of space preclude the type of detailed analysis undertaken on 'safety culture' in Chapter Five. The originality of that contribution has perhaps been recognised through its initial publication (Frosdick 1999b) and subsequent inclusion in a collection (Mars and Weir 2000a). But to set out such an analysis of 'project culture' would add little to knowledge since, as we saw at the end of Chapter Five, it is already well-established that 'project cultures differ' (Dingle 1997:250). So the objective here is simply to illustrate how such an analysis of 'project culture' might be developed for this research setting.

Chapter Two argued that Johnson and Scholes (1999) 'cultural web' (see Figure 2.3) was descriptive rather than analytical, and that what was needed was an analytical model to disaggregate the different types of paradigm to be found within the 'cultural web'. Cultural Theory provides such model. Thus a marriage can be proposed between the cultural web, as a well-established device for describing the factors which influence organisational culture, and Cultural Theory, as a model for disaggregated paradigm analysis. The key to such an analysis will be an examination of each of the six headings within the cultural web to determine those factors which suggest the relative strength of grid and group.

At first sight, the headings of *power structures*, *organisational structures*, *control systems* and *symbols*, have very clear dimensions of grid, whilst *routines* has a clear group dimension. *Rituals and myths* would seem to be signposts for deference to history and tradition indicating a cultural bias towards hierarchy. But on more detailed consideration, it is possible to argue that five of the six headings has both grid and group dimensions.

In drawing out the analysis, account will need to be taken of the grid group framework for cultural analysis proposed in Figure 5.1 in Chapter Five. This framework set outs the headings of space, time, objects, resources and labour; autonomy, reciprocity, insulation and competition; and frequency, mutuality, scope and boundary (see Mars 1994; Mars and Mars 1996).

Discussion: Cultural Factors[23]

Power Structures

The grid dimension describes the locus of power. If grid is extremely high, power is inherent in the system and no level of management has autonomy. This is only viable if the economic environment is static. More commonly, high grid means that control is held by senior management. Top management autonomy is high while middle management autonomy is low. Low grid means that middle managers are the locus of power. Top management autonomy is low, in that they must bring about changes by influencing middle managers, whose autonomy is high. Very low grid means that decision making is vested at the level of the first line supervisor.

The group dimension describes the importance of co-ordination versus individual autonomy. If group is high, individual action is discouraged,

---

[23] This section is derived from Frosdick (1997h).

power is centralised and co-ordination is required either vertically (in high grid organisations) or horizontally (where grid is low). If group is low, power is decentralised and individual action is encouraged. With low grid, this encourages individual middle managers to think of themselves as entrepreneurs running a 'business within a business'. Where grid is high, middle managers are free to individually follow their goals within boundaries set by those above them.

Organisational Structures

The most generally recognised structural types range from the *simple* and *functional* through to the more complex *multidivisional* and *matrix* structures. Whatever the type, an examination of the organisation chart will give a feel for the relative strength of grid and group at the macro organisational level.

Irrespective of the size and complexity of the organisation, the number of layers of management will give a good indication of grid in this context. Long chains and narrow spans of command suggest that grid is high, whilst wide spans and short chains imply lower grid. Thus a small organisation with a basic functional structure but multiple layers of management within each function may be higher grid than a large divisional organisation with a very flattened management pyramid or matrix structure.

Nomenclature, corporate identity and intra-organisational boundaries provide evidence of the extent of group. Asking the staff who they work for is key. Thus the multidivisional company operating under one brand name is relatively high group, whilst the holding company with subsidiaries retaining their own identities is relatively low group. The structures for meetings within the organisation provide a further indication of group. Regular inter-divisional and cross-functional meetings suggest that group is high, while purely departmental meetings imply lower group.

Control Systems

Key considerations under this heading will include the systems for formal control of space, time, resources and labour. High grid is suggested by rank related prescriptions in the use of space. Executive canteens and washrooms, designated parking spaces and bigger offices for more senior staff are common indicators here. The most senior personnel will frequently have access to their offices guarded by an ante-room and secretary.

Emphasising function over rank involves a very different approach to spatial use. With low grid, we find open access to all areas, an absence of symbolic load and a tendency to open plan and low level screening, for greatest visibility and access. Where group is also low, sectional competition may be expected to lead to the emergence of privately captured space. With low group, there will be no perceived requirement for public areas. On the other hand, the presence of communal space, for example meeting rooms, reception areas and an atrium or foyer with coffee facilities, provides a good indication of high group.

Formal time controls such as clocking-on, factory hooters, set tea breaks, lunch hours and even holidays, all indicate high grid, whereas flexi-time and control of diaries by individuals themselves suggest grid is low.

Gaskell and Hampton (1982) have demonstrated how different aspects of accounting procedures can be used to illustrate the relative strengths of grid and group in the context of resource management. High grid is indicated where capital expenditure proposals originate only from the top, where there is central control and compulsory use of resources and no accountability in respect of such use and where uncertainty in accounts is concealed. Low grid is the reverse. Blame absorption, belief in the accounts and lack of penalties for exceeding budgets all suggest the organisational group dimension is high. Again, low group is the reverse. Thus the existence of diverse cost/profit centres within an organisation is an indication of both low grid and low group.

As Mars (1994:24-28) has shown, the extent of control of labour depends on how the particular jobs within the organisation are organised 'on the ground'. Where grid is low, people have autonomy, can transact with a wide range of others and can carry out tasks in ways which they can define for themselves. Where grid is high, people may be tied to a defined place, time and mode of work where they are socially insulated from others and have no scope for competition. High group is derived from frequent and repeated face to face contacts with others in a mutually interconnecting network, across a range of activities. Low group is implied by isolated subordination (where grid is high) or individual entrepreneuriality (where grid is low).

Human resource management policies within the organisation will be further indicators. For example, performance-related pay and bonuses suggest competition between individuals and thus low grid. Similarly, the strength of group may be deduced from whether appraisals and objective setting are conducted on an individual or team basis.

Routines

Informal controls of space and time may be considered under this heading. New members of the organisation may unwittingly break unwritten high grid rules about who sits where in the canteen or who parks where in the car park.

The strength of a group is further increased as the scope of its activities becomes wider, perhaps through communal residence or habitual association outside work. Where grid is also high, individuals may be powerless to resist, for example, a three-line whip to go drinking after work on Fridays. Looking at how coffee is taken gives a helpful indication of group. The tea trolley coming round to individual offices suggests lower group than a ritual daily canteen or foyer meeting at a predetermined time.

Symbols

The symbolic and rank related size and quality of objects such as desks, furnishings and carpets etc. all suggest high grid. Where, on the other hand, such objects are functional rather than symbolic, we find that grid is low. Where grid and group are high, the public space will include large entrances, elaborate doorways and expansive reception areas and thus symbolically distinguish the inside from the outside. Communal use of objects may be evidence either of high grid, where such use is prescribed, or high group, where the communal use takes place by consensus.

Rituals and Myths

An emphasis on myths and stories, told repeatedly over coffee or at social functions, provides a strong suggestion of hierarchy, in which grid and group are both high.

Moving On To The Case Studies

Having established the viability – albeit not the reality – of an analysis of 'project culture' through the application of Cultural Theory, we have now achieved the objective set at the conclusion of Chapter Five of replicating the analytical structure adopted for the PAFs setting. We have therefore reached the point where we can move on into the area of analysis which (for reasons explained in Chapter Two) was not achieved for the PAFs setting. We therefore now turn to a consideration of the 41 case studies undertaken in the police programme and project research setting.

Following the design and methods for case study research set out by Yin (1994), the case study analysis will be set out in two passes. For the first pass, the remainder of this Chapter will present an extended case study of the NSPIS programme. Chapter Seven will then analyse the other 40 individual case studies in order to provide the first set of files needed for a grounded theory analysis (see Turner 1983). For the second pass, Chapter Eight will then go on to set out the cross-case analysis and so provide the second set of data required for the grounded theory approach.

The first case presented is an extended case study of the NSPIS programme. The choice of this case for the most detailed presentation arises for three reasons. First, it was the case for which I was involved for the longest period of time – four and a half years – from May 1995 to November 1999. Second, it was the case on which I expended the most days effort – 106.75 days – more than two and a half times more involvement than I expended in any other case. Third, the case is already in the public domain (see Frosdick and Odell 1996, Frosdick 1999b, 1999e, 2003) and there are thus no ethical difficulties about identifying it.

ANALYSIS: THE CASE OF THE NSPIS PROGRAMME[24]

Introduction

The background to the NSPIS programme has already been set out in the discussion of the police setting earlier in this Chapter.

The NSPIS programme provided a tremendous opportunity for creating significant improvements in police service information systems provision. But these would only come about when they were totally integrated into the business operation. Projects deliver products but it is only through their operational use that benefits are realised. Thus the programme needed a well co-ordinated benefits management regime. Conversely, the complexity and scope of the programme and its projects meant there was considerable potential for costs to escalate, timescales to slip and quality to disappoint. Thus in addition to benefits management, it was seen as essential that the management of risk formed an integral part of the management of the programme. Since the programme and its projects were using the CCTA programme and project management methodologies, it seemed logical for the CCTA guidelines on the management of risk (CCTA 1994b, 1995a, 1995b) to be adopted as the basis of the management of risk strategy.

Risk Framework and Approach

The overall CCTA framework for the management of risk has already been set in Figure 5.2 in Chapter Five. It comprises three main components and a number of subsidiary processes: risk analysis (identification, estimation and evaluation); risk management (planning, resourcing and controlling); and risk monitoring. And as we saw in Chapter Two, risk is defined by CCTA as 'the chance of exposure to the adverse consequences of future events' (Scarff *et al*. 1993:88). This framework and the very substantial set of definitions, explanations and process guidelines provided in support of them did seem to provide a most comprehensive regime for the management of programme and project risk.

---

[24] This section is derived from Frosdick and Odell (1996), Frosdick (1999b), Frosdick (1999e) and Frosdick (2003).

However, as we saw earlier in this Chapter in the discussion of the significance of the setting for research, there was one area in which the CCTA guidelines were considered to be deficient, namely in their failure to take sufficient account of the implications of research into risk perception. Taking a contrary view to CCTA, it was decided that it was important to capture as rich and diverse a range of risk perspectives as possible in the management of risk exercise. Research findings from psychology and from Cultural Theory showed that different people and groups of stakeholders perceived risk in entirely different ways. No one measure of risk could represent the perceptions of different individuals and groups of stakeholders. There were no right or wrong answers and nobody would be wrong either to perceive a particular matter as a risk, or to evaluate a risk in a particular way. Thus any risk exercise would be undertaken by a group of people, rather than just one or two. And representatives of each of the four groups proposed by Cultural Theory would be identified and invited to participate. This would include inviting known opponents of NSPIS to join in the exercise. They would not hesitate to articulate the risks some other people might prefer not to hear.

The Initial Management of Risk Strategy

The initial strategy for managing risk within the programme was therefore designed around the management framework and definitions offered by CCTA, together with the research findings on risk perception from Cultural Theory. Risk was thus defined as *perceived* exposure to the *perceived* adverse consequences of *perceived* future events. It was decided to combine the risk identification and estimation processes into a risk assessment workshop. It was then decided that risk evaluation would be a management decision for the Programme Director, the most senior executive involved in the programme. This decision would determine which risks would require countermeasures and which risks would be accepted as residual. Finally, it was decided to review the risk evaluation, plan the necessary countermeasures and allocate responsibility for them at a risk management workshop. In terms of philosophy, it was decided that operationalising Cultural Theory would offer an opportunity both to identify the adherents to each of the four cultural types which would inevitably be present within the overall organisational culture of the programme and to ensure that the full richness and diversity of a range of risk perspectives were captured in the workshops.

The Risk Assessment Workshop

Selection of Participants

Initial analysis revealed that the four cultural types were indeed fully represented within the programme's stakeholders, namely by the Police IT and Communications Suppliers Association (PITACSA), by recipient police forces, by the Home Office and Police Advisory Group IT (PAGIT) and by certain police forces vociferously opposed to the chosen implementation routes for NSPIS. Having identified the four constituencies, it was hypothesised that, if asked to articulate the risks to the programme, PITACSA might focus on commercial risks to the profitability of their businesses, whilst the Home Office and PAGIT would be more worried about threats to the programme's procedures and structures. Opponent police forces would identify how the programme threatened their right to determine their own local IS/IT strategy and therefore the future, whilst the majority of police forces would broadly accept the *fait accompli* of standard national applications. In order to maximise the chances of identifying and properly assessing all the sources of risk, it was therefore seen as essential that all four types should participate in the risk assessment as equal partners.

Equal numbers of representatives of each constituency were therefore invited to attend a risk assessment workshop at the Police Staff College, Bramshill, in August 1995. Whilst the actual attendees from each type were not quite equal in numbers on the day, nevertheless each group was represented. The introduction to the workshop emphasised the differences in risk perception and that there were no right or wrong answers. Equally importantly, all the participants were assured that nothing they could say would cause any offence, on the contrary, their candour would be welcomed and the validity of their views recognised.

Risk Identification Exercise

The risk identification exercise involved the consideration of potential risks arising from both the external and internal environments. The mnemonic PESTLE was used to facilitate the identification of political, economic, social, technological, legal and ecological risks arising from threats in the external environment. Risks arising from weaknesses in the internal environment were generated through consideration of the core business areas of infrastructure, human resources, finance, technology, logistics and marketing. These broad headings were intended to guide the participants in thinking about any possible matters which might have adverse consequences for the programme. Participants had been circulated with worksheets in advance of the workshop and asked to give some thought to the risks they might raise, feeling free to interpret the headings in any way they wished. Two examples were provided. The withdrawal of Government support for NSPIS might be listed as a risk arising from a threat in the external political environment. Similarly, the corruption of data on a computer hard disk might be listed as a risk arising from a weakness in the management of technology in the internal environment.

On the day of the workshop, after allowing participants some time to individually review the work they had (or in some cases had not) completed in advance, the participants were split into three groups; suppliers, Home Office/PAGIT and forces (recipient and opposing combined). The three groups were sent away for 90 minutes to discuss the headings and compile a list of risks to the programme from the perspective of their group. Each group was then allowed 30 minutes to present their findings to the whole workshop. Unsurprisingly, the lists of risks identified and reported back by each group were substantially different from each other and very much in line with the working hypothesis. The exercise resulted in the identification of almost 200 risks listed under the various broad headings. Very few duplicates were eliminated, but, on the basis that nobody was wrong to perceive a particular matter as a risk, no other risks, however improbable or inconsequential they appeared to anybody else, were removed from the list.

Risk Estimation Exercise

Each risk was then considered by the whole group, debated and a collective judgement made about the probability of the risk occurring. The probability was judged on a five point scale: none; low; low to medium; medium to high; or high. Judgement was then needed about the potential adverse consequences of the risk. It had been decided there were four types of adverse consequences to consider, namely that the programme or its projects: could not be completed at all and had to be cancelled; could not be completed on time; could not be completed within budget; or did not meet the quality required.

Different risks could have different levels of adverse impact. For example, the prolonged absence of a key member of staff might have a high impact on quality, a medium impact on timescales, a low impact on budgets and no impact at all on the overall survival of the programme. The constraints of time did not allow for all four types of consequences to be considered by the whole group. The participants were therefore split into four groups, with each constituency represented in each group, and each group allocated one of the four types of adverse consequences, for judging on the same five point scale. At the conclusion of the workshop, there was general agreement that the richness and diversity of the debate, conducted in an atmosphere of openness and respect for the views of others, had fully justified the chosen approach to the exercise.

Subsequent Paper Circulations

The workshop process resulted in the compilation of a draft risk register. In order to allow for review of the risks and to reach consensus on the scorings, the first, and later on, the second draft risk registers were circulated to participants for comments using a crude Delphi technique.

Risk Evaluation Process

Each of the 200 or so risks in the register was then plotted on a five by five matrix, as shown in Figure 6.3 on the next page.

Although adding to the complexity, a separate matrix was plotted for each of the four types of adverse consequences. The distribution of the risks on each matrix was then evaluated by the Programme Director. The Director evaluated the level of acceptable risk as shown by the wavy lines in Figure 6.4 on the next page and allocated an identifier to each of the four boxes above the line.

It is important to note that the Director's role was to decide on the level of acceptable risk, not to review the risks themselves to decide whether he agreed with them or not. The fact that a senior manager did not agree with a risk was fine but should not, it was felt, lead to any changes to the risk register. The risk might be something the senior manager would prefer to ignore or their own bias might simply mean they would not have thought of the risk. The whole point was to maximise the richness, diversity, honesty and objectivity of the risk register. The Programme Director fully accepted this argument.

After briefing and discussion at a private meeting, the Director decided that any risk appearing in box A in at least three of the matrices would be designated high risk and have to be addressed by a countermeasure. Any risk appearing above the line in at least one box would be designated as medium risk and might have to be addressed by a countermeasure, if the participants at the risk management workshop felt this was appropriate. The remaining risks would be designated as low risk.

A risk assessment report was prepared to reflect the Director's decision and as a working document to inform the participants at the risk management workshop.

Figure 6.3: Risk Matrix
(Source: Frosdick and Odell 1996:31)

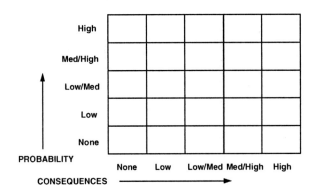

Figure 6.4: Risk Evaluation Decision
(Source: *ibid.*)

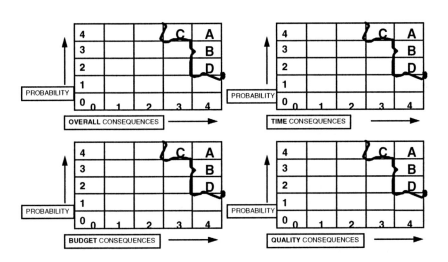

Risk Management Workshop

Selection of Participants

Whilst preference was to invite all the participants in the risk assessment workshop to participate in the risk management workshop, commercial and political realities meant it was not possible to invite the PITACSA representatives at that time.

Invitations were however extended to the remaining participants, although a number of them were not able to attend on the nominated day. Additional participants were invited from within the staff of the programme. Since it was they who would have to action the countermeasures identified, it seemed appropriate to ensure their ownership of the risks.

Deciding the Priority Risks

The introduction to the workshop, held in September 1995, emphasised that the risks identified were the product of a substantial and careful process and were not up for further debate in this forum. All the high risks, however uncomfortable people found them, were priorities and would require countermeasures to be identified and actioned. Any medium risks that the workshop agreed were also priorities would require similar action. The medium risks were reviewed and certain of them identified as needing countermeasures.

Taken together with the high risks, there was now a list of some 50 priority risks for which countermeasures were required.

Risk Management Decision Tree

In respect of each priority risk, the workshop participants were asked to consider what action could be taken to reduce the probability and/or consequences to a tolerable level. A decision tree (Figure 6.5 on the next page) was used to facilitate this process.

The actions defined and responsibilities allocated were recorded. The outcome of the process was the draft risk management plan, which again was circulated to workshop participants for comments before being finalised.

Outcomes

Key Areas of Risk

As a result of this very comprehensive, albeit preliminary, analysis, a number of key themes were identified as giving rise to risks which needed to be addressed to ensure the success of the programme.

Figure 6.5: Risk Management Decision Tree
(Source: adapted from Frosdick and Odell 1996:32)

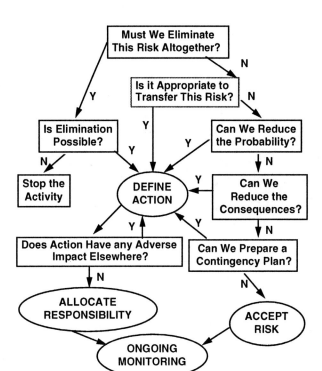

The management of risk approach adopted had, in effect, acted as a catalyst for precipitating the confrontation of some difficult and key issues, which it was felt would not have been brought out into the open other than as a result of the chosen approach.

These key areas of risk were articulated in a report to the Programme Board, as follows:

Decision Making: it was unclear who had responsibility to make decisions and under what circumstances. There was too much of an overlap between all the various groups within the Home Office, the Local Authority Associations and the Association of Chief Police Officers.

Programme Initiation: there was little evidence that the programme had been initiated other than through the lead force application projects. The projects were not centrally controlled. Infrastructure and organisational projects to support application projects had not been identified and only now, well in excess of a year after the initiation, were such projects being identified. The initiation phase of the programme had been overtaken by events, i.e. the desire to press on with application projects. Resources had been directed towards applications and insufficient had been left for non-technical infrastructure.

Police Service Commitment: this was not being demonstrated in that at that time more than 50% of police forces were not involved in any of the projects. Application developments which formed part of the programme were still being independently developed and procured by forces; resources for these projects would be better directed towards programme projects.

Changing Local Priorities: police service-wide priorities might or might not be the same for individual forces. Where priorities were not the same and there was an urgent need to replace an application or to divert money to other activities outside of IS/IT development, these could work against the objectives of the programme.

Securing and Retaining Funding (at both the local and national level): reduction in public expenditure, numerous initiatives, sometimes contradictory, both centrally and locally sponsored, and competition with the remit of the Association of Chief Police Officers Technical and Research Committee, created uncertainty about the viability of the programme.

Action Plans

The paper circulations subsequent to the risk management workshop resulted in a draft risk management plan containing over 60 different action plans to address the priority risks summarised above. Responsibility for progressing many of these actions had been identified as properly resting with senior members of the Programme Board. It was therefore decided to ask the Board to consider the plan as a draft document, bearing in mind that their approval of the draft would mean they were agreeing to progress the actions allocated within it. It was appreciated that this approval process would span at least two meetings of the Programme Board, and so, in the interim, it was decided to press on with designing and implementing a process for monitoring the progress of the management of risk strategy.

Initial Risk Monitoring Process

Review Workshop

It was considered that the management of risk process should be ongoing throughout the life of the programme to ensure that the risk implications of any changes in the external or internal environments were considered and appropriately acted upon. Accordingly, a one day review workshop back at the Police Staff College, Bramshill, was arranged in December 1995. The selection of the participants followed the same principles as before, and although the action plans would be being discussed, it was by now considered acceptable and appropriate to include the PITACSA representatives in all elements of the process. For a variety of logistical reasons, including the last minute withdrawal of some invitees and the attendance of deputies in place of others, the mix of participants was not as had been planned. In particular, the forces opposed to NSPIS were not represented, although the other three groupings were, albeit by different personalities. The review workshop resulted in a small increase in the number of priority risks, four of which had not previously been identified, together with the action plans needed to counter them.

Risk Products

The risk register, risk assessment and risk management plan, the draft of which had by now been approved, were now updated to reflect the discussions at the review workshop. At the same time, a database of the risks and action plans was developed to facilitate the monitoring process.

Action Plans Progress Report

All persons having overall or delegated responsibility for progressing risk management action plans were visited and a report on initial progress obtained. Report-by-dates were negotiated and the timescales within which the action plans would be progressed agreed. The database was updated accordingly.

Implications for the Projects

It was considered that the communication of risks between the programme and project levels should be a two-way process and a number of programme risks had already been identified from management of risk activities undertaken by individual projects. Similarly, several of the risk action plans required action at the project level. To reinforce the need for communication and to raise their awareness, the Project Managers of all the projects within the first tranche portfolio were visited. It was being argued that the more comprehensive risk regime now in place at the programme level meant that the management of risk at the project level could be more focused. Project concerns about programme matters could now be communicated to the Business Change Manager rather than addressed ad hoc. Each project manager was therefore provided with a copy of the programme risk products and the channel of risk communication formally opened. Project Managers were also formally requested to note the action plans requiring progress at the project level.

The visit was also used to identify and report on the management of risk activities and products at the project level. These were found to range between non-existent and comprehensive and it was noted that, the more recently the project had been initiated, the more comprehensive the management of risk regime in use within the project. This was entirely consistent with the timescales within which the programme level strategy had been developed and represented an encouraging sign for the rigour with which the management of risk was likely to be addressed by subsequent projects.

Subsequent Risk Monitoring Process

Notwithstanding the monitoring process, it proved to be a struggle to get people – many of them senior managers – to tackle their actions plans and progress was slower than had been hoped for. Nevertheless, the client felt it was important to show that we had confidence in the process and wished to repeat it. But first, to comply with procurement rules, I had to complete a tendering exercise. Between March 1996 and March 1999, subsequent reviews of the risk register and progress reporting in respect of action plans were undertaken within a planned programme of management of risk consultancy.

A review conducted in early 1998 concluded that the original risk analysis was a robust assessment of the risks to the programme but that the detail in the analysis was now excessive. The risk register database was therefore reorganised into the 17 key areas of risk shown in Table 6.9.

Table 6.9: Key Areas of NSPIS Programme Risk 1996-1998

Lack of corporatism in the British police service
Lack of commitment to the development of NSPIS products
Lack of commitment to the purchase of NSPIS products
Deficiencies in programme management
Deficiencies in project management
Deficiencies in procurement processes
Suppliers not finding a sufficient business case to tender

Lack of sustained funding
Lack of sufficient skilled staff
Post-contract development risks
Implementation and multiple implementation risks
Ineffective post-implementation functional change control
Business requirements not translated into technical architecture/infrastructure
External technological changes and developments
Inability to achieve technical interactions between applications
IT security risks
Configuration management and change control of technical
architecture/infrastructure

Each action plan was revised to include both a cross-reference to the relevant
key area of risk and a rationale showing the specific risks to be addressed by
the plan. Progress reports were commissioned and audits carried out with the
persons having overall or delegated responsibility for progressing the
relevant plans. The progress status of each plan was then noted as either 'Not
Started', 'Satisfactory', 'Ongoing' (for those plans which had become
institutionalised as practice), 'Not Satisfactory' or 'Completed' (including
discontinued plans).

Successive audits, summarised in Table 6.10, clearly showed the progress
made in eliminating unsatisfactory progress, in institutionalising planned
activities into practice, and in successfully completing plans or discontinuing
obsolete plans.

Table 6.10: Action Plans Progress Status
(Source: Frosdick 1999e:8)

	03/96	04/97	09/97	07/98	10/98	03/99
total plans	66	79	107	124	126	126
'not started'	4 (6%)	5 (6%)	18 (17%)	13 (10%)	5 (4%)	0 (0%)
'satisfactory'	24 (36%)	48 (61%)	38 (35%)	11 (9%)	16 (13%)	17 (13%)
'ongoing'	0 (0%)	0 (0%)	0 (0%)	35 (28%)	33 (26%)	31 (25%)
'not satisfactory'	23 (34%)	11 (14%)	12 (11%)	3 (2%)	0 (0%)	0 (0%)
'completed'	15 (23%)	15 (19%)	39 (36%)	62 (50%)	72 (57%)	78 (62%)

The risk analysis continued to be regarded as very robust – there was widespread consensus that it described accurately what could go wrong. But it continued to be very difficult to persuade the persons responsible for progressing the action plans to get on with progressing them. Table 6.10 shows that it took three years to get the number of action plans for which the progress status was 'unsatisfactory' or 'not started' down to zero.

It was a constant case of 'nice analysis – shame about the inactivity'. This was a clear reflection of the more political nature of the risk management process. The 'what could go wrong' (project risks) started to turn into 'what was going wrong' (project issues) and an analysis undertaken in 1998 noted that, 'In the case of those risk related issues which remain unresolved, the majority represent risks which have subsequently come true' (Frosdick 1998j:5).

Conclusion

This case study has described in some detail the rationale, processes and products adopted to manage risk within the National Strategy for Police Information Systems for England and Wales. It has demonstrated how taking account of research findings from Cultural Theory, combined with the use of concepts recommended by CCTA, has facilitated the capture of a broad range of risk perspectives and so maximised the richness and diversity of the risk assessment.

The case study has shown how the risks of most concern to the programme were prioritised, and action plans developed to deal with them. Whilst there were significant difficulties in progressing the action plans, nevertheless subsequent progress showed the whole process to have been worthwhile. Without this work, key areas of concern might not have been brought into the open, discussed, tackled and progressed.

The individual reports of the 40 other cases are set out in the next chapter.

CHAPTER SEVEN: POLICE PROJECTS RISK – PART II

SUMMARY

Following on from the extended case study of the NSPIS in Chapter Six, this Chapter explains the within-case sampling approach and presents the 40 other case studies undertaken in the police setting. These represent the application of Cultural Theory at the micro level of analysis, which has only rarely featured in previous Cultural Theory studies (for example see Mars and Mars 1996, which is itself unpublished).

ANALYSIS: INDIVIDUAL CASE STUDIES

Introduction

Case Data Sampling and Presentation

Since this book is not primarily an ethnographic study, there is no systematic or standardised approach to the presentation of the case studies in this Chapter. That standardisation is found in the case study protocol and coding frame (Appendix A) and in the Microsoft Access® database in which the case study data are recorded.

As we saw in Chapter Two, the analysis for this stage of the research has a particular focus on the participation (or non-participation) of stakeholders drawn from each of Cultural Theory's four social solidarities. It is not practicable to give an extended description of each of the 40 other case studies, which are presented in this Chapter as individual vignettes. The constraints of space and the stated purposes of this analysis mean that I have constructed these vignettes by reflexively and purposively sampling from *within* each case. Such reflexive and purposive sampling has its conscious elements, including a careful re-reading of and reflection on the original documents and files. But it also has its subconscious aspects.

Referring to sampling from within a case, Hammersley and Atkinson point out that, 'very often the sampling is not the result of conscious deliberation' (1995:45). In presenting the individual vignettes, I am therefore focussing on those aspects of the case experienced by me (the agent) that my 'whole life' experience of the research suggests to me (the researcher) to be relevant and important evidence on which to build the cross-case analysis in Chapter Eight.

Case Data Summary

The case data for the individual case studies are summarised in Table 7.1. This shows the case aliases (to preserve informant anonymity), start and end dates, days effort and the extent of stakeholder participation. Table 7.1 is sorted in chronological order of start date. In respect of stakeholder participation, 'A' refers to the more individualist supply chain constituency; 'B' to the more fatalist user community; 'C' to the more hierarchical governance constituency; and 'D' to the more egalitarian user special interest groups.

Table 7.1: Case Study Details – Sorted by Start Date

Case Alias	Start Date	End Date	Days Effort	Stakeholder Participation			
				A	B	C	D
Mike	07/04/1995	18/11/1996	42.00			✓	
November	26/05/1995	26/11/1999	106.75	✓	✓	✓	✓
Oscar	12/12/1995	22/12/1999	13.25			✓	
Victor	29/08/1996	18/09/1996	1.00			✓	
Whisky	28/09/1996	05/02/2001	31.75	✓	✓	✓	
X-Ray	08/12/1996	23/07/1999	28.00	✓	✓	✓	✓
Kilo	07/02/1997	05/03/1997	4.75			✓	
Delta	10/03/1997	10/03/1997	1.00			✓	
Echo	18/03/1997	18/04/1997	1.50			✓	
Broadway	25/04/1997	25/09/1997	12.25			✓	
Foxtrot	28/04/1997	10/10/1997	5.50	✓	✓	✓	
Juliet	06/05/1997	08/07/1997	6.50			✓	
Alpha	24/07/1997	31/03/1998	14.00	✓	✓	✓	
Charlie	15/09/1997	28/10/1997	3.75		✓	✓	✓
Bravo	15/10/1997	21/10/1997	5.50		✓	✓	
Lima	04/11/1997	22/04/1998	10.50		✓	✓	✓
Quebec	12/11/1997	03/02/1998	5.00		✓	✓	✓
Papa	02/12/1997	04/12/1997	1.50			✓	
Romeo	12/12/1997	12/12/1997	1.00	✓		✓	

Name	Start	End	Value				
Yankee	18/12/1997	17/02/1998	9.50	✓	✓	✓	
Zulu	23/04/1998	19/06/1998	24.50		✓	✓	✓
Trojan	11/06/1998	28/08/1998	7.75		✓	✓	
Uniform	19/08/1998	10/01/2000	11.50		✓	✓	✓
Purple	19/10/1998	14/12/1998	2.00		✓	✓	
Hunter	25/11/1998	14/07/1999	13.50	✓	✓	✓	✓
Golf	22/12/1998	05/02/1999	2.50			✓	
Hotel	12/02/1999	14/06/1999	11.00		✓	✓	✓
India	04/05/1999	09/06/1999	4.00			✓	
Sierra	08/05/1999	28/07/1999	11.00	✓	✓	✓	✓
Tango	22/06/1999	03/12/2000	17.50	✓	✓	✓	✓
Ranger	08/02/2000	26/04/2001	13.00	✓	✓	✓	✓
Central	18/03/2000	07/07/2000	2.50		✓	✓	
Amber	23/04/2001	12/06/2001	3.75	✓	✓	✓	
Orange	12/06/2001	02/11/2001	6.00	✓	✓	✓	✓
Uncle	29/11/2001	24/09/2002	15.50	✓	✓	✓	
Bluegrass	13/05/2002	31/03/2004	21.75	✓	✓	✓	✓
Harvard	13/06/2002	13/11/2002	12.75	✓	✓	✓	
Royal	22/11/2002	12/09/2003	6.25	✓	✓	✓	✓
Apple	08/04/2003	18/07/2003	2.25	✓		✓	
Zebra	12/05/2003	18/07/2003	9.00	✓	✓	✓	
Peter	12/12/2003	22/03/2004	3.25		✓	✓	

In terms of duration, 'long' refers to my input being 20 or more days (six cases). 'Medium' refers to more than ten but less than 20 days (12 cases). 'Short' refers to more than three but less than ten days (14 cases), whilst 'very short' refers to less than three days (nine cases).

Case Study 'Mike'

This long case was my first entry into this setting and involved risk-related work for a police IT project. I drafted the risk chapter for the project initiation document (PID), establishing the principle that,

> 'It is widely recognised that different people perceive risk in entirely different ways and that there are no right or wrong answers. It is therefore important to ensure that the business, user and technical communities are all adequately represented.'

But I was never really able to get to grips with the application of Cultural Theory. It was effort enough persuading my managers to adopt a process that was new to them. I facilitated a risk log for the start-up stage of the project but this involved only a type 'C' hierarchy of 'business' managers, 'technical' managers and junior staff – notionally 'user' representatives – but brought onto the project team to do the managers' bidding. I had not yet been able to apply the idea that 'user' more properly referred to the fatalist/egalitarian diagonal and that individualist suppliers could also be involved.

Subsequently, I facilitated a risk log for the overall project. This was regularly reviewed, formally updated on four occasions and eventually incorporated into a computer database. I also worked one-to-one with the managers of 13 of the project stages to produce their own stage risk logs. Lots of process, then, but what was really going on was my learning to apply the techniques and create relevant documentation.

Case Study 'November'

This was the long duration case of the NSPIS programme set out as an extended case study in Chapter Six.

Case Study 'Oscar'

This was a medium duration case involving a police IT project with which I was involved over four years and was the first case where I sought to replicate the approach developed for 'Mike'. I established the same principles in an identical risk chapter for the PID, but again the case was more about applying process and less about Cultural Theory. I facilitated a workshop of type 'C' (hierarchical) Project Board and project team members at which 177 threats were identified. These were risk assessed using the same kind of crude Delphi technique described in 'November' and risk managed at a separate workshop. After nine months, I facilitated a workshop review of the documentation, but the client was used to the process and it was inappropriate to suggest widening the approach. A further workshop review followed after a further nine months. I also facilitated a stage manager one-to-one to produce their own risk log.

The documentation I produced for this case was excessively complex, reflecting my focus on process. There was a risk methodology, a risk register, a risk assessment and a risk management plan. Later I would learn to combine all four into one document.

Case Study 'Victor'

This was an early but significant case of very short duration involving a police business project. The client was convinced of the value of Cultural Theory and we recorded in the risk log,

> 'An initial stakeholder analysis revealed four distinct groups whose views on risk needed to be taken into account, namely: those who were assumed to be committed to seeing the implementation process through, for example [name of force], Home Office and the team themselves; those who were opposed to the process, for example the Trade Unions and many of the staff affected; those who were ambivalent about the process, for example most users/customers, most managers not affected by the process, external bodies such as local authorities and the people of [name]; and those who would stand to benefit commercially from the process, for example existing and potential suppliers and contractors.'

This was an insightful analysis in which all four constituencies were clearly identified. But when it came to the initial workshop, only type 'C' (hierarchical) representatives from the project team were invited. In fact others were deliberately excluded. In a subsequent memorandum the client explained,

> 'Risk is a subjective issue. We were clear that at this stage there was no prospect of the Trade Union and Management sides taking the same view of some elements of the risk.'

The client planned to get the initial risk analysis approved and then undertake a more detailed process involving all four groups. Sadly, this foundered because of an organisational political decision to decline to authorise the next stage of the work. The hierarchical client did not want to engage with the other constituencies.

Case Study 'Whisky'

This was a long duration case over four and a half years involving seven risk-related assignments for a police IT project. For the first early assignment, I had now developed my case study protocol. This made an impact, since the work now had less of the process focus seen in 'Mike' and 'Oscar'. The use of the protocol, my increased confidence in the process and my repeated involvement over an extended duration, together allowed for increased emphasis on applying Cultural Theory.

The work explicitly introduced workshop participants to some simplified risk perception theory. I was showing slides and telling people it was to be expected they would have different perceptions of risk. The workshops were designed to involve type 'C' (hierarchical) business, technical, senior user and project team representatives and type 'B' (fatalist) users from the client police organisation. The client never wanted to involve type 'D' (egalitarian) representatives. But there was progressive involvement of type 'A' (individualism). An early workshop involved two consultants – one a technical advisor to the Project Board and the other a procurement specialist. They were outsiders raising a range of concerns about the project's parent programme and about the technical capabilities of the market. Their involvement added 23 strategy-related, technical and procurement-related risks to the log.

Once the contract had been awarded, the stakeholder analysis for the next review workshop added three type 'A' (individualist) representatives from the contracted supplier. The workshop also took account of the supplier's own risk analysis. However an interesting situation developed whereby the project experienced delays and each side began using their risk logs as a stick to beat the other with. Reviews of the police project risk log blamed failings in the supplier and vice versa. Table 7.2 shows an analysis of a fairly late version of the risk log. This shows that supplier-related risks formed 45% of the total and 60% of the risks evaluated as high.

Table 7.2: Risk Categories in Risk Log for Case Study 'Whisky'

Risk Category	High	Med.	Low	Total
Supplier Performance and Capability Risks	17	12	7	36
Project and Team Capability Risks	5	3	8	16
Programme Management Related Risks	5	5	6	16
Risks Arising From Other External Influences	0	4	2	6
Compliance-Related Risks	1	2	2	5
Column Totals	**28**	**26**	**25**	**79**

Subsequently, I was involved in efforts to bring the two the two sides together and negotiate a joint risk log. The idea was that they should stop blaming each other and jointly address the risks. This eventually happened after my own involvement had ceased.

Case Study 'X-ray'

This was my first involvement in a police business (as opposed to IT) project and was a long case involving three risk-related assignments extending over two and a half years.

The initial assignment was the most interesting. I visited the client group and gave a presentation which included a simple description of Cultural Theory. They were convinced from the outset and adopted the same PID chapter as 'Mike' and 'Oscar'. Our risk assessment workshop included all four constituencies. For the purposes of identifying risks, the participants were allocated to one of five distinct groups. The 'Project Team' and 'Business' groups represented type 'C' (hierarchy). 'Users 1' represented type 'B' (fatalism), 'Users 2' type 'D' (egalitarianism) and 'Suppliers' type 'A' (individualism). When assisting the client to identify participants for the type 'D' group, the client recognised the need to choose people who would 'give them a hard time'.

Each group worked individually to identify their risks under twelve headings[25], which they recorded on work sheets and prioritised. Thus for the first time I was able to keep a record of the source of the risks identified.

For the purposes of estimating the risks, the constituencies were mixed up so as to provide diversity of perception in each of four groups. Each group was allocated one quarter of the risks to assess in their group. This workshop groups design is shown in Table 7.3.

Table 7.3: Workshop Groups Design for Case Study 'X-Ray'

Groups 1 and C	Project Team Member
Groups 1 and D	Project Team Member
Groups 2 and A	Assistant Chief Constable
Groups 2 and B	Director of Support Services
Groups 2 and C	Divisional Commander

---

[25] External threats in the political, economic, social, technological, legal and ecological environments; internal weaknesses in managing infrastructure, finance, personnel, technology, logistics and communications.

Groups 3 and D	Head of Operational Support
Groups 3 and A	Civilian Divisional Communications Assistant
Groups 3 and B	Divisional Inspector
Groups 3 and C	Sergeant Divisional Operations Room
Groups 4 and D	Constable Police Federation
Groups 4 and A	Unison Representative/Enquiry Officer
Groups 4 and B	FOR Communications Assistant
Groups 5 and C	[Name of Consultancy Firm]
Groups 5 and D	[Name of Preferred Supplier]

The two subsequent assignments were paper reviews involving only members of the project team.

Case Study 'Kilo'

This was a short IT security case which was an offshoot of 'Whisky'. The timescales were very constrained because the client had been directed to undertake an IT security risk analysis using the CRAMM[26] methodology. I did not know how to do this but was asked by the client because it was risk-related, because it provided me with a development opportunity and because I would therefore do the work for a reduced fee! The whole focus was on getting the job done very quickly and I was learning to use CRAMM for the first time, assisted by a Home Office IT security manager. Thus, for expediency, only a few available type 'C' (hierarchy) project team members were involved in the analysis.

Case Study 'Delta'

This was a very short case involving a small police IT project. From exposure at the programme level, the client was aware of the Cultural Theory approach to risk perception, however they chose to produce the risk log alone. The risk log acknowledged the Cultural Theory approach but stated that,

> 'This approach has time and resource implications which are disproportionate to the benefits for a project of this scale and duration.'

---

[26] CRAMM is the CCTA Risk Analysis and Management Method for IT Security. CRAMM involves a system and data asset valuation using scorecards, a threat and vulnerability analysis using a structured questionnaire, the input of all the data into a software package and the software then 'recommending' a variety of technical and management controls to address the risks associated with data unavailability, data destruction, unauthorised data disclosure and unauthorised data modification.

The risk log also recognised that,

> 'It is inevitable that the analysis will lack the richness and diversity of the [Cultural Theory] approach.'

It is not known if the identified risk management actions were ever progressed since a planned review never took place. With hindsight, the client had been told they had to produce a risk log for their project and sought to do so as a one-off exercise.

Case Study 'Echo'

This was a very short case involving one-on-one work with a single police IT project team representative (type 'C') who had been given responsibility for project risk. Some training in risk perception theory was given but the person was uninterested, preferring to deal simply with the mechanical steps in the CCTA risk processes and to restructure their existing risk documentation accordingly. With hindsight, the project had felt they had to invite me in because of my involvement with their parent programme, but in truth they were not interested in addressing the implications of risk perception theory.

Case Study 'Broadway'

This was a medium duration assignment to facilitate an IT security risk analysis for the same client as 'Oscar'. Building on 'Kilo', this was my second application of the CRAMM methodology. Time was not an issue so I was able to apply the methodology in full. But again it was the application of method rather than Cultural Theory which drove the case. Only type 'C' (hierarchical) representatives were involved, although this time these were extended beyond the Home Office IT security manager and the project team to include other technical managers and the 'User Assurance Coordinator'. This latter person was a middle manager from an 'Assist' Force – so shades of type 'B' (fatalism) – but also a member of the type 'C' Project Board. The outcome was a more CRAMM-compliant analysis but still lacking any significant input from the fatalist/egalitarian user axis or from the more individualist supplier community.

Case Study 'Foxtrot'

This was a short case involving a police IT project. From exposure at the programme level, the client was convinced by the Cultural Theory approach to risk perception. Because the process would be new to their project team, the client wanted several of them involved, but was happy to have 'guests' from the other constituencies. So I set up a process which involved five hierarchical representatives (the project manager and four middle-ranking technical colleagues), one IT consultant and one police force user. The consultant worked for a major police IT supplier and was currently undertaking some contract work for the client. We felt this person could be briefed to represent the type 'A' (individualist) view. The user worked for a police force which might take product from the client's parent programme and its projects. The force had quality concerns and had appointed this user as their full-time 'intelligent customer'. The user had a reputation for being 'difficult' and we felt they could be briefed to play a hybrid type fatalist/egalitarian role.

Accordingly, I briefed the workshop on Cultural Theory and asked the attendees to think laterally and represent the known or likely views of identified stakeholders from all four constituencies. This they duly did and the workshop raised 174 different risks. The user played their role to the full, smugly announcing, 'I've got one' each time I asked if anyone wanted to raise a risk under a particular heading. At the conclusion, the participants expressed themselves very satisfied with the quality of the analysis. In particular, the user felt their concerns had been given a good airing. Indeed the user was so impressed by the approach that they subsequently invited me to do some work for them.

Case Study 'Juliet'

This was a short duration IT security assignment for the same client as 'Echo'. The client brought me in because (like 'Kilo') they had been directed to undertake an IT security risk analysis, but also because I had by now done CRAMM work for two other projects within the parent programme. I was thus the easiest way for them to 'tick the box'. I took the fee and did the work but only junior type 'C' (hierarchy) representatives from the project team and the Home Office IT security manager were involved. There was no interest from the client or attempt by me to apply Cultural Theory in the case.

Subsequently, the Home Office IT security manager combined the results of 'Kilo', 'Broadway' and 'Juliet' to produce a set of generic IT security countermeasures for police IT projects. These were of course derived from a largely type 'C' (hierarchical) perspective, with only shades of type 'B' (fatalism) from the junior 'user' representatives at the base of the hierarchical project teams.

Case Study 'Alpha'

This was a medium duration case involving a programme of police IT projects. From exposure elsewhere, the client was aware of and accepted the Cultural Theory approach, and the work first involved producing a risk strategy document, which was identical to the PID chapters for 'Mike', 'Oscar' and 'X-Ray'.

But the client's acceptance was less because of being convinced and more because, being a hierarch, they felt obliged to comply. The client was clearly anxious and this showed in three ways. First, when designing the risk assessment, the client asked for an initial process involving only their own type 'C' (hierarchy) staff. The resulting risk assessment would then be reviewed by a wider group. Second, the client asked me for a briefing note showing how they were complying with all the risk process directions issued by their own parent organisation. Third, when discussing the organisation of a risk management workshop involving types 'A' (individualism) and 'B' (fatalism), the client asked me, in an anguished voice, 'but do we have to do what they say?'

The client grew in confidence after the risk assessment involving twelve of their own staff. For the risk assessment review by the wider group, we invited a carefully designed 'focus group' of 12 persons: three type 'C's (hierarchy) from the client's own department, three type 'C's from other departments, three type 'A' (individualist) representatives from IT companies in the client's supply chain and three type 'B' (fatalist) representatives from police software projects which would take the client's products. Our prediction of the fatalist 'non agenda' was clearly evidenced by the fact that none of the three invited type 'B's turned up to the review! Nevertheless, the client subsequently stated how much he had valued the input from the three type 'A's – so much so that he invited them to nominate a representative to also attend the problem-solving risk management workshop. He now realised that, whilst he didn't have to 'do what they said', nevertheless he could benefit from hearing their point of view.

Going further, the client became an ambassador for a standing Cultural Theory focus group which could be drawn on by other departments. The heads of the other departments, not having experienced the process, declined the idea.

Case Study 'Charlie'

This was a short case involving a police business project. I met with the client's project manager and helped structure the logic tree for a failure modes analysis. We then carefully designed a review workshop to be attended by four groups: the project team, the police business, specialist advisors and police users. In Cultural Theory terms, I intended that the police business representatives, being those with governance of the project, were clearly type 'C' (hierarchy), as was the project team. I intended that the mix of users, including customers and trade unions, would represent a fatalist and egalitarian alliance. I intended that the specialist advisors, being consultants and police managers having governance of the specialism, would represent an alliance of individualism and hierarchy. Thus my careful design would ensure that all four Cultural Theory types were involved and that there were inbuilt tensions in the discussion.

Things did not go as planned. My consultant was replaced by a hierarchical manager so I lost my individualist perspective. But two additional users had been invited and so my fatalist/egalitarian alliance group was strengthened in numbers. The review workshop was fascinating in that three of the groups turned on the police business group (including my client) and blamed their decisions for many of the failure modes identified. Having commissioned the risk assessment, my client now found themselves beaten with it. I was not asked to facilitate any risk management work, which indeed never took place. And I think the risk assessment got buried. I did, however, subsequently pick up business from two of the participants.

Case Study 'Bravo'

This was a short case to facilitate an IT security risk analysis for a police IT project. I had won the business because I had by now undertaken three police CRAMM studies. The client did not have the CRAMM software, so I could only apply the principles of CRAMM and try to establish whether the generic Home Office IT security countermeasures appeared to be valid. The project was at pre-procurement, so it was not possible to interview the supplier, however I made an effort to access the more fatalist user perspective for this case. Thus, as well as three type 'C's[27], two junior 'users'[28] not involved with the project team were also involved in the analysis.

Interestingly, the results obtained were in line with the composite results from which the generic IT security countermeasures had been derived. This makes sense, since the fatalists have no particular perspective of their own. Brought into the project team context, junior 'user' representatives form the base of the hierarchy and so adopt its compliance perspective. This taught me that, in order to tease out an alternative 'user' perspective, I had to involve a fatalist and egalitarian axis of articulate type 'B's and representatives of type 'D' groups.

Case Study 'Lima'

This was a medium duration case involving a police IT project to implement the software being produced for 'Oscar'. But where 'Oscar' had been more

---

[27] The project manager, the Force Head of IT and a police officer member of the project team.

[28] A data protection administrator and a database administrator.

about process, two years later I was able to focus more on Cultural Theory. The client was convinced, particularly about the need to involve users. The risk assessment contained the statement that,

> 'Each of these stakeholder groups have different perspectives on risk, and involving them in the process allows the project to enjoy a richness and diversity in the risk assessment which would not otherwise be possible.'

Because we could draw on the risk assessment from 'Oscar' and the output from a briefing workshop involving 29 users from across the Force, we decided to prepare an initial risk assessment with a small group and have it reviewed by a wider group.

The initial risk assessment was prepared by the type 'C' (hierarchy) project team, together with two type 'B' (fatalist) users from other departments who would be affected by the project but knew little about it. 110 relevant risks were brought forward from 'Oscar' and the briefing workshop and 22 new risks were added.

For the review, the project team were joined by eleven further type 'B' users of mixed ranks and grades from across the Force, together with two type 'D' (egalitarian) representatives from the Police Federation and UNISON. This created a strong fatalist and egalitarian alliance, which added 11 further high and medium risks. Predictably, these were of the 'fitness for purpose' and 'impact on jobs' kind. They included concerns about abstractions for training, new functionality requiring users to collect more data and the risk that

> 'General uncertainty about future job direction, prospects, salary, career development, etc. will reduce morale, threaten efficiency and effectiveness, and lead to a loss of personnel.'

Risk management was then undertaken by the project team alone.

Case Study 'Quebec'

This was a short case which was a risk project in its own right. The client had been a participant in 'Charlie' and had been impressed with the approach. So they asked me to apply it in their own police force to identify the risks associated with a particular set of internal business processes.

As with 'Charlie', I helped the client's deputy to structure a four-level failure modes analysis and to carefully design a review process involving four groups. These were identified to all participants as the training department; the police business; operational staff; and special interest groups. This was a much more explicit Cultural Theory design. The three latter were clearly types 'C' (hierarchy), 'B' (fatalism) and 'D' (egalitarianism) respectively.

The training department was part of the hierarchy and thus type 'C', but with shades of type 'A' (individualism) in this context since they were the internal supplier.

This time, although two of the original review nominees had to be substituted, I was able to control who their replacements were because the client's deputy understood what I was trying to do and why. Table 7.4 on the next page shows the review participants.

One member of the predicted fatalist Group B (shown in italics) did not turn up.

Table 7.4: Review Workshop Participants for Case Study 'Quebec'

Group	Participant	Group	Participant
A	Head of Training	C	Assistant Chief Constable Support
A	Deputy Head of Training	C	Chief Inspector Support South Area
A	Trainer/Course Designer	C	Employment Services Officer
A	Police Inspector Training Delivery	C	Equal Opportunities Officer
B	Police Inspector Skills	D	Driving School Representative
B	Police Constable Central Area	D	Unison Representative
B	Specials Liaison Officer	D	Police Federation Representative
B	*Civilian Staff Member*	D	Health and Safety Officer

The review process required each group to discuss the initial four-level logic tree. A lively morning plenary was then held, driven by 'B' and 'D'. The changes made to the analysis show that the fatalist and egalitarian axis was expressing a lack of confidence in both policy-making by the business and the delivery capabilities of the training department.

Risk estimation of the level three failure modes was undertaken by the whole group during the afternoon plenary and again, the debate was lively, with clear differences in risk perception expressed particularly between groups 'C' and 'D'. Risk estimation of the level four failure modes was subsequently undertaken by paper circulation, individual scorings and aggregation, as with 'November' and 'Oscar'.

Finally, the risk analysis was presented to a senior management group, which made the risk evaluation decision and took responsibility for the risk management. I ceased involvement at that point but I subsequently learned that the force had taken significant decisions about the deployment of Special Constables and other volunteers based on the results of the risk analysis.

Case Study 'Papa'

This was a very short case involving the production of a risk log for a police IT project. The log used identical wordings to 'Delta' above, i.e. the Cultural Theory approach was acknowledged but considered disproportionate. But there were three key differences. First, the team member who invited my involvement had themselves been a recent participant in another case where Cultural Theory had been more fully deployed. They had seen it work – this was thus a Cultural Theory-inspired referral. Second, four type 'C' (hierarchy) members of the project team participated in the exercise, which identified 46 risks, 21 of which needed management. Third, in preparing the risk log, team members tried to think laterally and, as the risk log recorded,

> 'Take account of the known views of the following groups of stakeholders: the Chief Executive, who commissioned the project; staff, who are the end users of the project; Trade Union Side, who have an interest on behalf of their members; external bodies who will interface with the new system (police forces, suppliers and the general public) and; potential suppliers [of the new system].'

This was a succinct analysis identifying all four Cultural Theory constituencies. The lateral thinking approach allowed awkward risks to be raised in a neutral way as a known stakeholder rather than a personal perception.

Case Study 'Romeo'

This was a very short case where I was brought in to a police force IT project by a type 'A' (individualist) consultant project manager, whom I knew. I also worked with a type 'C' (hierarchy) police project manager, who insisted on being accompanied by their own rival type 'A' consultant.

My advice to involve one or more fatalist or egalitarian representatives was declined. I felt the consultant project manager had brought me in simply to 'tick the box' and 'do' a risk log but when I finished the work he commented, 'that was a really good process, I can see the value of it'. Although he grasped the process, he did not see the issue of risk perception. The police project manager was a reluctant participant and the consultant suspicious, expecting me to 'know' what the risks were rather than to seek to facilitate different perspectives. Nevertheless, I managed to persuade them to think laterally and consider the risks which might be raised by the type 'B' (fatalist) users on the project. One of the risks raised was that 'the Police Federation and Unison will decline to co-operate with the consultants'. This was an explicit admission that type 'D' (egalitarianism) had been excluded from the process.

Case Study 'Yankee'

This was a short case involving a police business project. One of the participants in 'Charlie' wanted to me to introduce my approach to a colleague and invited me to give a presentation. I turned up expecting to meet a potential client and found myself presenting to their whole department. As with 'X-Ray', I gave a short lecture on risk perception theory and its implications for the management of risk process. This was received with enthusiasm – a second successful use of Cultural Theory as sales pitch!

The stakeholder analysis was used to design four groups of participants in the risk assessment: the project team (type 'C'); the police business and its suppliers (an 'A/C' 'center' alliance); police users who would be affected by the project but knew little about it (type 'B'); and police and other users who were known to be concerned about the project (a 'B/D' 'border' alliance). The risk assessment workshop followed the same approach as 'X-Ray', with each group recording their risks under headings and prioritising them. The number of risks raised by each group and their subsequent evaluation is shown in Table 7.5.

Table 7.5: Numbers of Risks Raised By Groups in Case Study 'Yankee'

Project Team C					Business/Suppliers A/C					Police Users B					Police/Other Users B/D				
X	L	M	H	=	X	L	M	H	=	X	L	M	H	=	X	L	M	H	=
32	0	6	8	46	0	6	6	10	22	5	2	2	4	13	31	4	2	10	47

X – Not Assessed; L – Low Risk; M – Medium Risk; H – High Risk; = Total Risks

There was insufficient time to assess all the risks and the project team deliberately held back, wanting to hear the concerns of the other groups. The key point in Table 7.5 is the difference between the well informed and critical users (47 risks) and the more fatalist ones (13 risks). As I visited the groups to check on progress, I found that the police/other users group were working intensely whilst the police users were struggling with the exercise.

The client invited the users to nominate one representative to participate in the subsequent risk management workshop. The client and I made a point of asking the nominee's opinion throughout the workshop, ensuring a full user contribution to the problem-solving discussion.

Case Study 'Zulu'

This was a long case involving a CRAMM analysis for a police IT project being undertaken by the same client as 'Bravo'. The case had a strong hierarchical base: CRAMM is a compliance-based methodology – the higher the risk, the more stringent the controls; the generic police IT countermeasures had been derived from a largely type 'C' perspective; and the client was a middle manager in a hierarchical police organisation. So they took readily to CRAMM and had now bought the software. We could not involve type 'A' (individualism) as the project was pre-procurement. But I explained the need to involve users on the fatalist and egalitarian axis as well as type 'C's from the hierachy. 'Why do we need to involve the Federation?', the client asked, and I was able to draw and explain the 'four views of nature' (see Figure 3.2). Now the client understood.

Data asset valuation interviews were carried out with three type 'C's (hierarchy) but also with one type 'B' (fatalism) and one type 'D' (egalitarianism). The results of the interviews were then reviewed by a mix of type 'B' users and type 'C' business representatives. The threat and vulnerability analysis questionnaire was completed by a group of type 'C' technical experts. Users and business representatives simply would not have understood it – I hardly did myself. The various participants in these processes are shown in Table 7.6.

Table 7.6: Participants in Case Study 'Zulu'

Data Asset Valuation Interviewees
A Police Sergeant from a Division, who was also a Police Federation Representative
A Police Superintendent Divisional Commander, who was also a Senior User on the Project Board
A Police Inspector from the Communications Room
The Assistant Chief Constable (Operations)
A Police Constable from a Division
Data Asset Valuation Review Workshop Participants
The Assistant Chief Constable (Management Services)
A Chief Inspector from a Division
A Police Inspector from the Communications Room
A Police Sergeant from Headquarters
A Police Constable from a Division;
A Shift Manager from the Communications Room

The Information Security Officer
Threat and Vulnerability Exercise Participants
A Police Superintendent who was also the Senior Technical on the Project Board;
The Communications Officer
The IT Support Manager
The Information Systems Development Manager
The Information Security Officer
The Data Protection Officer

The differences in individual risk perception were clearly evident from the records of the interviews and the review workshop. For example, on the question of the consequences for personal safety of the new system being unavailable for 15 minutes, the Federation Sergeant thought that officers would be put at risk. The Divisional Commander disagreed but thought that public safety could be at risk, as did the Assistant Chief Constable and the Police Constable. The fatalist and hierarchical focus was on the public whilst the egalitarian focus was on the Federation's members.

The criticality of the new system meant that some risks were perceived to be higher than had been the case on 'Kilo', 'Broadway' and 'Juliet'. Thus the controls recommended by CRAMM were more stringent than those in the generic police IT security countermeasures, although the project manager subsequently rejected some of these on grounds of cost and practicability.

Case Study 'Trojan'

This was a short case involving an IT security risk analysis for a police IT project. The contract had been awarded and the software was under development by the supplier. Thus I had the chance to engage type 'A' (individualism) in the analysis. However the client did not want this since they were in dispute with the supplier about both timescales and quality. As the project manager put it, '[Name of supplier] are the enemy'.

I also had the chance, as with 'Zulu', to involve type 'D' (egalitarian) users but the client rejected this since the project manager felt they would 'have no understanding of the issues'. I did, however, persuade the client to go beyond the project team and invite two type 'B' (fatalist) user experts to contribute to the analysis.

The sensitive nature of some of the data in the application led the expert users to perceive very high levels of risk associated with unauthorised data disclosure. As a result, CRAMM recommended very stringent access controls for the application which, as with 'Zulu', the project manager subsequently rejected on grounds of cost and practicability.

Case Study 'Uniform'

This was a medium case of risk assessment, risk management, risk monitoring and risk review activities for a police business project. This was repeat business, with the same client as 'X-ray', and the client was already convinced of the value of Cultural Theory.

The chronology and derivation of the work was set out in the risk register as follows:

> 'The 52 risks identified in an initial SWOT (strengths, weaknesses, opportunities and threats) analysis undertaken by the Project Director, Project Manager and Project Officer in August 1998;
>
> A risk assessment workshop held in October 1998, involving the Project Director, Project Manager and Corporate Projects personnel, together with the Constabulary's Director of Support Services. This workshop reviewed the initial SWOT analysis and assessed a further 38 risks perceived by the workshop participants;
>
> A quality review workshop held in November 1998, involving a range of the project's stakeholders. This workshop reviewed the risk assessment and assessed six further risks perceived by the workshop participants;
>
> A re-evaluation (downwards) of 16 of the risks as a result of the risk management progress reports obtained during January 1999;
>
> A risk assessment review workshop held in September 1999 and risk management review process undertaken during October 1999; and
>
> A risk management review undertaken in January 2000.'

The SWOT analysis and initial risk assessment involved only hierarchical type 'C's. The SWOT analysis noted that it took,

> 'Only limited account of the views of the many other organisations who have a stake in the policing of [name]. Ways will in due course be explored to seek to ensure that these perspectives are properly captured and assessed.'

The initial risk assessment then promised that,

> 'We shall be involving a range of other stakeholders in a subsequent review of our analysis.'

There was no type 'A' (individualist) involvement, however the type 'B' (fatalist), 'C' (hierarchy) and 'D' (egalitarian) composition of the review group is shown in Table 7.7.

All levels of the hierarchy were represented but careful effort had been made to involve front-line users and special interest groups.

Table 7.7: Risk Review Group for Case Study 'Uniform'

Assistant Chief Constable	Project Director	Type 'C'
Police Superintendent	Project Manager	Type 'C'
Civilian Staff Member	Project Team Member	Type 'C'
Civilian Staff Member	Project Team Member	Type 'C'
Police Sergeant	Project Team Member	Type 'C'
Civilian Staff Member	Project Support Office	Type 'C'
Member	Police Authority	Type 'C'
Member	Police Authority	Type 'C'
Member	Police Authority	Type 'C'
Head of Department	Support Department	Type 'C'
Detective Superintendent	Crime Department	Type 'C'
Police Superintendent	Divisional Commander	Type 'C'
Civilian Staff Member	Unison Representative	Type 'D'
Police Sergeant	Police Federation Representative	Type 'D'
Police Sergeant	General Patrol Officer	Type 'B'
Police Chief Inspector	Operational Department	Type 'B'
Civilian Staff Member	Support Department	Type 'B'

For the project closedown evaluation I reported that,

> 'The risk assessment and risk management methodologies followed … were based on the premises that assessing risk involves sharing perceptions of uncertainty and that managing risk involves ownership and accountability.
>
> The management of risk on the project went well. The various stakeholders involved in the initial risk assessment and the subsequent formal risk reviews gave feedback which suggested they were impressed with the robustness of the process and appreciated the opportunity to share their concerns. The senior managers allocated ownership of the various risks were co-operative and happy to be held accountable for progress with their risk management plans. The risk-related papers presented to the Project Board appeared to be well received. Most importantly, nothing seems to have gone wrong with the [description of organisational change].'

Case Study 'Purple'

This was a very short case to prepare a risk log for a police IT project and was referral business from 'Alpha'. The client had been told they had to prepare a risk log and I was the logical choice for the work.

The client showed little enthusiasm for or understanding of Cultural Theory but agreed to involve some users. Participants in the one-day workshop were nine type 'C' (hierarchy) members of the client's own organisation and three police users who were type 'B' (fatalist) in this context because they knew little about the project but would be affected by it. As the risk assessment process unfolded, one particular user became quite frustrated at the project team, scoffing at the planned duration of the project, which would deliver too late for police forces. The same user also noted that the project had been initiated as somebody's good idea but did not have either an approved business case or an ACPO sponsor. This was a good example of the differences in perceptions of quality between types 'B' (fatalism) and 'C' (hierarchy) – fitness for purpose versus compliance with specification.

Case Study 'Hunter'

This was a medium case which was a risk project in its own right. The work involved an assessment of the risks associated with a criminal investigation policing function. The work was delayed as the client changed twice. As with 'Charlie' and 'Quebec', I worked with the second client and three members of their team to structure the logic tree for a failure modes analysis. The second client accepted that this represented only their team's type 'C' (hierarchical) view and knew that I had planned from the outset with the first client to have the initial analysis reviewed by relevant stakeholders.

By the time we got to designing the review process, a third client had taken over the work. The third client accepted the principles of Cultural Theory but preferred a hybrid design for the review, which comprised three groups: the police business and academe (an 'A/C' hybrid); customers in police forces and other parts of the client's organisation (a 'B/C/D' hybrid); and operational detectives (a 'B/D' hybrid).

The review process was fascinating. The academic raised concerns about methodology. Some of the police customers were defensive of their own organisations and critical of the client's. The operational detectives gelled from a set of individual type 'B's (fatalists) into a type 'D' (egalitarian) group, and also turned against the client. The upshot of the review was recorded in the report as follows:

> 'The review workshop considered that ... the use of a consultancy methodology had been too lean for such a complex research problem.

Much more time needed to be taken to identify the problem and to investigate its causes.

The review workshop felt that the review process should also have involved divisional crime managers and crime desk managers in respect of volume crime, others involved in the Administration of Justice and researchers specialising in volume crime. There should also have been a series of consultations with other high interest high impact stakeholders, for example victims of crime and the staff associations.'

This clearly shows how antagonisms between the four constituencies can play out in practice.

Case Study 'Golf'

This was a very short case involving a programme of police support function projects. The client had participated in a previous case and had liked the process.

The client was a strong character and, although they listened to my explanation of risk perception theory, they wanted to do things their own way – 'Oh no we don't want to ask the Federation'. The seven participants who joined the client at the workshop were all hierarchical type 'C's from the particular support function, albeit they came from different levels and different parts of the organisation.

The process designed was too complex, requiring the workshop participants to identify hazards by constructing 'If X then Y' statements and then estimating the probability of 'X' and the financial cost consequences of 'Y'. The client was the most senior figure present at the workshop, the most notable feature of which was the client 'showing off' how clever they were, both with the process and with the hazards they raised.

We were unable to complete the planned risk management at the workshop, and the work was never done to my knowledge. But the client was happy – they had shown themselves to be smart and had been seen to have consulted within the hierarchy.

Case Study 'Hotel'

This was a medium duration case which was a risk project in its own right, involving the assessment and management of the risks associated with a major policing operation. The client's overarching concern was that the Force would 'be unable to cope effectively with the demands placed upon it.' So we worked with 13 type 'C' (hierarchical) operations managers from across the Force to analyse the failure modes leading up to this scenario. Our logic tree had three levels: 102 contributory risks; ten major categories of risk and one overarching failure.

The client accepted that our analysis was derived from a purely type 'C' middle manager perspective. Accordingly, we designed a formal review process which involved two type 'B' (fatalist) Police Constables from operational shift-work, two type 'D' (egalitarian) representatives of the Police Federation and UNISON, and a range of type 'C' (hierarchy) managers who had not been involved in the initial analysis. The review process resulted in ten minor amendments to the existing risks and in the identification and assessment of six new risks. There was nothing Cultural Theory constituency-specific in the six new risks.

An interesting feature of the review was the way the two type 'B' (fatalist) Constables warmed to their task. Initially uncertain as to their role, they grew in confidence as spokespersons for the front-line and began to offer opinions prefaced with statements such as 'but from an operational point of view ...'.

The risk management planning reverted to the group of type 'C' (hierarchy) middle managers. Countermeasures were designed where appropriate, however the bulk of the work involved deciding which one of twelve graded tactical options would be implemented as a contingency plan for the occurrence of each risk.

Case Study 'India'

This was a short case to produce a risk log for a police business project. The Cultural Theory approach was acknowledged but proved impracticable. This was because of non-availability of stakeholder representatives and because the publications of two separate but highly relevant government reports had been delayed.

The data for the risk log was gathered at a workshop attended by four 'C' (hierarchy) project representatives. The context was highly political. The project team knew their preferred direction but there had been divergent views in submissions to the two government enquiries and in other relevant reports. There was thus a focus on thinking about alternative scenarios for the project, the risks these posed for the organisation and the countermeasures needed.

None of this was either explicitly or implicitly informed by Cultural Theory. The whole exercise was part of ongoing political in-fighting between the individual hierarchies within a macro hierarchical context.

Case Study 'Sierra'

This was a long case which was a risk project in its own right, involving the assessment and management of the risks associated with a major national policing operation. Following the work on 'Hotel', I was invited by the President of the Association of Chief Police Officers (ACPO) to replicate the analysis, but this time on a national scale.

The client was very interested in the Cultural Theory approach and asked for a full theoretical explanation. So I provided a copy of Mars and Frosdick (1997). I then met with the client and we identified four groups of stakeholders and their risk agendas, as shown in Table 7.8.

Table 7.8: Risk Assessment Design for Case Study 'Sierra'

Group 1 Participants: Risk As Deviance – "We Must Get Our Act Together"
- One nominee from [Name of Government Department]
- One nominee from Her Majesty's Inspectorate of Constabulary (HMIC)
- Three nominees from [Name of ACPO Committee]

Group 2 Participants: Risk As System Blame - "You Haven't Got Your Act Together"
- One nominee from the Police Federation
- One nominee from the Superintendents Association
- One nominee from UNISON
- Two nominees from Police Forces which think they are ahead of the game

Group 3 Participants: Risk As Acts Of God - "Thank You For Asking Us What We Think"
- Three nominees from Forces identified by HMIC as ill-prepared for the operation
- One nominee from the Association of Police Authorities
- One nominee from the Local Government Association

Group 4 Participants: Risk As A Random Chance Events - "It'll Be Alright On The Night"
- One nominee from the Police IT Organisation
- One Police Force IT Manager
- One nominee from the Emergency Planning Society

Groups 1,2, 3 and 4 were explicitly Cultural Theory types 'C' (hierarchy), 'D' (egalitarianism), 'B' (fatalism) and 'A' (individualism) respectively. The risk perceptions predicted were explicitly in line with Cultural Theory's four views of nature (see Thompson *et al.* 1990, p.27 and Figure 2.1 in Chapter Two).

We convened a two-day workshop. The attendees were not identical to the design but the integrity of the four Cultural Theory groups was carefully preserved. The groups were asked to review the work undertaken for 'Hotel', together with other pieces of work which had already been undertaken at a national level. This work was presented under six main headings: policing emergencies, co-ordinating emergency response, managing death, dealing with offences and incidents, maintaining public order and providing policing services.

One notable feature of this review was that, following the group discussions, the Group 2 (type 'D' egalitarian) participants raised a new heading which they felt had been completely overlooked. This was to do with the internal capability of the police service to manage and resource the major national policing operation. This was typical type 'D' system blame and the group were quite vociferous in making their views known to the other participants. The review expanded the 'Hotel' work and 192 threats were now identified under seven key headings, now including internal capability.

Following the risk identification, the participants were placed into three mixed groups, each group containing all four Cultural Theory types, to estimate the probabilities and consequences. This was the same approach as used for 'X-ray'.

The work concluded with a national conference where I presented the risk assessment and recommended risk management controls to over 100 delegates representing more than 60 police and other emergency services organisations. The analysis was subsequently taken into use across the UK police service. This was the most significant piece of work of my career and it was solidly underpinned by Cultural Theory.

Case Study 'Tango'

This was a medium duration case involving risk assessment, risk management and risk review activities for a programme of police projects in the field of racial diversity. The client was themselves completing a PhD and so was happy to engage with theory. The client was convinced by the Cultural Theory approach and we invited four representatives from each of the four constituencies to attend a workshop.

On the day, we had four type 'A' (individualist) consultants in diversity matters. We had four type 'B' (fatalist) representatives from police forces – people working in the field of diversity but who were unfamiliar with our programme. We had four type 'C' (hierarchy) representatives with governance of diversity responsibilities from ACPO, HMIC, the host organisation and the Home Office.

But only two of the type 'D' (egalitarian) group representatives – the Police Federation and the Public and Commercial Services Union – turned up. The invited representatives from two visible ethnic minority pressure groups were missing. One of the consultants commented, 'we're talking about black issues, but everyone in the room is white'.

We completed the risk assessment exercise, but the draft risk log noted,

> 'The participants noted with regret that, despite the Project Manager's efforts to secure their attendance, the invited representatives from [name] and [name] did not attend the workshop. This meant that none of the workshop participants were drawn from visible minority ethnic communities, which participants felt would inevitably diminish the quality of the analysis.'

The risk management process then involved a type 'A/C' 'center' alliance of the client, a consultant and an HMIC representative.

Accepting that the type 'D' (egalitarian) perspective had not been fully captured, the client and I designed a quality review process involving all four constituencies. This time, neither the type 'B' (fatalist) police force representative nor the type 'D' minority group representative turned up. So we went and visited one of the type 'D' representatives to review the work with them and sent copies of the risk log to a variety of relevant minority group organisations.

A year later, we held a formal review of the risk assessment following the same workshop design. This time there were members of minority groups present. We placed the participants in four explicitly Cultural Theory groups: Group A (individualism) – Consultants; Group B (fatalism) – the User Community; Group C (hierarchy) – the Police Business; and Group D (egalitarianism) – Advisory Groups. We briefed them on our predicted risk perceptions for their group and encouraged them to play to their different roles.

The four groups worked independently to review the risk log and I then facilitated a discussion. For one risk, three of the groups agreed that nothing had changed. When I asked the egalitarian Group D their view, the chair played their part beautifully and responded, 'You won't be surprised to hear that we disagree'.

The review of the risk management plans then also involved representatives from all four groups. The whole review worked very well and several of the participants commented on how inclusive the process had been. Subsequently, I was asked to do work for one of the consultancy firms present. Later on, I was also asked by another attendee to design a risk training course for their organisation.

Case Study 'Ranger'

This was a medium duration case involving risk assessment and risk management activities for a programme of police organisational change projects. The client was familiar with the Cultural Theory approach from previous work I had done for their organisation and indeed the final risk log included the sentence, 'The analysis drew on Grid Group Cultural Theory to reveal five key groups of Programme stakeholders'.

At out initial meeting, a brief analysis revealed a large number of different stakeholders from each of the four constituencies[29]. There were too many for a workshop, and the client was reluctant to leave any of them out, so we decided instead to undertake semi-structured interviews with representatives of the stakeholders.

The client identified nine type 'C' (hierarchy) interviewees, five drawn from their own organisation and four from bodies having oversight of policing, including ACPO, HMIC and the Home Office. The research design was thus skewed towards hierarchy. However the client was fully cognisant of Cultural Theory and the interviewee list also included three type 'D' (egalitarian) organisations (Police Federation, Superintendents Association and Unison), four type 'A's (individualists) from within the supply chain and four type 'B' (fatalist) customers in police forces – managers who had to use whatever services the organisation provided.

A briefing note on the programme was circulated to each interviewee. Each interview was then semi-structured around the process shown in Table 7.9 on the next page.

The interviewees spoke frankly and openly about their concerns and the interviews resulted in the identification of some 200 perceived threats or issues of concern regarding the programme[30].

---

[29] The detailed stakeholder analysis for Case Study 'Ranger' is set out in Table 6.5 in Chapter Six.

[30] Through my company, I engaged associate staff known to the client to undertake the interviews. The quality of the interviews was disappointing as the writing up, although sufficient for the consultancy, was generally scant. I have not therefore undertaken a secondary data analysis of the interviews for this account of the case.

Table 7.9: Semi-Structured Interview Process for Case Study 'Ranger'

Thank you for agreeing to be interviewed as part of the risk assessment process. The interview will last approximately 60 to 90 minutes and no special preparation is required. We are simply asking you to reflect on the [Name] Programme and to share with us any thoughts you may have on how or why the programme might go awry.

The interview will be in five stages. We will ask you:

* to consider a list of adverse outcomes of the programme and to change, add or delete anything you feel appropriate.

* to list your own 'top ten' threats which could give rise to those adverse outcomes.

* to say how likely it is that each of these threats will happen.

* to say how bad the adverse outcomes would be if the threats did happen.

* to make any other comments you wish.

Thank you for your help.

A content analysis of the interviews then revealed 19 key areas of threat. The risk log noted that,

> 'It was recognised that, from the perspective of the stakeholder interviewees, each of these 19 threats posed a high risk to the programme. It was also recognised that these were genuine perceptions which would require careful management.'

Some of the 19 areas concerned the capability and credibility of the organisation. This was uncomfortable for the interim Chief Executive, but they convened a meeting of their senior staff. Highlighting the importance of risk as perception rather than reality, the Chief Executive told them, 'If they [the stakeholders] say we're crap, we're crap'.

I then briefed the meeting on the 19 key threats and facilitated the senior staff to estimate the risks using the same type of Delphi technique as 'November' and 'Oscar'. My client then took the risk evaluation decision and I facilitated them to determine the risk management controls required. There were 30 risk management controls identified in the risk log as, 'critical for the success of the Programme'.

As a validity check, the risk log was then circulated to the 20 interviewees for their comments. One type 'D' (egalitarian), one type 'B' (fatalist) and two type 'C's (hierarchy) responded. They concurred with the analysis.

Six months later, I assisted the client with a review of the risk log. Partly because of the risk work and partly because a new Chief Executive had arrived, the change programme was now much less ambitious. Eight additional controls had been implemented and, of the 38 controls, 15 were ongoing, 12 had been completed, and 11 had been remitted from the programme to the operational business. Critically, these 11 controls dealt with the organisation's capability and credibility but the operational business managers never implemented them – all too difficult.

The organisation continued to lose credibility with its customers, its Chief Executive resigned following a scandal and the Home Office later cut its budget by nearly a third.

Case Study 'Central'

This was a very short case involving a mooted police IT project. The case involved two workshops (Northern and Southern) with three purposes – benefits analysis, user requirements and risk assessment.

The project was the client's 'good idea' for a networked information repository and they wanted to see what their user community thought of it. Thus the workshops design was focussed on nine type 'C' (hierarchy) members of the client's organisation, together with 17 user representatives of various ranks and roles within the client's UK police customer base. These were type 'B's (fatalists) because they had no agenda – they did not know anything about the project and had no views on it – until they were asked.

Interestingly, the users in both workshops formed into cohesive groups – the type Bs thus acquired shades of type 'D' – and it became clear that they did not think much of the client's idea. They raised lots of risks but could see few benefits, suggesting instead that the client should put the information on a CD-Rom.

The users were not involved in the subsequent risk evaluation and risk management, which were undertaken with the client alone. The risk management plans were never progressed because the idea for the project was shelved. This was a good example of how the type 'B/D' (fatalist/egalitarian) user input can result in a risky project being stopped at an early stage.

Case Study 'Amber'

This was a short case involving the assessment and management of the risks associated with organising a police event. For the workshop, the client and I took a dual approach. First we invited event management consultants (type 'A' – individualism), members of the organising committee (type 'C' – hierarchy) and type 'B' (fatalist) representatives from the venue for the event, who might become type 'D' (egalitarian) if vociferous in their concerns about the disruption the event would cause to their site.

Second, we suggested to the participants the predicted risk concerns of four groups of stakeholders, as shown in Table 7.10.

Table 7.10: Predicted Risk Concerns for Case Study 'Amber'

Governance – Organising Committee Concerns (Type 'C' – Hierarchy)
- Threats to the security of the event
- Health and safety hazards

User – Delegate Concerns (Type 'B' – Fatalism)
- Threats to the delegate experience (facilities, accommodation, catering, programme, social events)

User – Host Site Concerns (Type 'B/D' – Fatalist/Egalitarian)
- Disruption to normal activities on the site
- Disruption to the local community

Consultants – Commercial Concerns (Type 'A' – Individualist)
- Threats to the commercial viability of the event

These four perspectives were directly derived from analysis set out in the PAFs setting towards the end of Chapter Five and thus provide a direct link between the two research settings.

The approach worked well. The participants engaged in some useful lateral thinking and identified over fifty risks, together with a list of over 60 control measures which needed to be implemented. Some of these controls had a significant impact on the management and infrastructure of the site, as well as on the organisation of the event. Following the event, I received a letter from the client's boss which said, 'I was not convinced initially of the need for the risk assessment exercise but am now wholly convinced and grateful for being pushed towards it'.

Case Study 'Orange'

This was a short case involving a police business project. The client had been a participant in 'Amber', had seen the Cultural Theory approach work, and wanted the process replicated for their own project. So we tried the dual approach of stakeholder analysis and predicted risk concerns, albeit in a project rather than an event context.

The four stakeholder groups (commercial providers, user community, the organisation itself and staff associations) and their predicted risk concerns were explicitly Cultural Theory.[31] We then convened a risk workshop with three or four representatives of each group. As with 'Tango', I made it explicit that each group was being asked to play a role – one that Cultural Theory would predict would come naturally to them.

The group work risk identification and subsequent facilitated risk estimation proved very time-consuming and only 14 risks were assessed on the day. The estimates of probability and consequences were consensually agreed through independent voting, lengthy discussion of differences in perceptions between the four groups and, where necessary, aggregation. At the conclusion of the workshop, participants all commented on how valuable they had found the process. Each group agreed to nominate one person to participate in the subsequent risk management workshop. In an aside, one commercial provider commented on the riskiness of the client's procurement approach and told me, 'I expect this has given [name of client] lots of good reasons not to do this'.

The participants' notes were retained and used to identify eight additional risks. These were assessed by the client alone. The client also took the risk evaluation decision alone. For the risk management session, the type 'B' (fatalist) user community representative sent their apologies, reflecting a fatalist 'why bother' attitude, but the type 'A' (individualist) commercial provider and the type 'D' (egalitarian) staff association representative did attend. At the conclusion of a worthwhile session, which identified 34 essential controls, the commercial provider commented to me,

> 'I've learned such a lot through this process – seeing things from other points of view. I used to be blinkered and just look at things from a business perspective, but now I can see the need to think more widely'.

---

[31] The detailed stakeholder analysis and predicted risk concerns for Case Study 'Orange' are set out in Table 6.7 in Chapter Six.

Case Study 'Uncle'

This was a medium duration case involving the risks associated with organising a series of police events. The client was someone who had been involved in five previous cases and was thus very familiar with the Cultural Theory approach.

The research design for the risk assessment used the stakeholder analysis, semi-structured interviews and coding and analysis approach first used for 'Ranger' but in this case the number of interviewees was ten[32]. There were two type 'A' (individualist) commercial providers within the supply chain for the events, two type 'C' (hierarchy) managers responsible for the proper governance of the organisation, two type 'C' staff responsible for the organisation of the events, and four type 'B' (fatalist) customers in police forces (police managers who might attend or send people to the events). Type 'D' (egalitarian) organisations were not consulted, however one of the four type 'B' customers selected was known to have been very critical of the organisation's previous events, and thus represented something of a hybrid 'B/D' perspective.

A secondary analysis of the interview data reveals which of the three groups (commercial type 'A', governance type 'C' and customers type 'B' with a hint of 'D') raised threats which were coded within the 16 key risks identified. This analysis is set out in Table 7.11.

Table 7.11: Risk Identification Interview Sources for Case Study 'Uncle'

No.	Key Area of Risk	Commercial	Governance	Customers
1	Event topics and objectives	7	5	11
2	Organisation, planning and co-ordination	9	4	1
3	Financial viability	6	9	3
4	Event location and timing	0	2	2
5	Quality of venue	2	1	1
6	Audi-visual systems	2	1	1

---

[32] Through my company, I commissioned an associate to undertake the interviews. The account of this case is therefore based on a secondary data analysis of the interviews.

7	Internal venue threat to safety and security	4	2	0
8	External threat to safety and security	3	4	1
9	Public disorder at venue	3	1	0
10	Security of property and information	3	2	0
11	Speaker's expectations	1	0	0
12	Non-attendance of speakers	1	1	2
13	Quality and content of speakers' presentations	4	5	3
14	Legal and ethical aspects of speakers' presentations	1	4	4
15	Delegates attitude and behaviour	1	1	1
16	Competition	0	3	1
	Total Mentions	*47*	*45*	*31*
	Number of Interviewees	*2*	*4*	*4*
	Average Number of Mentions Per Interviewee	*23.5*	*11.25*	*7.75*

Whilst the number counts are small, four interesting features emerge from Table 7.11.

First is the agreed perception of all three groups of the importance of getting the subject matter right (see risks 1, 13 and 14). Second was the relative absence of customer perceptions of financial and security compliance-related risks (see risks 2, 3 and 7 to 10), which are more of a 'center' concern. Third is the distribution of the threats raised. The six 'A/C' center alliance interviewees raised an average of 15.3 threats each, whilst the type 'B' with a hint of 'D' customers were about half that, confirming their more fatalist perspective – they had less to say. Fourth was the relative lack of any risks raised uniquely from a customer perspective. A greater focus on the inclusion of more than one 'border' type customer might have changed this situation.

Risk estimation, risk evaluation and risk management planning were undertaken by the client alone and resulted in the identification of 21 critical risk management controls. I do not know how well these were implemented since my involvement with the case ceased after I had written up the risk log.

Case Study 'Bluegrass'

This was a long case involving risk assessment, risk management, risk monitoring and ongoing risk reviews for a multi-million pounds programme of police business projects which will take many years to complete. At my initial meeting with the client, I presented the Cultural Theory research design developed through 'Ranger' and 'Uncle'. The client invited me to submit a proposal for the work, which they then commissioned.

We undertook a stakeholder analysis and selected twelve interviewees, three from each of four constituencies: the police business, the user community, 'advisory' groups and providers and advisors[33]

The interview process was identical to 'Ranger' (see Table 7.9 above). The interview data were supplemented by a brainstorming exercise involving type 'C' (hierarchy) implementation team personnel drawn from across the organisation. The interviews and 'brainstorm' resulted in the identification of 195 concerns. The analysis aggregated these into 73 threats and then into 17 key areas of risk[34]. These were then presented to the Programme Board, on which all four Cultural Theory types were represented. One further key area of risk was then added.[35] If these key risks materialised, the analysis suggested 20 different adverse outcomes which might ensue.

I then worked with the two type 'C' representatives of the client to estimate and evaluate the risks and to allocate responsibility for controlling them to named type 'C' post-holders. Subsequently, I interviewed those post-holders to help them decide on the appropriate risk management controls.

The management of risk model for the programme is shown at Figure 7.1 on the next page.

---

[33] The detailed stakeholder analysis for Case Study 'Bluegrass' is set out in Table 6.6 in Chapter Six.

[34] Through my company, I commissioned an associate to undertake the interviews. I then worked with the associate on the brainstorm and the coding and analysis.

[35] This addition was a duplicate added against my wishes but at the personal insistence of the Chair of the Police Authority. It was removed at a subsequent review and has been discounted for the purpose of this analysis.

Figure 7.1: Management of Risk Model for Case Study 'Bluegrass'

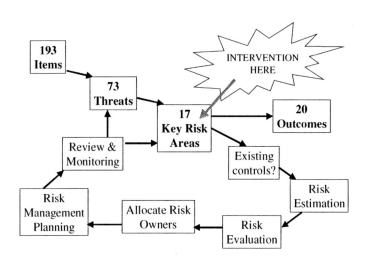

Following the development of the Programme Risk Log, I provided a management of risk training session for the Programme Board. Thereafter, I ran a 'How to Manage Project Risk' training course for the project managers within the programme. To the present day I continue to work with the two type 'C' representatives of the client to facilitate quarterly reviews of the Programme Risk Log, updates of which are presented to the Programme Board, and to monitor and advise on the risk logs produced by the trained project managers.

As with 'Uncle', a secondary analysis of the interview data reveals which of the four constituencies raised threats which were coded within the 17 key risks first identified. This analysis is set out in Table 7.12.

Table 7.12: Risk Identification Interview Sources for Case Study 'Bluegrass'

No.	Key Area of Risk	Risk	A*	B*	C*	D*	T*
1	Fit with operational capability	Medium	8	5	1	2	1
2	Key supporters	Low	5	2	3	2	3
3	Communication and consultation	Low	3	3	7	6	3
4	Changes in the policing environment	Low	4	2	3	1	1
5	Asset impairment	Medium	6	0	5	3	3
6	Strategic procurement	High	6	0	3	0	6

7	Asset exploitation	Low	2	0	0	1	0
8	Funding and cash flow	Medium	6	2	7	2	2
9	Programme management/monitoring	Medium	2	0	4	2	8
10	Management skills and capability	Medium	6	0	7	3	3
11	Locations of facilities	Low	3	7	2	6	4
12	Space requirements specification	Low	5	3	2	1	3
13	Amenities requirements specification	Medium	5	3	2	5	0
14	Health, safety and security	Low	1	2	2	4	1
15	Custody specific	Low	5	4	4	2	0
16	Joined-up criminal justice	Medium	1	2	2	0	0
17	Partnership working	Low	1	6	1	0	0
	Total Mentions		*69*	*41*	*55*	*40*	*38*
	Number of Interviewees		*3*	*3*	*3*	*3*	*-*
	Average Mentions Per Interviewee		*23*	*13.7*	*18.3*	*13.3*	*-*

*Key: A = Providers and Advisors, B = the User Community, C = the Police Business, D = Advisory Groups, T = the Implementation Team Brainstorm.

As with 'Uncle', the number counts are small, nevertheless Table 7.12 reveals six interesting points.

First is again the comparatively smaller mentions of concern from both the user community and the advisory groups, although this time we can see that it is both constituencies which have less to say, not just the fatalist 'B's. Second is the areas of concern perceived by the 'B/D' alliance. More than half the mentions by the fatalist 'B's are on four risks (1, 11, 15 and 17) which affect their working environment. And more than half the mentions by the egalitarian 'D's are on four risks (3, 11, 13 and 14) which raise matters which affect their members' jobs.

Third is the relative lack of perception by the police business of most of the risks of most concern to the 'B/D' alliance (risks 1, 11,13, 14 and 17). Fourth is the vice versa, i.e. the relative lack of perception by the 'B/D' alliance of the risks of most concern to the 'center' 'A/C' alliance (risks 2, 5, 6, 8, 9, 10). In fact the only 'high' risk (6) is not mentioned at all by the 'B's or 'D's. Fifth, then, is the distinctive perception of the providers/advisors (risks 1, 6 and 12). Interestingly and sixth, there is only one risk (9) for which the predominant perception is the hierarchical type 'C', i.e. the police business supplemented by the 'brainstorm'. These findings clearly illustrate the differences in risk perception between the two diagonal alliances as well as between the four individual constituencies.

Case Study 'Harvard'

This was a medium duration case involving a police IT project. I was brought into the project as part of an external consultancy team. The consultant's project manager was not interested in Cultural Theory and simply wanted a risk log producing. Both the consultancy days and timescales were limited so I offered a scaled down version of the stakeholder interviews approach adopted for 'Ranger', 'Uncle' and 'Bluegrass'. However, due to procurement rules, I was not permitted to interview the likely supplier, who the client organisation did not rate, but was instead provided with a copy of the supplier's own risk log. My suggestion of the need for type 'D' (egalitarian) interviews was rejected so I ended up with eight interviews with type 'B' (fatalist) users of the existing system and type 'C' (hierarchy) managers of relevant business functions within the organisation.

The analysis of the supplier risk log and the interviews yielded 69 pieces of data, which were coded into 15 key threats. I was also able to rank the adverse consequences in order of perceived seriousness. I then facilitated the client project manager and IT manager to assess the risks, evaluate them and determine the necessary controls. Of the 15 controls, five directly reflected the client organisation's suspicions about the likely supplier's capability.

Thus despite the consultant project manager's lack of interest in the Cultural Theory approach, I was able to deploy the interviews methodology and include type 'A' (individualism), 'B' (fatalism) and 'C' (hierarchy) perceptions in the risk log, which was well received by the client organisation. Subsequently, that organisation engaged me directly for three further assignments, two of which were risk-related and are included in this set of case studies.

Case Study 'Royal'

This was a short case in a criminal justice context. The client had been required to produce a risk log as part of a tendering process and the timescales were very constrained. The client's project team were very bright and would be interested in theory. So I sat down with the client and did a Cultural Theory stakeholder analysis[36].

We then convened a workshop of project team members, briefed them on Cultural Theory and then asked them to reflect on the risks facing the project from each of four different perspectives in turn. These perspectives, their

---

[36] The detailed stakeholder analysis for Case Study 'Royal' is set out in Table 6.8 in Chapter Six.

associated risk 'agendas' and predicted risk concerns are set out in Table 7.13.

Table 7.13: Fourfold Risk Perspectives for Case Study 'Royal'

Hierarchy – governance perspective (compliance agenda) – on time, to budget, to specification

Individualism – supplier perspective (commercial agenda) – profitability, sustainability, reputation

Fatalism – customer/user perspective (no particular agenda) – fitness for purpose, study 'experience'

Egalitarianism – 'representatives' perspective ('political' agenda) – terms and conditions, workloads.

The project team did this lateral thinking very well. On four separate passes, they completed 'post-it' notes setting out the hazards they perceived from the particular perspective. The 'post-it' notes were then coded and analysed into key risks, each of which was then risk assessed as it was felt that perspective would assess it. Risk management controls were suggested immediately where appropriate.

Cultural Theory was overt throughout the whole process and was mentioned by name in the Risk Log, which was favourably received by the project team, the client and the client's client. Subsequently, the client won the contract and the risk log was reviewed and updated throughout the life of the project, although now only from a type 'C' (hierarchical) Project Board and project team perspective.

Case Study 'Apple'

This was a very short case to produce a risk log for a police event. The work was commissioned at the insistence of the events management consultant whom I had previously worked with on 'Amber' and 'Uncle'. The client reluctantly agreed and promptly stalled. Two months passed before we were allowed to start. I then worked with the consultant using the generic events risk log produced in 'Uncle' to draft the risk assessment. The event organisation was going wrong and the consultant wanted to shuttle the blame onto the client.

A further month passed before a review was arranged – and by now the event was only two months away. The review was attended by four type 'C' (hierarchy) members of the project team and two type 'A' (individualist) consultants. Only minor changes were made to the analysis. Risk management controls considered essential by the consultants were devised but never progressed. And a planned review with one month to go was cancelled at short notice.

The risks were identified but not managed. The event did not go well and one of the two consultants resigned because of the negative experience.

Case Study 'Zebra'

This was a short case involving a police business project[37]. The approach replicated the methodology developed through 'Ranger', 'Uncle' and 'Bluegrass' but on a smaller scale.[38]

The client's project manager was briefed on Cultural Theory and the stakeholder analysis revealed the four Cultural Theory constituencies of the commercial supply chain (one interviewee selected), police and public users of the project's products (two police and one public interviewees selected), the governance of the project (one pair of interviewees selected) and representative groups. For the latter, my associate e-mailed me to report that the client's project manager was unwilling to involve any representative groups 'because of the political issues surrounding the project. They do not want to let the cat out of the bag yet!' This was a deliberate exclusion of the type 'D' (egalitarian) perspective.

However I was able to persuade the client's project manager to allow my associate to interview an acknowledged expert in the field, well known in public life, who had a distinctive perspective. In the particular context of this project, this person displayed aspects of all three active Cultural Theory types – so a hint of type 'D' system blame.

The interviews were supplemented by a variety of source documentation produced by those having governance of the project. The interviews and documents yielded 101 concerns which were coded into 13 key threats. It is not appropriate to give any further details of the risk analysis.

---

[37] This project was confidential for reasons of national security and the details in the case are therefore deliberately vague.

[38] Through my company, I commissioned an associate to undertake the interviews and produce the first draft of the risk analysis. The account of this case is therefore based on a secondary analysis of the interview data.

As with 'Uncle' and 'Bluegrass', the risk estimation, risk evaluation and risk management planning were then undertaken by the hierarchical type 'C' client alone. When I presented the risk log to the Project Board, the key point was that the highest risk to the project had been contributed by the expert. This risk challenged and changed the client's thinking in the field addressed by the project.

Case Study 'Peter'

This was a short case to produce a risk log for a police IT project. The client was very experienced in the management of risk and I had worked with them extensively since 1995. I proposed an approach which would involve eight interviews, two with each constituency. But the client told me, 'This is a low risk project – three interviews will be enough: the senior user, a techie and a couple of users, who you can see together'.

This was a challenge since I had no way of determining how extensive the risk assessment work on any project should be. I had previously used the scale of the project – the bigger the project the more risk-related work. So for the first time outside the training room I used the OGC Project Profile Model[39] (PPM) to check this overall risk perception. The model 'agreed' it was a low risk project.

I was now beginning to formulate the idea that the PPM could provide a more useful filter than scale alone. Thus an overall high risk project could imply a full-blown risk assessment through stakeholder interviews or a large scale focus group. An overall medium risk project could suggest a small focus group doing some lateral thinking, whilst an overall low risk project could be more perfunctorily risk-assessed.

Thus a small-scale risk assessment was undertaken through interviews with two hierarchical type 'C's and two fatalist type 'B' users. The risk evaluation decision and risk management measures were drafted for the client and approved by them with only minor amendment.

---

[39] The OGC Project Profile Model is a structured questionnaire within a Microsoft Excel® Worksheet. Like CRAMM, it is a bureaucratic method produced by bureaucrats for bureaucrats. The answers to the questions are numerical and, on the basis of the answers given, the software calculates an overall 'risk' score for the project. This is a decision support tool which enables a project manager to provide some supporting evidence for their 'gut feel' about how risky the project is.

CONCLUSION

The data sampled from the 41 case studies and set out above represent the first set of data required for a case study-based grounded theory analysis. Chapter Eight will open with the cross-case analysis which provides the second set of data required for the grounded theory approach. The theoretical propositions emerging from the analysis will then be drawn out and substantiated.

CHAPTER EIGHT: CONCLUSION

SUMMARY

This Chapter opens with the cross-case analysis which provides the second set of data required for the grounded theory approach. It continues by considering the theory that emerges from and is grounded in the research data and offers seven theoretical propositions. Finally, the Chapter introduces new Cultural Theory-based methodologies for consulting in and training on the management of risk.

ANALYSIS: THE CROSS CASE REPORT

Introduction

This second pass at the case study data begins by referring again to the date order in which the cases were undertaken. This was set out in Table 7.1 in Chapter Seven and is replicated in Table 8.1 below for ease of reference.

In respect of stakeholder participation, 'A' refers to the more individualist supply chain constituency; 'B' to the more fatalist user community; 'C' to the more hierarchical governance constituency; and 'D' to the more egalitarian user special interest groups.

Table 8.1: Case Study Details – Sorted by Start Date

Case Alias	Start Date	End Date	Days Effort	Stakeholder Participation A	B	C	D
Mike	07/04/1995	18/11/1996	42.00			✓	
November	26/05/1995	26/11/1999	106.75	✓	✓	✓	✓
Oscar	12/12/1995	22/12/1999	13.25			✓	
Victor	29/08/1996	18/09/1996	1.00			✓	
Whisky	28/09/1996	05/02/2001	31.75	✓	✓	✓	
X-Ray	08/12/1996	23/07/1999	28.00	✓	✓	✓	✓
Kilo	07/02/1997	05/03/1997	4.75			✓	
Delta	10/03/1997	10/03/1997	1.00			✓	
Echo	18/03/1997	18/04/1997	1.50			✓	
Broadway	25/04/1997	25/09/1997	12.25			✓	
Foxtrot	28/04/1997	10/10/1997	5.50	✓	✓	✓	
Juliet	06/05/1997	08/07/1997	6.50			✓	

Alpha	24/07/1997	31/03/1998	14.00	✓	✓	✓	
Charlie	15/09/1997	28/10/1997	3.75		✓	✓	✓
Bravo	15/10/1997	21/10/1997	5.50		✓	✓	
Lima	04/11/1997	22/04/1998	10.50		✓	✓	✓
Quebec	12/11/1997	03/02/1998	5.00		✓	✓	✓
Papa	02/12/1997	04/12/1997	1.50			✓	
Romeo	12/12/1997	12/12/1997	1.00	✓		✓	
Yankee	18/12/1997	17/02/1998	9.50	✓	✓	✓	
Zulu	23/04/1998	19/06/1998	24.50		✓	✓	✓
Trojan	11/06/1998	28/08/1998	7.75		✓	✓	
Uniform	19/08/1998	10/01/2000	11.50		✓	✓	✓
Purple	19/10/1998	14/12/1998	2.00		✓	✓	
Hunter	25/11/1998	14/07/1999	13.50	✓	✓	✓	✓
Golf	22/12/1998	05/02/1999	2.50			✓	
Hotel	12/02/1999	14/06/1999	11.00		✓	✓	✓
India	04/05/1999	09/06/1999	4.00			✓	
Sierra	08/05/1999	28/07/1999	11.00	✓	✓	✓	✓
Tango	22/06/1999	03/12/2000	17.50	✓	✓	✓	✓
Ranger	08/02/2000	26/04/2001	13.00	✓	✓	✓	✓
Central	18/03/2000	07/07/2000	2.50		✓	✓	
Amber	23/04/2001	12/06/2001	3.75	✓	✓	✓	
Orange	12/06/2001	02/11/2001	6.00	✓	✓	✓	✓
Uncle	29/11/2001	24/09/2002	15.50	✓	✓	✓	
Bluegrass	13/05/2002	31/03/2004	21.75	✓	✓	✓	✓
Harvard	13/06/2002	13/11/2002	12.75	✓	✓	✓	
Royal	22/11/2002	12/09/2003	6.25	✓	✓	✓	✓
Apple	08/04/2003	18/07/2003	2.25	✓		✓	
Zebra	12/05/2003	18/07/2003	9.00	✓	✓	✓	
Peter	12/12/2003	22/03/2004	3.25		✓	✓	

Whilst I do not want to engage in any attempt at formal quantitative correlations, Table 8.1 does show that I have got better at involving more Cultural Theory constituencies in the cases.

If we exclude the most recent case and band the remaining 40 cases in Table 8.1 into sets of ten, we can see that the participation of stakeholders has progressed as shown in Table 8.2.

Table 8.2: Chronological Increase in Stakeholder Involvement in Cases

Cases	A	B	C	D	=
'Mike' to 'Broadway' (1995 to 1997)	3	3	10	2	18
'Foxtrot' to 'Yankee' (1997 to 1998)	4	7	10	3	24
'Zulu' to 'Tango' (1998 to 2000)	3	8	10	5	27
'Ranger' to 'Zebra' (2000 to 2003)	9	9	10	4	32

Since my clients have all been organisations, type 'C' inevitably features in all the cases. But it is clear that I have improved my ability to persuade clients to involve types 'A' and 'B' in the management of risk. The improvement in respect of type 'D' is less evident but we have seen from the individual cases that some hierarchies struggle to reach out to those who may oppose them.

Sorting the case studies in order of days effort (Table 8.3), it is also clear that, the greater my involvement, the more stakeholder constituencies have been involved.

Table 8.3: Case Study Details – Sorted By Days Effort

Case Alias	Start Date	End Date	Days Effort	Stakeholder Participation			
				A	B	C	D
November	26/05/1995	26/11/1999	106.75	✓	✓	✓	✓
Mike	07/04/1995	18/11/1996	42.00			✓	
Whisky	28/09/1996	05/02/2001	31.75	✓	✓	✓	
X-ray	08/12/1996	23/07/1999	28.00	✓	✓	✓	✓
Zulu	23/04/1998	19/06/1998	24.50		✓	✓	✓
Bluegrass	13/05/2002	31/03/2004	21.75	✓	✓	✓	✓
Tango	22/06/1999	03/12/2000	17.50	✓	✓	✓	✓
Uncle	29/11/2001	24/09/2002	15.50	✓	✓	✓	
Alpha	24/07/1997	31/03/1998	14.00	✓	✓	✓	

Name							
Hunter	25/11/1998	14/07/1999	13.50	✓	✓	✓	✓
Oscar	12/12/1995	22/12/1999	13.25			✓	
Ranger	08/02/2000	26/04/2001	13.00	✓	✓	✓	✓
Harvard	13/06/2002	13/11/2002	12.75	✓	✓	✓	
Broadway	25/04/1997	25/09/1997	12.25			✓	
Uniform	19/08/1998	10/01/2000	11.50		✓	✓	✓
Hotel	12/02/1999	14/06/1999	11.00		✓	✓	✓
Sierra	08/05/1999	28/07/1999	11.00	✓	✓	✓	✓
Lima	04/11/1997	22/04/1998	10.50		✓	✓	✓
Yankee	18/12/1997	17/02/1998	9.50	✓	✓	✓	
Zebra	12/05/2003	18/07/2003	9.00	✓	✓	✓	
Trojan	11/06/1998	28/08/1998	7.75		✓	✓	
Juliet	06/05/1997	08/07/1997	6.50			✓	
Royal	22/11/2002	12/09/2003	6.25	✓	✓	✓	✓
Orange	12/06/2001	02/11/2001	6.00	✓	✓	✓	✓
Bravo	15/10/1997	21/10/1997	5.50		✓	✓	
Foxtrot	28/04/1997	10/10/1997	5.50	✓	✓	✓	
Quebec	12/11/1997	03/02/1998	5.00		✓	✓	✓
Kilo	07/02/1997	05/03/1997	4.75			✓	
India	04/05/1999	09/06/1999	4.00			✓	
Charlie	15/09/1997	28/10/1997	3.75		✓	✓	✓
Amber	23/04/2001	12/06/2001	3.75	✓	✓	✓	
Peter	12/12/2003	22/03/2004	3.25		✓	✓	
Golf	22/12/1998	05/02/1999	2.50			✓	
Central	18/03/2000	07/07/2000	2.50		✓	✓	
Apple	08/04/2003	18/07/2003	2.25	✓		✓	
Purple	19/10/1998	14/12/1998	2.00		✓	✓	
Echo	18/03/1997	18/04/1997	1.50			✓	
Papa	02/12/1997	04/12/1997	1.50			✓	
Delta	10/03/1997	10/03/1997	1.00			✓	
Romeo	12/12/1997	12/12/1997	1.00	✓		✓	
Victor	29/08/1996	18/09/1996	1.00			✓	

Table 8.4 presents the cases in Table 8.3 banded into three groups of ten and one of eleven.

Table 8.4: Days Effort and Stakeholder Involvement in Case Studies

Cases	*A*	*B*	*C*	*D*	*=*
'November' to 'Hunter' (10 cases – 106.75 to 13.50 days)	8	9	10	6	33
'Oscar' to 'Zebra' (10 cases – 13.25 to 9.00 days)	5	8	10	5	28
'Trojan' to 'Charlie' (10 cases – 7.75 to 3.75 days)	3	7	10	4	24
'Amber' to 'Victor' (11 cases – 3.75 to 1.00 days)	3	4	10	0	17

Again without wishing to attempt any formal quantitative correlation, it is evident from the numerical sequences that, the more I have been involved in the cases, the greater the extent to which Cultural Theory has been operationalised. There is a sequential decrease in the involvement of types 'A', 'B' and 'D' commensurate with my reduced involvement in the cases.

To continue this second pass at the case study data, I now want explore the cases with reference to the main headings in the coding frame at Appendix A.

Organise the Project

In analysing the case data and coding the cases, I have considered whether I made use of Cultural Theory as a heuristic in pitching for the business or otherwise during the initial meeting with the client. For 15 of the cases, I decided that I had not and for the remaining 26 cases, I decided that I had.

For 15 of these 26 cases, I simply outlined Cultural Theory to the client and explained its significance for informing the design of a management of risk process[40]. For four of the cases, I gave a formal presentation to the client and their team. The other seven cases were repeat or referral business, where the client was already aware of the Cultural Theory approach and wanted it deployed on a new case.

Whilst I am again deliberately avoiding any formal quantification, the clarity of the correlation between the use of Cultural Theory as a heuristic and the extent of stakeholder participation in the cases is marked.

Table 8.5 sets out the 41 cases sorted by extent of stakeholder participation.

Table 8.6 then highlights (in bold) the 26 cases where Cultural Theory featured in organising the work.

---

[40] See the section on 'Explaining Cultural Theory' in Chapter Six.

Table 8.5: Case Study Details – Sorted by Stakeholder Participation

Case Alias	Start Date	End Date	Days Effort	A	B	C	D
November	26/05/1995	26/11/1999	106.75	✓	✓	✓	✓
X-ray	08/12/1996	23/07/1999	28.00	✓	✓	✓	✓
Bluegrass	13/05/2002	31/03/2004	21.75	✓	✓	✓	✓
Hunter	25/11/1998	14/07/1999	13.50	✓	✓	✓	✓
Ranger	08/02/2000	26/04/2001	13.00	✓	✓	✓	✓
Tango	22/06/1999	03/12/2000	17.50	✓	✓	✓	✓
Sierra	08/05/1999	28/07/1999	11.00	✓	✓	✓	✓
Royal	22/11/2002	12/09/2003	6.25	✓	✓	✓	✓
Orange	12/06/2001	02/11/2001	6.00	✓	✓	✓	✓
Whisky	28/09/1996	05/02/2001	31.75	✓	✓	✓	
Uncle	29/11/2001	24/09/2002	15.50	✓	✓	✓	
Alpha	24/07/1997	31/03/1998	14.00	✓	✓	✓	
Harvard	13/06/2002	13/11/2002	12.75	✓	✓	✓	
Yankee	18/12/1997	17/02/1998	9.50	✓	✓	✓	
Zebra	12/05/2003	18/07/2003	9.00	✓	✓	✓	
Foxtrot	28/04/1997	10/10/1997	5.50	✓	✓	✓	
Amber	23/04/2001	12/06/2001	3.75	✓	✓	✓	
Zulu	23/04/1998	19/06/1998	24.50		✓	✓	✓
Uniform	19/08/1998	10/01/2000	11.50		✓	✓	✓
Hotel	12/02/1999	14/06/1999	11.00		✓	✓	✓
Lima	04/11/1997	22/04/1998	10.50		✓	✓	✓
Quebec	12/11/1997	03/02/1998	5.00		✓	✓	✓
Charlie	15/09/1997	28/10/1997	3.75		✓	✓	✓
Apple	08/04/2003	18/07/2003	2.25	✓		✓	
Romeo	12/12/1997	12/12/1997	1.00	✓		✓	
Trojan	11/06/1998	28/08/1998	7.75		✓	✓	
Bravo	15/10/1997	21/10/1997	5.50		✓	✓	
Peter	12/12/2003	22/03/2004	3.25		✓	✓	
Central	18/03/2000	07/07/2000	2.50		✓	✓	
Purple	19/10/1998	14/12/1998	2.00		✓	✓	
Mike	07/04/1995	18/11/1996	42.00			✓	
Oscar	12/12/1995	22/12/1999	13.25			✓	

Broadway	25/04/1997	25/09/1997	12.25	✓
Juliet	06/05/1997	08/07/1997	6.50	✓
Kilo	07/02/1997	05/03/1997	4.75	✓
India	04/05/1999	09/06/1999	4.00	✓
Golf	22/12/1998	05/02/1999	2.50	✓
Echo	18/03/1997	18/04/1997	1.50	✓
Papa	02/12/1997	04/12/1997	1.50	✓
Delta	10/03/1997	10/03/1997	1.00	✓
Victor	29/08/1996	18/09/1996	1.00	✓

Table 8.6: Cultural Theory as a Heuristic and Stakeholder Participation

Case Alias	Start Date	End Date	Days Effort	Stakeholder Participation			
				A	B	C	D
November	26/05/1995	26/11/1999	106.75	✓	✓	✓	✓
X-ray	08/12/1996	23/07/1999	28.00	✓	✓	✓	✓
Bluegrass	13/05/2002	31/03/2004	21.75	✓	✓	✓	✓
Hunter	25/11/1998	14/07/1999	13.50	✓	✓	✓	✓
Ranger	08/02/2000	26/04/2001	13.00	✓	✓	✓	✓
Tango	22/06/1999	03/12/2000	17.50	✓	✓	✓	✓
Sierra	08/05/1999	28/07/1999	11.00	✓	✓	✓	✓
Royal	22/11/2002	12/09/2003	6.25	✓	✓	✓	✓
Orange	12/06/2001	02/11/2001	6.00	✓	✓	✓	✓
Whisky	28/09/1996	05/02/2001	31.75	✓	✓	✓	
Uncle	29/11/2001	24/09/2002	15.50	✓	✓	✓	
Alpha	24/07/1997	31/03/1998	14.00	✓	✓	✓	
Harvard	*13/06/2002*	*13/11/2002*	*12.75*	✓	✓	✓	
Yankee	18/12/1997	17/02/1998	9.50	✓	✓	✓	
Zebra	12/05/2003	18/07/2003	9.00	✓	✓	✓	
Foxtrot	28/04/1997	10/10/1997	5.50	✓	✓	✓	
Amber	23/04/2001	12/06/2001	3.75	✓	✓	✓	
Zulu	23/04/1998	19/06/1998	24.50		✓	✓	✓
Uniform	19/08/1998	10/01/2000	11.50		✓	✓	✓

				A	B	C	D
Hotel	**12/02/1999**	**14/06/1999**	**11.00**		✓	✓	✓
Lima	**04/11/1997**	**22/04/1998**	**10.50**		✓	✓	✓
Quebec	**12/11/1997**	**03/02/1998**	**5.00**		✓	✓	✓
Charlie	**15/09/1997**	**28/10/1997**	**3.75**		✓	✓	✓
Trojan	**11/06/1998**	**28/08/1998**	**7.75**	X	✓	✓	X
Bravo	*15/10/1997*	*21/10/1997*	*5.50*		✓	✓	
Peter	**12/12/2003**	**22/03/2004**	**3.25**		✓	✓	
Central	*18/03/2000*	*07/07/2000*	*2.50*		✓	✓	
Purple	*19/10/1998*	*14/12/1998*	*2.00*		✓	✓	
Apple	*08/04/2003*	*18/07/2003*	*2.25*	✓		✓	
Romeo	*12/12/1997*	*12/12/1997*	*1.00*	✓		✓	
Mike	*07/04/1995*	*18/11/1996*	*42.00*			✓	
Oscar	*12/12/1995*	*22/12/1999*	*13.25*			✓	
Broadway	*25/04/1997*	*25/09/1997*	*12.25*			✓	
Juliet	*06/05/1997*	*08/07/1997*	*6.50*			✓	
Kilo	*07/02/1997*	*05/03/1997*	*4.75*			✓	
India	*04/05/1999*	*09/06/1999*	*4.00*			✓	
Golf	**22/12/1998**	**05/02/1999**	**2.50**		X	✓	X
Echo	*18/03/1997*	*18/04/1997*	*1.50*			✓	
Papa	*02/12/1997*	*04/12/1997*	*1.50*			✓	
Delta	*10/03/1997*	*10/03/1997*	*1.00*			✓	
Victor	**29/08/1996**	**18/09/1996**	**1.00**	X	X	✓	X

But for five of the cases, ('Harvard', 'Trojan', 'Peter', 'Golf' and 'Victor') this would be a perfect correlation.

And all five cases can be explained. For 'Harvard', we saw in Chapter Seven that I was able to deploy Cultural Theory notwithstanding the client's lack of interest. For 'Trojan', we saw that the client deliberately chose to exclude types 'A' and 'D', whilst for 'Peter', we saw that a risk-experienced client perceived the project as low risk and chose to pare down the process. For 'Golf', the client wanted to do things their own way and excluded types 'B' and 'D', whilst for 'Victor', we saw that the client deliberately excluded all except type 'C'.

Risk Strategy Document

For three early cases (Mike, Oscar and X-ray), all before 1997, I produced a risk methodology for the client's project initiation document. This was because I had not yet combined the methodology, risk assessment and risk management plans into a single document. But it was from these early cases that I derived the reference to risk perception included in each subsequent risk log. In the generic risk log my company uses this is that,

> 'It is widely recognised that different people perceive risk in entirely different ways. Risk assessment is not an exact science but seeks to draw out shared perceptions of uncertainty. It is therefore important to ensure that a broad range of stakeholders is adequately represented in the risk assessment exercise.'

These words refer directly to Cultural Theory and have provided the guiding principle for my work from the very outset.

For 'November', as we saw in Chapter Six[41], I produced a strategy paper in May 1997. This affirmed the same principle and also set out the baseline risk activities to be undertaken by each of the programme's projects. One activity required a written methodology, thus I produced such a document for 'Alpha' in August 1997.

Stakeholder Analysis

Stakeholder analysis featured in 27 of the 41 cases. In other cases Cultural Theory may have informed the design, but the case data do not record a formal stakeholder analysis. Chapter Six[42] includes examples of the different stakeholder analyses undertaken for the cases of 'November', 'Ranger', 'Bluegrass', 'Orange' and 'Royal'. The individual reports in Chapter Seven additionally refer to the stakeholder analyses for 'Victor', 'X-ray', 'Quebec', 'Papa', 'Uniform', 'Sierra', 'Tango', 'Amber' and 'Uncle'. There is thus a good body of evidence to support the discussion in Chapter Six[43] of the four different Cultural Theory constituencies revealed through the cases.

Risk Assessment

Chapter One argued that 'risk analysis' and 'risk assessment' were synonymous and represented the sum of the three sub-processes of risk

---

[41] See the section on 'The Impact of the Research on the Setting'.

[42] See the sections on 'Explaining Cultural Theory' and 'Stakeholder Analyses'.

[43] See the section on 'Discussion: Cultural Theory Constituencies'.

identification, risk estimation and risk evaluation. These are therefore addressed in turn.

Risk Identification

The cases have used a variety of methods and tools to tease out the threats or hazards perceived by the various participants. The methods have ranged from one-on-one interviews with a single participant, through workshops involving anything from four to twenty stakeholders, to semi-structured interviews with up to twenty stakeholder representatives. The tools have included mnemonics, checklists, logic trees and critical paths. However, as we have seen, these techniques are insufficient in themselves.

The key to richness and comprehensiveness in risk identification has been recognition of the fact that Cultural Theory posits four different ways of perceiving risk. This point clearly emerges in sixteen of the 41 cases.

In the extended account of the NSPIS ('November'), the risks raised were in line with the working hypothesis about fourfold risk perception which informed the selection of the participants. In 'Victor', there was clear recognition that management (type 'C') and unions (type 'D') would see things differently. The value of the type 'A' commercial perspective was clear in 'Whisky' and 'Orange', The type 'D' perspective added a whole new category to the risk analysis in 'Sierra', and in 'Lima', content was added by the involvement of a type 'B/D' alliance in a risk review. In 'Romeo', the deliberate exclusion of type 'D' featured in one of the risks raised, whilst the differences in awareness between well informed and critical users and their more fatalist colleagues were clear in 'Yankee'. In 'Hunter', a type 'B/D' alliance rejected type 'C's initial analysis and in 'Tango', type 'D' played up nicely to their 'we disagree' role – once the client and I managed to get them to participate. In 'Ranger', the type 'C' Chief Executive accepted the critical perceptions coming from the other constituencies. The methodology used for 'Uncle' and 'Bluegrass' allowed for an analysis of the perceptual differences in the interview data. Finally, the approach adopted for 'Papa', 'Royal' and 'Amber' showed the value of asking participants to engage in lateral thinking to consider all four Cultural Theory points of view.

Risk Estimation

Since this book argues against the myth of scientific objectivity and in favour of risk as a subjective perception, it follows that none of the cases feature any attempt to use 'objective' numerical estimates. Rather the cases have used a variety of scales which participants have been invited to use to make subjective judgements.

In all cases probabilities have been Bayesian estimates using three-point or more usually five-point scales. Such scales have been a matter of individual client preferences and examples are shown in Table 8.7.

Table 8.7: Examples of Probability Estimation Scales

'Bluegrass'	*'November'*	*'Whisky'*	*'Royal'*
1 = Very Unlikely	0 = None	0 = None	Green = Low
2 = Unlikely	1 = Low	1 = Low	Amber = Medium
3 = Possible	2 = Low/Medium	2 = Medium	Red = High
4 = Probable	3 = Medium/High	3 = High	
5 = Very Probable	4 = High	4 = Very High	

Similarly, the estimation of adverse consequences has in all cases been subjective and made with reference to various scales negotiated with the client. Examples are shown in Table 8.8.

Table 8.8: Examples of Consequences Estimation Scales

'Bluegrass'	*'November'*	*'Whisky'*	*'Royal'*
1 = Minor	0 = None	0 = None	Green = Low
2 = Moderate	1 = Low	1 = Low	Amber = Medium
3 = Serious	2 = Low/Medium	2 = Moderate	Red = High
4 = Severe	3 = Medium/High	3 = Severe	
5 = Fatal/Devastating	4 = High	4 = Critical	

We saw in the case of the NSPIS 'November' that I asked the workshop participants to make four estimates of adverse consequences: one each for overall failure, timescales, costs and quality. This approach was applied for most of the early cases.

As I grew in experience through the cases, I increasingly realised that stakeholders perceived a whole range of adverse outcomes, many of which went beyond the programme or project, as we saw for example in Table 6.2

in Chapter Six. This had twenty adverse outcomes, a number which it would clearly be impracticable to score individually for each threat.

So I began simply to use a five-point scale and to ask participants to think about the whole range of adverse outcomes and estimate 'how bad would it be if X actually happened?'

Participants sometimes found this difficult, so, as the cases progressed, I used my experience of the CRAMM methodology to help me to develop a single scale which took account of a range of adverse outcomes and could be customised to reflect the particular circumstances of each case. I began to provide this scale as a handout to assist participants in making their estimates. An example is set out in Table 8.9.

Table 8.9: Example Multiple Consequences Estimation Scale

1   Minor, e.g.
  - Cost over-runs within tolerance
  - Time over-runs from tolerance up to three months
  - Quality reductions within tolerance
  - Minor distress to an individual
  - Financial losses of up to £10,000
  - Inefficient policing in one part of the organisation
  - Very minor lobbying/disruption at one site
  - Minor loss of goodwill confined to an individual site

2   Moderate, e.g.
  - Cost over-runs of £10,001 to £100,000
  - Time over-runs of three months to six months
  - Minor quality reductions
  - Minor illness/injury
  - Minor distress to more than one person
  - Civil damages/criminal penalty of up to £10,000
  - Financial losses of £10,001 to £100,000
  - Inefficient policing across the organisation
  - Minor disruption or protest at one site
  - Loss of goodwill but with no effects beyond an individual site

3   Serious, e.g.
  - Changes which undermine the strategic vision
  - Cost over-runs of £100,000 to £1,000,000
  - Time over-runs of six months to twelve months
  - Moderate quality reductions
  - Serious illness/injury/threat to life, restricted to an individual

- Substantial distress to one or more persons
- Civil damages/criminal penalty of £10,001 to £250,000/up to 10 years imprisonment
- Financial losses of £100,001 to £1,000,000
- Undermining policing in one part of the organisation
- Disruption or protest in the local community
- Damage to reputation/credibility extending beyond an individual site

4 Severe, e.g.
- Radical changes to or the abandonment of the strategic vision
- Cost over-runs above £1,000,000
- Time over-runs above twelve months
- Serious quality reductions
- Serious illness/injury/threat to life involving more than one person
- Financial losses above £1,000,000
- Unlimited civil damages/criminal penalty or imprisonment in excess of ten years
- Undermining policing across the organisation
- Disruption or protest with nationally felt effects
- Significant damage to reputation/credibility resulting in widespread adverse publicity

5 Fatal/Devastating, e.g.
- Loss of life
- Seriously impeding national policing

The problem with this approach was in the subsequent design of risk management controls. Whilst controls designed to reduce high probability were straightforward, in the case of high adverse consequences the single number estimate meant it was not possible to tell which outcomes one was seeking to mitigate.

For the cases where the risk identification was undertaken by way of semi-structured interviews, I addressed this problem by asking each interviewee to say whether they thought there was a causal link between the threat they were raising and each one of a set of adverse consequences. In the subsequent coding and analysis, I was thus able to show which adverse outcomes were considered by the interviewees to be likely to be caused by each threat. I was also able to count the number of mentions received by each adverse outcome and so highlight to the client the rank order of seriousness with which outcomes were perceived. An example from 'Bluegrass' is shown in Table 8.10.

Table 8.10: Example Adverse Outcomes Frequency Analysis

This table shows fifteen adverse outcomes identified by the twelve interviewees and the frequencies with which each interviewee associated each of their concerns with each outcome.

The fifteen adverse outcomes are shown as letters **a** to **o**.

The twelve interviewees are shown as letter **A** to **L**.

Totals are shown at the end of each column and row.

The rank order for each adverse outcome is shown in the final row R.

	a	b	c	d	e	f	g	h	i	j	k	l	m	n	o	=
A	1	2	2	1	1	0	6	2	2	2	1	2	0	3	2	32
B	5	3	3	2	2	2	6	8	1	7	3	8	5	2	2	65
C	0	0	0	0	0	0	0	0	2	7	4	5	0	1	0	22
D	2	3	0	2	1	1	1	4	0	1	1	2	2	2	1	28
E	2	1	2	0	0	0	4	3	2	3	5	0	0	3	1	30
F	2	3	1	4	5	5	6	4	1	1	2	0	0	3	7	54
G	4	4	4	1	5	1	3	8	6	6	4	6	1	1	5	63
H	5	4	5	3	3	3	1	11	6	6	4	4	2	5	3	74
I	1	13	3	1	2	2	2	5	1	1	4	1	1	5	1	44
J	3	7	2	3	2	1	2	2	2	3	1	1	5	5	1	48
K	4	5	3	3	1	2	5	8	0	1	0	6	6	1	4	50
L	0	0	0	9	0	0	2	9	1	1	0	2	2	0	1	28
=	29	45	25	29	22	17	38	64	24	39	29	37	24	31	28	
R	7	2	11	7	14	15	4	1	12	3	7	5	12	6	10	

Throughout the cases, I have used one of five methods to get participants to make their estimates. One method, used for example for 'Oscar' and 'Ranger', was a crude Delphi technique involving paper circulations, individual scorings and aggregation. This has generally been used when a workshop has focussed on risk identification and run out of time for estimation. This method has weaknesses since it does not allow for discussion of differences in perception and the aggregation process drags scorings towards the mean. A second method has involved working one-to-one with the client to simply get their own estimates. This clearly has significant weaknesses since it completely ignores risk perception theory, however it was sometimes the only option where the client was not prepared to pay the costs of a stakeholder workshop.

The other three methods have sought to avoid 'group-think' by individual simultaneous voting. This has been either by pointing to laminated A4 cards with numbers printed on them, by the holding up of red, amber and green cards (for three-point scales), or by 'five finger scoring' (for five-point scales).

The key point here is the wide variations in perceptions which emerge through such voting processes. In more than half of all the risks raised at workshops, these differences (for example some people voting 1 and others 5) have been so marked that I have had to facilitate a discussion of the differences in perception. Because I have been facilitating such workshops as a consultant, it has not been practicable to keep data on which Cultural Theory constituency representatives have voted differently from each other. However the overarching experience has been that the exchanges of views has been very informative for participants, and views have often been changed on the basis of new information received. This all supports the view that risk perception is a product of familiarity and dread (see Slovic 1991 and Figure 1.4 in Chapter One). A repeated comment from my clients has been how valuable it was for their own understanding of the risks to listen to different stakeholders debating probabilities and consequences.

Risk Evaluation

From the discussion in Chapter One of more democratic and participative risk evaluation techniques, it is possible that Cultural Theory might have been applied within the cases to facilitate risk evaluation by a mixed group. But this has not happened. My clients have all been type 'C' managers and have without exception all seen the making of the risk evaluation decision as a management decision-making responsibility. The decision has been variously taken by the client and their project manager either alone, together, or in consultation with one or more senior managers. Thus the application of Cultural Theory does not feature at all in the risk evaluations undertaken within any of the 41 cases.

In 13 of the cases there has been no risk evaluation decision to make. One case ('Echo') did not get as far as risk evaluation. Six cases were the IT security studies where the risk evaluation was automated within the CRAMM software. And six cases ('Amber', 'Royal', 'Peter', 'Romeo', 'Mike' and 'India') featured a pre-coded three-by-three cross impact matrix where the estimates of probability and consequences determined the risk evaluation. An example of such a matrix is shown in Figure 8.1 on the next page.

For three of the cases ('Charlie', 'Quebec' and 'Hunter'), the risk evaluation has involved the banding of calculated cumulative probabilities within a logic tree. But for the remaining 25 cases, the process has involved plotting the risks on a five-by-five matrix (see Figure 5.4 in Chapter Five and Figure 6.3 in Chapter Six) and facilitating the decision-maker(s) to determine where to draw the boundaries of high, medium and low risk.

Figure 8.1: Pre-Coded Risk Evaluation Matrix

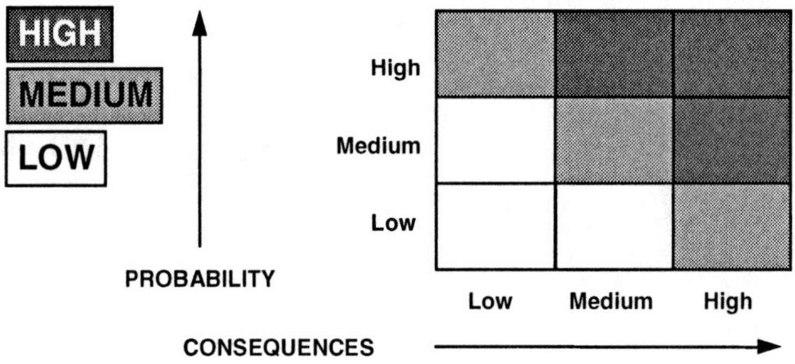

Risk Management

Risk management features in all of the cases bar four ('Charlie', 'Hunter', 'Golf' and 'Echo'). We saw in Chapter Seven that all four of these cases foundered before the risk management stage. In two other cases, the client took over responsibility and compiled the risk management controls without my help.

Of the remaining cases, 29 involved my facilitating the risk management problem-solving with only combinations of the client, their project manager and other senior managers. The decision tree tool I have used to support this process dates back to the extended case of the NSPIS ('November') and is set out in Figure 6.5 in Chapter Six. I have found no need to change it since 1995.

In the six other cases, my clients have been prepared to invite different stakeholders to participate in the risk management process. This participation has been far less extensive than in the risk assessment process and the extent of stakeholder involvement is shown in Table 8.11.

Table 8.11: Stakeholder Involvement in the Risk Management Process

Case Alias	Start Date	End Date	Days Effort	Stakeholder Participation			
				A	B	C	D
November	26/05/1995	26/11/1999	106.75	✓	✓	✓	
Alpha	24/07/1997	31/03/1998	14.00	✓		✓	
Yankee	18/12/1997	17/02/1998	9.50		✓	✓	
Tango	22/06/1999	03/12/2000	17.50	✓		✓	
Amber	23/04/2001	12/06/2001	3.75	✓	✓	✓	
Orange	12/06/2001	02/11/2001	6.00	✓		✓	✓

None of the cases have successfully involved all four Cultural Theory constituencies – although we have come close, particularly for 'November' and 'Amber'. For the NSPIS ('November') we saw that the type 'D' opponent police forces were invited but did not participate. For 'Orange' we saw that the type 'B' users did not turn up, whilst for 'Tango' neither the type 'B' users nor the type 'D' advisory groups responded to the invitation. 'Yankee' managed to involve type 'B' users and well as members of the hierarchy, whilst for 'Alpha', a single type 'A' commercial representative was invited to join a workshop of type 'C' representatives.

Chapter One argued that there was growing evidence of the need for dialogue and participation in decision-making, however the extent to which this has been implemented in the case studies is limited. As was the case with risk evaluation, the great majority of my clients have seen risk management decision-making as a management responsibility rather than a participative process. For example, for case study 'Uniform', the risk documentation emphasised the need for senior managers to take ownership of the risks and to be accountable for determining and progressing the risk management controls.

We saw that in some of the cases that the nominated risk owners did not do enough in this regard. I categorised this in Chapter Six as 'nice analysis, shame about the inactivity'. This problem was clear in the extended case of the NSPIS ('November'), where it was initially difficult to get senior managers to take ownership of their action plans. Indeed, we saw in Table 6.10 that progress with 34% of the plans was initially 'not satisfactory'. In 'Delta', we saw that there were doubts about whether the risk management actions were ever progressed at all. In 'Ranger', we saw the severe consequences of a failure to implement controls dealing with the organisation's capability and credibility.

In other cases, we saw that the implementation of the risk management controls had been effective. For example, 'Quebec' resulted in changes in the deployment of Special Constables and other volunteers. 'Uniform' resulted in a successful organisational change and 'Amber' led to changes in the management and infrastructure of a site. Most significantly, 'Sierra' resulted in a massive national policing operation passing off successfully.

Quality Review

Quality assurance or review is a project management concept which involves people formally reviewing a product – in this case a risk-related document – to determine whether it is fit for purpose and can be signed-off. The process often consists of nothing more than a document being circulated for comments and amended if necessary. For significant products, however, it is good (if expensive) practice for the product to be formally reviewed against the acceptance criteria specified in the product description or terms of reference for the work.

For all bar three of the cases, such assurance of the risk documentation has been undertaken informally by the client or by a combination of the client and their Project Board. However for 'Zulu', formal quality review processes for both the disaster recovery strategy and the system security policy were held at the request of the client – who was willing to pay for them. The reviews and reviewers were controlled by the client and Cultural Theory did not feature in their design.

However, now I had experienced the process, I was able to offer it to those of my clients who were willing to pay the additional costs involved. Only two have ever been so willing ('Uniform' and 'Hotel'), but for both these Cultural Theory has informed the design. In both cases the quality reviews have involved representatives of types 'B', 'C' and 'D', however there has been nothing Cultural Theory specific in the outcomes of those reviews.

Risk Monitoring

For the majority of the cases, my role as a consultant has meant I have gone in to help the client by facilitating the risk assessment and risk management planning and drafting the risk log. It has then been the client's responsibility to ensure that the nominated risk owners progress the relevant risk management controls. The key point here is that these risk owners have almost without exception been senior type 'C' managers carrying the authority to resource and take the necessary actions.

For seven of the cases, my company has been involved with the risk monitoring process. This involvement has taken three forms. For the early cases of 'Mike' and 'November' (both large-scale), I was myself the risk manager and therefore responsible to the project manager for progress chasing the risk owners[44]. For the very recent cases of 'Royal' and 'Peter' (both small-scale), having advanced in my career, I have been the project manager and so carried the responsibility myself. The other three cases ('X-ray', 'Uniform' and 'Bluegrass') have all been within the same police organisation where their preferred method of working has been for me to periodically interview each of the senior type 'C' risk owners and report on their progress with implementing the controls.

Risk Review

We saw in Chapter Seven that several of the cases had been commissioned by clients who simply wanted to 'tick the box' that they had compiled a risk log (see for example 'Delta', 'Echo', 'Juliet', 'Golf' and 'Apple'). These clients have shown no interest in risk perception and have also chosen to ignore the standard form of words included in my risk logs, namely that,

> 'Management of risk is not a one-off process to be forgotten as soon as it is completed. Rather it underpins decision-making on an ongoing basis. Effective risk management will result in risk reduction, and environmental scanning will result in the identification and assessment of new risks. Regular monitoring is therefore important.'

In other cases, the clients have accepted the need for review but, because my involvement as a consultant had ceased, I do not know whether any review activity took place or not. However in twelve of the cases, the clients have brought me back to facilitate reviews of the risk documentation, in some

---

[44] For 'November', I employed an associate to undertake the monitoring and report back to me.

cases on several occasions over several years. The review process has generally involved three stages: checking the risk assessment and progress with action plans for the high and medium risks; checking the risk assessment for low risks; and assessing any new risks which were now perceived.

For two of the cases ('Royal' and 'Peter'), I have been the project manager and so brought myself back, therefore we shall discount these cases.

Unsurprisingly, there is a clear correlation between my days effort on a case and the occurrence of review activities.[45] Taking this together with the apparent correlation between days effort and the extent of stakeholder involvement (see Table 8.4), we can see that some of these cases (for example 'November', 'Whisky', 'Tango', 'Uniform', 'Ranger', 'X-ray' and 'Bluegrass') have provided some of the most valuable insights for the research. These insights complement but do not add to the analysis set out in the 'Risk Assessment' section above.

THE GROUNDED THEORY

Introduction

So where does this all leave us? What can now be deduced from the work I have undertaken since 1992 in these two research settings? What explanation can now be said to emerge from and be grounded in the analysis presented in this book?

If we go back to Chapter Two, we see that the principal aim of the research has been to bridge the gap between theory and practice by testing the practical applicability of Cultural Theory. The research problem was framed as a study of whether Cultural Theory could be applied as a lean management of risk method through the practical application of grid-group: as a heuristic for explanation to clients; as a tool for stakeholder analysis and as a framework for disaggregated analysis.

The concluding part of Chapter Five hypothesised a practical approach to the management of risk which would apply Cultural Theory in the PAFs research setting. This would take account of different risk perceptions and seek to negotiate between them. It also tentatively suggested the practical application of Cultural Theory in the wider context of project management and the strategic management of major organisational change. This would help to assess and manage competing perceptions of risk in a new and revealing way.

---

[45] Nine of the ten cases feature in the first 15 places in the list of cases in Table 8.3.

Thus the conclusion to Chapter Five may be seen as an early attempt to suggest the theory that might emerge in this book.

The early ideas have been more fully developed through the shift to the second research setting and the 41 case studies undertaken. In addition to the analytical framework, the heuristic and the tool for stakeholder analysis, the research has revealed the practical contribution Cultural Theory makes within elements of the management of risk process. So I want to come towards a conclusion by suggesting that there are seven theoretical propositions which can be expounded from and justified by the analysis in this book.

Seven Theoretical Propositions

1. Management of Risk Techniques are Insufficient in Themselves

The first theoretical proposition is overarching and was first suggested in the literature review in Chapter One. This argued that management of risk techniques were insufficient without a sound understanding of risk theory, particularly risk perception theory and specifically Cultural Theory.

In Chapter One, we saw that the techniques of risk identification were insufficient for two key reasons. First, they rely on hindsight, from which lessons are often not learned, and which cannot in any case predict the future risks we face. Second, the simple application of the techniques overlooks the influences of cultural bias on risk perception. Those influences were clearly evident in the analysis of risk perception in PAFs towards the end of Chapter Five, in the extended case study of the NSPIS in Chapter Six and in several of the later cases (for example see 'Yankee', 'Amber', 'Uncle' and 'Bluegrass') in Chapter Seven.

Chapter One also suggested four reasons why the techniques of risk estimation are insufficient in themselves. Definitions of probability differ. There are question marks against the reliability of the data behind quantified estimates. Different expressions of quantified risk affect subsequent risk perception. And anyway, risk is a subjective social construct largely incapable of being objectively estimated as the physical scientists claim. The idea of differences in probability estimation is very clearly supported by the risk estimation experience in workshops for the case studies.

More tentatively, Chapter One argued that the techniques of risk evaluation are insufficient if they do not allow for risk as something which is collectively, socially and culturally constructed. And that having assessed and evaluated risk, simply applying the techniques of risk management is not enough. Risk management is a contested area of debate. Risk management decisions are political. The responsibility for making such decisions rests with managers, however there is growing evidence of the need for dialogue

and participation in decision-making. The hypothetical process offered in the
conclusion to the first research setting in Chapter Five suggested that there
would be value to be had from involving more than the hierarchical
constituency in risk management decision-making. This proposition however
has not been substantiated though the case studies undertaken in the second
research setting.

Nevertheless, as Chapter One concluded, theories of risk need to be
understood and then applied in practice. Whether in a safety, project or some
other risk context, this means recognising risk as a multiplicity of perceptions
about the source and level of threat or danger from future events or hazards
and about the variety of adverse consequences to which such events may give
rise. Effective management of risk requires the exercise of practical
management judgement, informed by a sound understanding of risk and risk
perception.

2. Cultural Theory as a Framework for Disaggregated Analysis

We saw in Chapter Two that Cultural Theory has enjoyed a breadth of
application, noting that, 'the idea is to go into some specific setting ... and use
the analytical scheme to sort out the various actors according to how grouped
and gridded they are' (Thompson *et al* 1999:3). We also noted Mars and my
published comment that, despite its demonstrated effectiveness, Cultural
Theory was 'still called upon to justify its claims with yet further examples of
empirical support' (Mars and Frosdick 1997:115).

The detailed Cultural Theory grid-group analysis of the British PAFs industry
in Chapter Four and the discussion of risk stakeholders in the police
programme and projects setting both offer such further empirical examples at
the macro level. The risk in PAFs business is dominated by hierarchical
organisations for who safety means compliance with rules. Those involved in
owning football clubs, developing PAFs and playing the game itself have an
individualist bias, whilst stadium communities and football supporters
occupy the egalitarian to fatalist axis. The analysis in Chapters Six and Seven
show that hierarchy refers to the police business and governance community,
who commission, pay for and have oversight of the work. The individualist
solidarity is represented by the commercial world, from which consultants,
potential tenderers and contracted suppliers are drawn. Egalitarianism refers
to pressure or 'advisory' groups, whilst fatalists are the front line user
community.

Further empirical examples at the micro level were offered through the
analysis of PAFs 'safety culture' in Chapter Five and of Cultural Theory as
organisation theory in Chapter Six. Chapter Five applied a grid-group

framework to explain how individual organisations provide the sub-cultures which interact to create the overall 'safety culture' at a particular venue. The relative strength of the grid aspect was determined by analysing the use of space, time, objects, resources and labour; whilst aspects of group were considered under the headings of frequency, mutuality, scope and boundary. Chapter Six illustrated how an analysis of 'project culture' might be developed by examining the six headings in Johnson and Scholes (1999) 'cultural web' to determine those factors which suggest the relative strength of grid and group.

These four empirical examples provide good supporting evidence for the second proposition – referred to in the original research problem – namely that the Cultural Theory's grid-group schema can be effectively applied as a framework for disaggregated analysis at a variety of levels.

3. Cultural Theory as a Heuristic

The research problem also sought to establish whether Cultural Theory's grid-group schema could be used as a heuristic – and the third theoretical proposition in this conclusion is that indeed it can.

Consider Figure 1.5 in Chapter One, Figure 2.1 in Chapter Two, Figure 6.2 and the discussion on 'explaining Cultural Theory' in Chapter Six, the cases in Chapter Seven, the cross-case discussions of 'organising the project' and the 'stakeholder analysis' earlier in this Chapter. Taken together, these sources in this book provide clear evidence of the effective application of Cultural Theory. This application has taught people that risk perception theory matters. It has persuaded them to permit the application of Cultural Theory for the design of their management of risk work. And it has played a major part in the application of the grounded theory through the development of the 'How to Manage Project Risk' training course outlined below.

4. Cultural Theory for Stakeholder Analysis

As well as the heuristic and the framework for disaggregated analysis of contexts, the research problem also posed the question whether Cultural Theory would work as a tool for disaggregated stakeholder analysis. The fourth proposition in this conclusion is that it does so work. This has been clearly evidenced earlier in this Chapter in the discussion of 'stakeholder analysis' in the cross-case report, which referred back to named cases in Chapter Six and Seven.

Further evidence comes from the discussion of cultural conflict in PAFs set out in Chapter Five. Regulatory perceptions of risk as breaking safety rules are predominant. PAFs owners and operators give priority to commercial risks such as access control, pirate merchandise, ticket touting, cash handling and ambush marketing. Spectator and local residents pressure groups are more concerned with quality and environmental risks, whilst the majority of fatalist spectators have to accept their lot.

This proposition builds on the second and third propositions, in the sense that the stakeholder analysis process demonstrated in this book has three main stages. The first stage requires the use of the heuristic so that the client can understand the framework for the analysis. The second stage requires the application of the grid-group schema to the setting in order to locate the four Cultural Theory constituencies and the organisations which represent them. The third stage provides for the identification of named individuals within those organisations. Those individuals can then be invited to participate in the various management of risk processes to be undertaken within the work. This process was hypothesised in the conclusion to Chapter Five, substantiated through the case studies in Chapters Six and Seven and forms a major part of the new risk consultancy and training methodologies outlined below.

5. Cultural Theory for Risk Identification

The next proposition is that Cultural Theory offers a valuable tool to support the risk identification process. This proposition is supported by the evidence from 16 of the case studies in Chapter Seven, summarised in the cross-case report above. These cases showed the impact on risk identification of the participation, non-participation or deliberate exclusion of one or more of the four Cultural Theory constituencies.

6. Cultural Theory for Risk Estimation

In a similar vein, the sixth proposition is that Cultural Theory can also be applied as a valuable tool to support the process of risk estimation. This is fully evidenced in the discussion within the cross-case report above so I will not repeat it here.

7. Risk Evaluation and Risk Management as Management Decision-Making

The final proposition is secondary to the first six, but nevertheless worth airing. We have seen that Cultural Theory was not applied for the risk evaluation for any of the cases. We have also seen that for 13 of the cases there was no risk evaluation decision to make. For the remaining 28 cases, the risk evaluation involved management decision-making. I have often emphasised to clients and trainees that there are no right or wrong answers here, only management judgements – indeed I have found on training courses that pairs of trainees will make different risk evaluation decisions using identical data. The consistent point that emerges from facilitating managers through the process is that, for the purposes of accountability, they have an audit trail and feel satisfied that their risk evaluation decisions are robust and defensible. Looking back to the discussion of 'Issues in Risk Evaluation' in Chapter One we can see that this is the type of good management judgement referred to by Smallman in his call for 'intelligent quantificationism' (1996:258).

We have also seen that, notwithstanding the tendency mooted in the literature towards more participative risk management decision-making, the process within the cases has again been largely a question of management judgement. There has been some involvement of other Cultural Theory constituencies but the data is limited and there is no apparent link between this involvement and any successful or ineffectual outcomes in the cases.

APPLYING THE GROUNDED THEORY

Introduction

Much academic work concludes with the presentation and justification of theoretical explanation. But I want to go further and now show that I have sought to apply the grounded theory. Of course the ideal application would have been back in the first research setting – the British PAFs industry – but the simple truth is that I have not been able to secure any relevant consultancy or training assignments. Accordingly, the attempted application has been confined to the police programme and projects setting.

The grounded theory has been applied in two ways. First is through the development of a 'Managing Risk' consultancy methodology. Second is through the design, delivery and evaluation of a 'How to Manage Project Risk' training course.

Consultancy Methodology

'Managing Risk'

The 'Managing Risk' consultancy methodology evolved during the course of the 41 case studies and has been in place since case study 'Orange'. The method is supported by a detailed menu of tasks and activities derived from the case study protocol at Appendix A. The key proposition behind the method is that 'Managing risk is about managing perceptions. Different individuals and groups of stakeholders can and do perceive risk in entirely different ways. It is therefore important to ensure a broad range of perspectives is adequately represented in any risk activity.'

On three recent occasions I have sat with clients and amplified this proposition by sketching out a figure which combines Figures 1.5 (Chapter One), 2.1 (Chapter Two) and 6.2 (Chapter Six). This has allowed me to offer a basic explanation of the four Cultural Theory types, their four different ways of perceiving risk and where the four types can be found in the context of police programmes and projects. On all three occasions, the clients have completely understood and accepted the proposition and invited me to submit proposals to undertake the work. Not unusually in the consultancy business, only one of the three prospects resulted in any paid work.

In the first case, the potential client was a chief police officer who wanted to improve the corporate governance of their organisation. I submitted a proposal, which was well-received by the chief officer, who, having initiated things, now wanted to delegate the oversight of the work to their organisation's full-time risk manager. I met with this individual but, not having any understanding of risk perception theory, they were obstructive about the proposed work. They had their own hierarchical perspective on what the risks were and did not want to change any of their own processes for the estimation, evaluation and 'treatment' (management) of the risks. Corporate governance for them was about complying with known management of risk processes and they could not see that these were insufficient in themselves.

To avoid conflict with the chief officer who was my sponsor, the risk manager cleverly scuppered my proposal by suggesting that the potential value of the contract meant that the organisation should go out to tender for the work. Two local organisations (who would have no travelling costs) were invited to bid against me and I was not surprised when I did not win the contract.

In the second case, the potential client was a public sector body which had been required by government to implement a large change management programme. A risk manager had been appointed who, on their own admission, knew nothing about risk whatsoever! I met with this individual and submitted a proposal for them to take to their Board of Directors (Heads of Department). The individual argued strongly for the proposal but it was turned down. Two reasons were given. First, the Directors could guess what would be raised and so some of them did not like the idea of asking the staff and representative groups about the risks to the programme. Second, they had not thought about costs and baulked at the price of the work.

The third prospect involved a police force which was seeking to replicate the work done for case study 'Bluegrass'. I met with the client but in view of the probable costs of the work, I declined to submit a proposal pending the potential client coming out to tender for the work. Internal politics delayed this process, however I was eventually invited to tender and in due course won the business.

For all three prospects, the potential clients were convinced of the value of the Cultural Theory approach. The first two, however, were unable to convince their organisational hierarchies of the need to go beyond risk process compliance.

Training Course

'How to Manage Project Risk'

The overall aim of the 'How to Manage Project Risk' course is to ensure that project managers and others within the client organisation have the necessary knowledge and skills to manage risk within a project. The learning outcomes are that, on completion of the training, students will be able to:

- Understand and be able to apply relevant theories of risk in the context of project management.
- Understand and apply the terms 'risk analysis' and 'risk management'.
- State and understand who has responsibility for risk in respect of projects.
- Determine at what stage to initiate and review the risk process.
- Use a recognised process and template document to:
  ⇒ Identify, estimate and evaluate the risks associated with a project.
  ⇒ Decide whether existing controls are adequate or whether more should be done.
  ⇒ Devise and implement additional controls as required.
- Maintain a Project Risk Log.

The first learning outcome is key, since it relies on the successful application of Cultural Theory as a heuristic for the students, who then seek to apply the theory for themselves. They do this by undertaking a stakeholder analysis for a case study project chosen by the client organisation. This analysis is used to identify twelve stakeholders, three from each of the four Cultural Theory constituencies. The students then role play a risk assessment workshop, each taking one of the twelve parts identified through the stakeholder analysis.

The definitive course document opens with the rationale for the course, together with the course programme. This is then unpacked into individual sessions. For each session, the document gives the objectives and learning outcomes, the teaching and learning process, the support materials and handouts and the assessment methods used.

The outline timetable for the course is shown in Table 8.12 on the next page.

Table 8.12: 'How to Manage Project Risk' Course Timetable

Times	Day One	Day Two
0845-0900	Arrival and Refreshments	Arrival and Refreshments
0900-0915	Introductions	Review of Day One
0915-0930	Aims/Objectives/Programme	Exercise: Risk Assessment –
0930-0945	Lecture: The Essence of	'Focus Group' Session 1
0945-1000	Project Management	(example + 4 students)
1000-1015	Exercise: Group Discussion	
1015-1030	and Feedback	
1030-1045	Refreshment Break	Refreshment Break
1045-1100	Lecture: Introduction to the	Exercise: Risk Assessment –
1100-1115	Management of Risk	'Focus Group' Session 2
1115-1130		(4 students)
1130-1145		
1145-1200	Briefing: Case Study Project	Exercise: Risk Evaluation
1200-1215	Briefing: Terms of Reference	
1215-1230	Questions and Discussion	
1230-1245	Lunch	Lunch
1245-1300		
1300-1315		
1315-1330	Exercise: Stakeholder	Briefing: Risk Management
1330-1345	Analysis for the	Exercise: Risk Management
1345-1400	Case Study Project	Session 1 – Countermeasures
1400-1415	Briefing: Organise Workshop	and Contingencies
1415-1430	Exercise: How Risky is the	
1430-1445	Case Study Project?	Exercise: Risk Management
1445-1500	Briefing: Different Approaches	Session 2 – Monitoring
1500-1515	Refreshment Break	Refreshment Break
1515-1530	Exercise: Risk Assessment –	Course Evaluation
1530-1545	'Quick and Dirty' Session 1	
1545-1600	(example + 1 student)	Review and Closing Remarks
1600-1615	Break	Close
1615-1630	Exercise: Risk Assessment –	
1630-1645	'Quick and Dirty' Session 2	
1645-1700	(3 students)	
1700	Close	

'How to Manage Project Risk' has been delivered seven times for two different clients and the evaluation reports have been very positive.

GENERALISABILITY?

To what extent can these research findings be generalised beyond the two research settings? This is an important question for contemporary social policy in a 'risk society' since Prime Minster Tony Blair has said that, 'what counts is what works, and that the current Labour Government is committed to evidence-led policy' (Tilley 2001). Whilst qualitative work such as this book might be seen as at the bottom of a hierarchy of evidence, with randomised control trials at the top, nevertheless an evaluation of 'what works' by the Kings Fund (2004) found that such experimental models were unlikely to be appropriate for evaluating complex social policy initiatives involving multiple stakeholders.

So do the research findings from this book suggest 'what works'? This book has demonstrated through grounded theory that management of risk techniques need to be informed by a sound understanding of risk perception theory; and that Cultural Theory 'works' as a framework for disaggregated analysis of context, as a heuristic, as a tool for stakeholder analysis and to bring richness to the processes of risk identification and risk estimation. Cultural Theory has been shown to do these things in two different management of risk settings – British PAFs and British police programmes and projects.

The generalisability question, however, is this. Would Cultural Theory 'work' in the same ways in other management of risk contexts? In the conclusion to Chapter Five, I argued that the cultural and organisational complexity revealed in the analysis of the PAFs setting seemed likely to be archetypal of the complicated structures to be found in other management of risk scenarios. I suggested that the operationalisation of Cultural Theory offered a method of assessing and managing competing perceptions of risk in a new and revealing way. The generalisability of those conclusions was then at least partly evidenced by replicating the analysis in the police projects setting. The management of risk consultancy method and the 'How to Manage [Project] Risk' training course, derived from the research in both settings, are designed to be generic and thus capable of application in yet other management of risk situations. Given the wide range of existing applications of Cultural Theory outlined in Chapter Two (and see Thompson *et al.* 1990:14; 1999:5), it seems entirely plausible to hypothesise that these Cultural Theory-based approaches ought indeed to be capable of such application.

One piece of supporting evidence for this proposition comes from two presentations on corporate governance which I have given on opposite sides of the world, first to senior officers of the Mauritius Prison Service (Frosdick

2003f) and second to the Commissioners of the new Independent Police
Complaints Commission (IPCC) in London (Frosdick 2004e). Both
presentations have showcased the application of Cultural Theory in the
context of the corporate governance of the organisation. In the case of the
IPCC, I was able to challenge the Commissioners to work in small groups to
apply Cultural Theory to address two key questions. Who are IPCC's key
stakeholders and what expectations will they have of IPCC corporate
governance? And how will IPCC's emerging corporate culture address issues
of corporate governance?

CLOSING REMARKS

In bringing this book to a close, I want to summarise the contributions which
this book makes to knowledge. Of course there have been some limitations in
the approach taken, not least of which was the need, part way through, to
revise the research design. Nevertheless, there are five key contributions
which can be highlighted.

First, the chronology of disasters, inquiries, reports, legislation and continued
near misses set out in Chapter Four clearly demonstrated the importance of
improving risk assessment and risk management in PAFs. The revised Green
Guide (Department of National Heritage 1997) and new national Training
Package for Stewarding at Football Grounds (Frosdick 1996e; Frosdick and
Sidney 1997; Frosdick 2003d) were examples of efforts in this direction. The
application of the Cultural Theory-based management of risk approach
outlined in Chapter Five would represent a further improvement.

Second, setting out a similar history of disasters, audit reports and lessons not
learned in programmes and projects, Chapter Six showed how Government
have repeatedly called for improved management of risk in this context (for
example see Scarff *et al.* 1993; CCTA 1994b; 1995a; 1995b; ILGRA 1996;
HM Treasury 2001; OGC 2002c, 2004). The grounded theory, consultancy
methodology and training programme derived from the empirical research in
this book offer ways in which such improvements might take place in the
practical management of programme and project risk.

Third, referring to the Selby rail crash in February 2001, Marston (2001)
quotes a senior adviser from the Royal Society for the Prevention of
Accidents, who said that it was misleading to describe the incident as a freak
occurrence, when 'almost all accident investigations show how the event
could have been prevented, or its consequences mitigated, by better risk
management and risk assessment'. Extrapolating this argument to more
general social policy in a 'risk society', this book provides an evidence base
to show that the practical application of Cultural Theory 'works'.

In addition to these three practical contributions, there are also two more theoretical contributions. We saw in Chapter Two that Cultural Theory has been criticised as lacking empirical support compared with psychological work on risk perception (see Royal Society 1992:113-114). The 'live' application of Cultural Theory in two practitioner settings in this book adds to other empirical work since 1992 and so lends weight to the contention that this criticism is now outdated.

Finally, the case studies in Chapters Six and Seven provide good empirical evidence of the practical application of Cultural Theory at the micro level of analysis, which, as we saw at the beginning of Chapter Seven, has only rarely featured in previous Cultural Theory studies.

This book shows that Cultural Theory offers useful, generic, practical support for improving the management of risk. Future research might usefully seek to further test the application of the theory. For example, an ideal for the present author would be to go back into the PAFs setting and apply the consultancy methodology to a case study. Other research might also further demonstrate the usefulness of Cultural Theory at a variety of levels of analysis, particularly the micro level.

REFERENCES

6, P. (1997) 'Recent Critiques of Cultural Theory', email Contribution to the Grid-Group Cultural Theory Discussion Forum, 20 November 1997.

Adams, J. (1985) *Risk and Freedom: the Record of Road Safety Regulation.* London: Transport Publishing Projects.

Adams, J. (1995) *Risk.* London: UCL Press.

Adams, J. (1997) 'Virtual Risk and the Management of Uncertainty', *Science, Policy and Risk.* London: The Royal Society.

Adams, J. (1999a) *Cars, Cholera and Cows.* Washington: CATO Institute.

Adams, J. (1999b) *Risky Business – The Management of Risk and Uncertainty.* London: Adam Smith Institute.

Adams, J. and Thompson, M. (2002) *Taking Account of Societal Concerns About Risk: Framing the Problem.* Research Report 305. Sudbury: HSE Books.

Alexander, J. (1985) 'Positivism' in A. Kuper and J. Kuper (eds.) *The Social Science Encyclopedia*, pp. 631-633. London: Routledge and Kegan Paul.

Arnold, T. (1991) 'Rich Man, Poor Man: Economic Arrangements in the Football League', in J. Williams and S. Wagg (eds.) *British Football and Social Change - Getting into Europe,* pp. 48-66. Leicester: Leicester University Press.

Ashby, W. R. (1968) 'Variety, Constraint, and the Law of Requisite Variety'. In W. Buckley (ed.) *Modern Systems Research for the Behavioral Scientist*, pp. 129-136. Chicago: Aldine.

Au, S., Ryan, M., Carey, M. and Whalley S. (1993) *Managing Crowd Safety in Public Venues: a Study to Generate Guidance for Venue Owners and Enforcing Authority Inspectors.* Health and Safety Executive Contract Research Report 53/93. Sudbury: HSE Books.

Baldwin, R. and Anderson, R. (2002) *Rethinking Regulatory Risk.* London: DLA and the London School of Economics.

Bale, J. (1990) 'In the Shadow of the Stadium: Football Grounds as Urban Nuisances'. *Geography*, 75(329): 325-334.

Bale, J. (1991) 'Playing at Home: British Football and a Sense of Place', in J. Williams and S. Wagg (eds.) *British Football and Social Change - Getting into Europe,* pp. 130-144. Leicester: Leicester University Press.

Bale, J. (1993) *Sport, Space and the City*. London: Routledge.

Beck, U. (1992) *Risk Society: Towards a New Modernity*. London: Sage.

Becket, M. (2003) 'Change of Heart on Corporate Killing', *The Daily Telegraph*, 26 May 2003, p. 29.

Bertalanffy, L von (1973) *General System Theory : Foundations, Development, Applications*. Harmondsworth: Penguin.

BRTF (2004) *Better Routes to Redress*. London: Better Regulation Task Force.

Boholm, O. (1996) 'Risk Perception and Social Anthropology: Critique of Cultural Theory'. *Ethnos* 61: 64-84.

Bond, D. (1999) 'Arsenal Homing in on New Stadium'. Retrieved 13 February 2001 from *http:/www.arsenal-world.net/forsale/230799.htm*.

Borodzicz, E (1996) 'After Disaster: Risk Communication for Social Services and Voluntary Agencies'. Paper presented and included in the proceedings of Second International Conference: *Local Authorities Confronting Disasters and Emergencies*. Amsterdam, Holland.

Bower, T. (2003) *Broken Dreams: Vanity, Greed and the Souring of British Football*. London: Simon and Schuster.

Brewin, C. (1992) 'Support for All', *When Saturday Comes*, December 1992, pp. 20-21.

Brewster, B. (1992) 'Architecture and Morality', *When Saturday Comes*, November 1992, pp. 20-22.

British Safety Council (2000) 'Safety Council Slates Shelving Of Corporate Killing Law', Press Release, 6 December 2000. Retrieved 09 February 2001 from *http://www. britishsafetycouncil.co.uk/Profile/Press/Campaigns/CorporateKilingLaw.htm*

British Standards Institution (1991) *Quality Vocabulary. BS4778 (Part 3 Section 3.2 = IEC 1990 50(191))*. London: BSI.

Business Continuity Institute (2001) 'Business Guide to Continuity Management'. Retrieved on 09 February 2001 from *http://www.thebci.org/bgcm.htm*.

Canter, D., Comber, M. and Uzzell D. (1989) *Football in its Place: An Environmental Psychology of Football Grounds*. London: Routledge.

Carnibella, G., Fox, A., Fox, P., McCann, J., Marsh, J. and Marsh, P. (1996) *Football Violence in Europe: A Report to the Amsterdam Group*. Oxford: The Social Issues Research Centre.

CCTA (1990) *PRINCE Reference Manuals*. Oxford: NCC Blackwell Ltd.

CCTA (1993) *An Introduction to Programme Management*. London: HMSO.

CCTA (1994a) *PRINCE User's Guide to CRAMM*. London: HMSO.

CCTA (1994b) *Management of Project Risk*. London: HMSO.

CCTA (1995a) *Management of Programme Risk*. London: HMSO.

CCTA (1995b) *An Introduction to Managing Project Risk*. London: HMSO.

CCTA (1998) *Managing Successful Projects With PRINCE2*. London: The Stationery Office.

Chapman, C. and Ward, S. (1997) *Project Risk Management: Processes, Techniques and Insights*. Chichester: John Wiley and Sons.

Coe, S. (2000) 'New Regulations Must Not Spoil the Event', *The Daily Telegraph*, 13 March 2000, p. S9.

Cohen, S. (1987) *Folk Devils and Moral Panics: The Creation of the Mods and Rockers* (New Issue of the Second Edition). Oxford: Basil Blackwell.

Collins, T. with Bicknell, D. (1997) *Crash: Ten Easy Ways to Avoid a Computer Disaster*. London: Simon and Schuster.

Coote, A., Allen, J. and Woodhead, D. (2004) *Finding Out What Works*. London: The King's Fund.

Cox, S. (1992) *Building Regulation and Safety*. Report to the Building Research Establishment.

Cox, S. and Tait, N. (1991) *Reliability, Safety and Risk Management (An Integrated Approach)*. Oxford: Butterworth-Heinemann.

Cracknell, D. (2001) 'Government Advisers Call For Indemnity Over MMR', *The Sunday Telegraph*, 11 February 2001, p. 2.

Crick, M. (2000) 'Shareholders United Against Murdoch'. *Soccer and Society*, 1(3): 64-69.

Critcher, C. (1991) 'Putting on the Style: Recent Aspects of English Football' in J. Williams and S. Wagg (eds.) *British Football and Social Change - Getting into Europe* pp. 67-84. Leicester: Leicester University Press.

Crowd Management Strategies (2004). Retrieved on 26 April 2004 from *http://www.crowdsafe.com/new.html*.

Curl, J. (1993) 'Ambush!' *Panstadia International Quarterly Report*, 1(2): 18 & 67.

Dake, K. (1991) 'Orienting Dispositions in the Perception of Risks, an Analysis of Contemporary World Views and Cultural Biases'. *Journal of Cross-Cultural Psychology*, 22(1): 61-82.

Dake, K. (1992) 'Myths of Nature: Culture and the Social Construction of Risk. *Journal of Social Issues*, 48(4): 21-37.

Daniels, K. (1992) *Cognitive Approaches to Risk and Implications for Risk Management and Risk Communication.* Unpublished paper, Cranfield University School of Management.

Deloitte and Touche (2000) 'Highlights of the Annual Review of Football Finance', August 2000. Retrieved on 13 February 2001 from *http://www.footballfinance.co.uk/Publications/FBB002.asp*.

Denzin, N. (1978) *The Research Act: A Theoretical Introduction to Research Methods.* New York: McGraw-Hill.

Denzin, N. and Lincoln, Y. (2000) *The Handbook of Qualitative Research* (Second Edition). London: Sage Publications.

De Quidt, J. (1997) 'The Origins and Role of the Football Licensing Authority', in S. Frosdick and L. Walley (eds.) S*port and Safety Management*, pp. 68-81. Oxford: Butterworth-Heinemann.

De Quidt, J. and Frosdick, S. (2002) 'L'Expérience Britanique Comme Exemple Pour L'Europe?' All-day seminar presented at the conference *Sécurité Evénementielle: Expériences et Perspectives Européennes*, Université de Technologie de Troyes, France, 26 March 2002.

Department of Culture, Media and Sport (2000) 'Safety at Sports Grounds'. Retrieved on 22 December 2000 from , *http://www.culture.gov.uk/sport/culture_bill.html*.

Department of Education and Science (1968) *Report of the Committee on Football (Chairman D. N. Chester CBE)*. London: HMSO.

Department of National Heritage and Scottish Office (1997) *Guide to Safety at Sports Grounds*. London: HMSO.

Department of the Environment (1984) *Report of an Official Working Group on Football Spectator Violence*. London: HMSO.

Dingle, J. (1997) *Project Management: Orientation for Decision Makers*. London: Arnold.

Dixon, M. (2000) *Project Management Body of Knowledge* (Fourth Edition). High Wycombe: Association for Project Management.

Douglas, M. (1978) 'Cultural Bias', Royal Anthropological Institute, Occasional Paper 35. Reprinted in Douglas, M. (1982) *In the Active Voice*, pp. 183-254. London: Routledge and Kegan Paul.

Douglas, M. (ed.) (1982) *Essays in the Sociology of Perception*. London: Routledge and Kegan Paul.

Douglas, M. (1985) *Risk Acceptability According to the Social Sciences*. New York: Russell Sage Foundation.

Douglas, M. (1986) *How Institutions Think*. London: Routledge and Kegan Paul.

Douglas, M. (1990) 'Risk as a Forensic Resource', *Daedalus*, 119(4):1-16.

Douglas, M. (1992a) 'Risk and Blame', in *Risk and Blame: Essays in Cultural Theory*, pp. 3-21. London: Routledge.

Douglas, M. (1992b) Review on 10 November 1992 of Schrader-Frechette K. (1991) *Risk and Rationality: Philosophical Foundations for Populist Reforms*. Berkeley: University of California Press.

Douglas, M. (2001) 'The Persistent Problem of the Top Left Quadrant', email Contribution to the Grid-Group Cultural Theory Discussion Forum, 13 October 2001.

Douglas, M. (2003a) 'Being Fair to Hierarchists (Part I – Grid-Group Method)', *University of Pennsylvania Law Review*, 151(1349): 1352-1360.

Douglas, M. (2003b) 'New Publications', email Contribution to the Grid-Group Cultural Theory Discussion Forum, 28 May 2003.

Douglas, M. and Wildavsky, A. (1982) *Risk and Culture*. Berkeley: University of California Press.

Dunning, E. (1989) 'The Economic and Cultural Significance of Football', *Proceedings of Football into the 1990s*, pp. 13-17. University of Leicester: Sir Norman Chester Centre for Football Research.

Dunning, E., Murphy, P. and Williams, J. (1988) *The Roots of Football Hooliganism - An Historical and Sociological Study*. London: Routledge and Kegan Paul.

Dunphy, E. (1986) *Only a Game?- The Diary of a Professional Footballer*, (Second Edition). London: Viking.

Edwards, A. (2004) 'Has Bath Burst Its Bubble?' *The Daily Telegraph*, 3 July 2004, p. W1.

Elliott, D. (1996) Unpublished PhD Thesis, University of Durham.

Elliott, D., Frosdick, S. and Smith, D. (1997) 'The Failure of "Legislation by Crisis"', in S. Frosdick and L. Walley (eds.) *Sport and Safety Management*, pp. 11-30. Oxford: Butterworth-Heinemann.

Elliott, D. and Smith, D. (1993) 'Football Stadia Disasters in the United Kingdom: Learning From Tragedy?', *Industrial and Environmental Crisis Quarterly*, 7(3): 205-229.

Ellis, R. (1993) 'The Case for Cultural Theory: Reply to Friedman', *Critical Review* 7(1): 81-127.

Fairlie, H. (1989) 'Fear of Living', *The New Republic*, 23 January 1989, pp. 14-19.

Fiorino, D. (1989) 'Technical and Democratic Values in Risk Analysis', *Risk Analysis*, 9(3): 293-299.

FLA (1992) *Guidance on Safety Certificates*. London: The Football Licensing Authority.

FLA (1996) Miscellaneous Press Reports Held in the Archives of the Football Licensing Authority, London.

FLA (2003) *Accessible Stadia*. London: The Football Stadia Improvement Fund and the Football Licensing Authority.

Football Association (1999) *England 2006*. London: The Football Association.

Football into the 1990s (1989), *Proceedings of a Conference held at the University of Leicester, 29-30 September 1988*. University of Leicester: Sir Norman Chester Centre for Football Research.

Football League, Football Association and FA Premier League (1995) *Stewarding and Safety Management at Football Grounds*. Lytham St Annes: The Football League Ltd.

Football League, Football Association and FA Premier League (1998) *Safety Management at Football Grounds*. Lytham St Annes: The Football League Ltd.

Football Task Force (1999) *Investing in the Community*. London: Stationery Office.

Ford, A. (1994) 'Crossing the Thin Blue Line', *Football Management*, 11 April 1994, pp. 16-17.

Foster, C (1996) 'Risk Management: An Economist's Approach', in Hood, C. and Jones, D. (eds.) *Accident and Design: Contemporary Debates in Risk Management*, pp. 155-160. London: UCL Press.

Frankfort-Nachmias, C. and Nachmias, D. (1996) *Research Methods in the Social Sciences* (Fifth Edition). London: Arnold.

Friedman, J. (1991) 'Accounting for Political Preferences: Cultural Theory Versus Cultural History', *Critical Review* 5(3): 325-351.

Frosdick, S. (1993a) *Public Safety Risk Management in Stadia and Sporting Venues: A Holistic Approach*. Unpublished MSc Thesis, Cranfield University School of Management.

Frosdick, S. (1993b) *Guidelines for the Surveying, Planning and Operation of Stewarding Services in Stadia and Sporting Venues*. Worcester: British Security Industry Association.

Frosdick, S. (1995a) 'Organisational Structure, Culture and Attitudes to Risk in the British Stadia Safety Industry', *Journal of Contingencies and Crisis Management*, 3(1): 115-129.

Frosdick, S. (1995b) 'Safety Cultures in British Stadia and Sporting Venues', *Disaster Prevention and Management - An International Journal*, 4(4): 13-21. Reprinted in G. Mars and D. Weir (eds.) (2000) *Risk Management - Volume II*, pp. 283-291. Aldershot: Dartmouth.

Frosdick, S. (1995c) 'Managing Risk as a Futures Threat', paper presented to the *Policing Futures Forum*, Centre for Public Services Management and Research, Staffordshire University Business School, 10 October 1995

Frosdick, S. (1995d) 'The Failure of Reactive Approaches to Safety Management', paper presented at the *Safety in Sports and Leisure Seminar*, Centre for Public Services Management and Research, Staffordshire University Business School, 07 November 1995.

Frosdick, S. (1996a) 'Managing Risk in Running Your Stadium', paper presented at the *FC Magazine Running Your Stadium Seminar*, Anfield, Liverpool, 15 February 1996.

Frosdick, S. (1996b) ''Safety Cultures': Risk Identification and Cross-Organisational Collaboration for Safety at British Sports Grounds', paper presented at *International Perspectives on Crime, Justice and Public Order*, a conference organised by the John Jay College of Criminal Justice, The City University of New York, in Dublin, Ireland, 21 June 1996.

Frosdick, S. (1996c) 'Sports and Safety: Leisure and Liability', paper presented at *Free Time and Quality of Life for the 21st Century*, the World Leisure and Recreation Association Fourth World Congress, in Cardiff, Wales, 16 July 1996.

Frosdick, S. (1996d) 'Risk and Responsibility', *Panstadia International Quarterly Report*, 3(4): 34-36.

Frosdick, S. (1996e) *Training Package for Stewarding at Football Grounds*. The Football League, The Football Association, The FA Premier League and The Football Safety Officers Association: Staffordshire University.

Frosdick, S. (1996f) 'Training Package for Stewarding at Football Grounds', paper presented to the *Ad Hoc Working Party on Stewarding, European Convention on Spectator Violence at Sporting Events and in particular at Football Matches*, Council of Europe, Strasbourg, France, 03 October 1996.

Frosdick, S. (1996g) 'Managing Risk in Public Assembly Facilities', paper presented at a research seminar for staff and students, Durham University Business School, 27 November 1996.

Frosdick, S. (1996h) 'Venues of Extremes: The PAF Approach', *Stadium and Arena Management*, 1(1): 26-30.

Frosdick, S. (1996i) 'Watching the Crowd', *Football Management*, 4(1): 28-30.

Frosdick, S. (1997a) 'Beyond Football Hooliganism', in S. Frosdick and L. Walley (eds.) S*port and Safety Management*, pp. 3-10. Oxford: Butterworth-Heinemann.

Frosdick, S. (1997b) 'Risk as Blame', in S. Frosdick and L. Walley (eds.) S*port and Safety Management*, pp. 33-40. Oxford: Butterworth-Heinemann.

Frosdick, S. (1997c) 'Cultural Complexity in the British Stadia Industry', in S. Frosdick and L. Walley (eds.) S*port and Safety Management*, pp. 115-135. Oxford: Butterworth-Heinemann.

Frosdick, S. (1997d) 'Safety Cultures in British Sports Grounds', in S. Frosdick and L. Walley (eds.) S*port and Safety Management*, pp. 136-154. Oxford: Butterworth-Heinemann.

Frosdick, S. (1997e) 'Designing for Safety', in S. Frosdick and L. Walley (eds.) S*port and Safety Management*, pp. 157-171. Oxford: Butterworth-Heinemann.

Frosdick, S. (1997f) 'The Strategic Development of Sports Safety Management', in S. Frosdick and L. Walley (eds.) S*port and Safety Management*, pp. 255-272, Oxford: Butterworth-Heinemann.

Frosdick, S. (1997g) 'Managing Risk in Public Assembly Facilities', in S. Frosdick and L. Walley (eds.) S*port and Safety Management*, pp. 273-282, Oxford: Butterworth-Heinemann.

Frosdick, S. (1997h) *Introduction to Cultural Theory*, Unit Eight of Module One, Distance Learning MSc in Risk, Crisis and Disaster Management, Scarman Centre for the Study of Public Order, University of Leicester.

Frosdick, S. (1997i) 'Venues of Extremes: The Inner Zones', *Stadium and Arena Management*, **1**(2): 34-36.

Frosdick, S. (1997j) 'Danger, Disruption, Finance and Fun', *Stadium and Arena Management*, **1**(3): 34-36.

Frosdick, S. (1997k) 'Keep Off the Grass', *Stadium and Arena Management*, **1**(4): 26-28.

Frosdick, S. (1997l), 'The Techniques of Risk Analysis are Insufficient in Themselves', *Disaster Prevention and Management - An International Journal*, **6**(3): 165-177.

Frosdick, S. (1997m), 'Problems on the Pitch?', *Football Management*, **5**(3): 12-14.

Frosdick, S. (1997n) 'Playing it Safe?', *Police Review*, **105**(5440): 20-21.

Frosdick, S. (1997o) 'Royal Dutch: Integrated Ticket System', *Stadium and Arena Management*, **1**(6): 32-36.

Frosdick, S. (1997p) 'Slide Arena: Gelredome's Moving Story', *Stadium and Arena Management*, **1**(7): 32-36.

Frosdick, S. (1997q) *NSPIS Programme Level Management of Risk Strategy*, NSPIS Programme Board paper 2/97, London: Home Office Local Police Systems Directorate.

Frosdick, S. (1998a) 'Sports and Safety: Leisure and Liability', in Collins, M. and Cooper, I. (eds.) *Leisure Management: Issues and Applications*, pp. 197-210, Oxon: C.A.B. International.

Frosdick, S. (1998b) *Strategic Risk Management in Public Assembly Facilities*, paper presented at 'Stadia 2000 - the 1st International Conference on Design, Construction and Operation of Stadia, Arenas, Grandstands and Supporting Facilities', organised by the Concrete Society in Cardiff, Wales, 01 to 03 April 1998.

Frosdick, S. (1998c) 'Strategic Risk Management in Public Assembly Facilities', in Thompson, P., Tolloczko, J. and Clarke, J. (eds.) *Stadia, Arena and Grandstands: Design Construction and Operation*, pp. 65-76, London: E and FN Spon.

Frosdick, S. (1998d), 'A Different League', *Football Decision*, **9**: 22-24.

Frosdick, S. (1998e) 'Being There!', *Stadium and Arena Management*, **2**(1): 6-10.

Frosdick, S. (1998f) 'Standing Up Again?', *Football Management*, March 1998: 8-10.

Frosdick, S. (1998g) *Alcohol in Stadiums: To Drink or Not to Drink?*, paper presented at the European Stadium Managers Association 4th Annual Convention, in Paris, France, 04 to 06 June 1998.

Frosdick, S. (1998h) 'Drink or Dry?', *Stadium and Arena Management*, **2**(4):20-24.

Frosdick, S. (1998i) *Introduction to the Management of Risk*, paper presented at the National Strategy for Police Information Systems (NSPIS) Business Change Management Forum, at National Police Training, Bramshill, Hampshire, 16 November 1998.

Frosdick, S. (1998j) *National Strategy for Police Information Systems (NSPIS): Programme Issues Register – Analysis and Recommendations* (Version PIR003), Report to the NSPIS Business Change Co-ordinator, Cirencester: Redfern Consultancy Ltd.

Frosdick, S. (1999a) 'The New University of Portsmouth Certificate of Higher Education in Stadium and Arena Safety', *Football Management*, Winter 1999: 2.

Frosdick, S. (1999b) *Introduction to the Management of Risk*, Distance Learning Unit, Institute of Criminal Justice Studies, University of Portsmouth.

Frosdick, S. (1999c) *Guidance on Safety at Sports Grounds*, Distance Learning Unit, Institute of Criminal Justice Studies, University of Portsmouth.

Frosdick, S. (1999d) *Sport and Safety Management*, Distance Learning Unit, Institute of Criminal Justice Studies, University of Portsmouth.

Frosdick, S. (1999e) *National Strategy for Police Information Systems (NSPIS): Management of Risk Strategy Progress Report* (Version RSK012), Report to the NSPIS Business Change Co-ordinator, Cirencester: Redfern Consultancy Ltd.

Frosdick, S. (2001a) 'Completely Safe', *Panstadia International Quarterly Report*, **7**(3): 70 & 72.

Frosdick, S. (2001b) 'Danger: Men at Work', *Stadium and Arena Management*, February 2001: 33-34.

Frosdick, S. (2001c) 'Safety Techniques Shared', *Stadium and Arena Management*, June 2001: 4.

Frosdick, S. (2001d) 'Constructing in Tight Corners', *Stadium and Arena Management*, June 2001: 18-20.

Frosdick, S. (2001e) 'Switch to Safety', *Stadium and Arena Management*, October 2001: 9-10.

Frosdick, S. (2001f) *Catastrophes, Désordres et de Gestion des Risques*, paper presented at the Conference 'Un Stade Dans la Ville: Espace de Passion ou Zone de Tension', Université de Technologie de Troyes, France, 30 March 2001.

Frosdick, S. (2001g), *Lower Profile Policing and Higher Profile Stewarding: An Evaluation*, paper presented at 'Stadia & Arena 2001', London Arena, 7 June 2001.

Frosdick, S. (2001h) *First Principles in Venue Safety and Security: What's Changed After September 11?* Panel Discussion Chair, 'International Sports Facilities Forum, London, 5 December 2001.

Frosdick, S. (2002a) 'Unthinkable', *Panstadia International Quarterly Report*, **8**(3): 14-15.

Frosdick, S. (2002b) 'Security Pendulum', *Stadium & Arena Management*, June 2002: 9-10.

Frosdick, S. (2002c) 'Violent Behaviour', *Stadium & Arena Management*, October 2002: 25-27.

Frosdick, S. (2002d) *Lessons From Europe: Security Update From the United Kingdom*, paper presented at 'Venue Safety and Security', Phoenix AZ, USA, 21 February 2002.

Frosdick, S. (2002e) *Sports Venue Safety and Security*, paper presented at 'Disaster Management: Lessons and Contemporary Issues', National Operations Faculty, National Police Training, Bramshill, 7 March 2002.

Frosdick, S. (2002f) *Causes of Spectator Violence: An International Review*, paper presented at 'Stadia & Arena 2002', Lisbon, Portugal, 6 June 2002.

Frosdick, S. (2002g) *Spectator Violence and Football Hooliganism*, Distance Learning Unit, University of Portsmouth: Institute of Criminal Justice Studies.

Frosdick, S. (2003a) 'Standing Debate', *Stadium & Arena Management*, June 2003: 25-26.

Frosdick, S. (2003b) *Planning for Safety and Security at Sporting Events*, presentation to the Commissioner and senior officers of the Mauritius Police Force, Vacoas, Mauritius, 8 May 2003.

Frosdick, S. (2003c) *Dealing With Racism in Football*, paper presented at 'Stadia & Arena 2003', Geneva, Switzerland, 4 June 2003.

Frosdick, S. (ed.) (2003d) *Training Package for Stewarding at Football Grounds* (Second Edition), Preston: The Football League, The Football Association, The FA Premier League and The Football Safety Officers Association.

Frosdick, S. (2003e) *Strategic Risk Management*, Distance Learning Unit, Institute of Criminal Justice Studies, University of Portsmouth.

Frosdick, S. (2003f) *Introduction to Risk and Corporate Governance*, seminar presented to the Acting Commissioner and senior officers of the Mauritius Prison Service, Beau Bassin, Mauritius, 6 May 2003.

Frosdick, S. (2004a) 'Tale of Two Cities – Part I', (Crowd Segregation at High-Risk Matches), *Stadium & Arena Management*, August 2004, pp. 23-24.

Frosdick, S. (2004b) 'Tale of Two Cities – Part II', (Crowd Segregation at High-Risk Matches), *Stadium & Arena Management*, October 2004, pp. 30-31.

Frosdick, S. (2004c) 'Ten Years of Seating', (the Tenth Anniversary of All-Seated Stands) *Stadium & Arena Management*, December 2004, p. 15.

Frosdick, S. (2004d) *Crowd Segregation and Control: Case Histories of Local Derbies*, paper presented at 'Stadia & Arena 2004', Milan, Italy, 9 June 2004.

Frosdick, S. (2004e) *Good Governance*, presentation to the Commissioners of the Independent Police Complaints Commission, London, 11 February 2004.

Frosdick, S. (2005) *First Principles in Strategic Risk Management*, paper presented to the UK Stadium Managers Association, Birmingham, 18 May 2005.

Frosdick, S. and Capon, N. (2003) *Project Management*, Distance Learning Unit, University of Portsmouth: Institute of Criminal Justice Studies.

Frosdick, S. and Chalmers, J. (2005) *Safety and Security at Sports Grounds*. Rothersthorpe: Paragon Publishing.

Frosdick, S. and Highmore, M. (1997), 'Ewood Effect', *Football Decision*, 7: 20-24.

Frosdick, S. and Mars, G. (1997) 'Understanding Cultural Complexity', in S. Frosdick and L. Walley (eds.) S*port and Safety Management*, pp. 108-114. Oxford: Butterworth-Heinemann.

Frosdick. S. and Marsh, P. (2005) *Football Hooliganism.* Cullompton: Willan Publishing.

Frosdick, S. and Newton, R. (2004) *The Nature and Extent of Football Hooliganism*, paper presented at 'Criminology, Governance and Regulation', The British Society of Criminology Conference, 8 July 2004.

Frosdick, S. and Odell, A. (1996) 'Practical Management of Programme Risk: The Case of the National Strategy for Police Information Systems for England and Wales', *Information Management and Computer Security*, 4(5): 24-34.

Frosdick, S. and Sidney, J. (1996a) 'Safe Cracking', *Football Decision*, 2: 48-51.

Frosdick, S. and Sidney, J. (1996b) 'Stewards Training Goes Multi-Media', *Football Management*, 4(3): 26.

Frosdick, S. and Sidney, J. (1997) 'The Evolution of Safety Management and Stewarding at Football Grounds', in S. Frosdick and L. Walley (eds.) S*port and Safety Management*, pp. 209-220. Oxford: Butterworth-Heinemann.

Frosdick, S. and Smith, B. (1997) 'On the Fence: Balancing the Risks', *Stadium and Arena Management*, 1(5): 30-32.

Frosdick, S. and Vaughan, A. (2003) 'Racism in Retreat', *Stadium & Arena Management*, 7(5): 29-31.

Frosdick, S. and Walley, L. (eds.) *Sport and Safety Management*, Oxford: Butterworth-Heinemann.

Frosdick, S., Holford, M. and Sidney, J. (1997) 'Playing Away in Europe', in S. Frosdick and L. Walley (eds.) *Sport and Safety Management*, pp. 221-238. Oxford: Butterworth-Heinemann.

FSADC (1991a) *Football Stadia Bibliography 1980 – 1990*. London: The Sports Council (Football Stadia Advisory Design Council).

FSADC (1991b) *Seating - Sightlines, Conversion of Terracing, Seat Types*. London: The Sports Council (Football Stadia Advisory Design Council).

FSADC (1992) *Digest of Stadia Criteria*. London: The Sports Council (Football Stadia Advisory Design Council).

FSADC (1993) *Terraces - Designing for Safe Standing at Football Stadia*. London: The Sports Council (Football Stadia Advisory Design Council).

FSC (2001) Federation of Stadium Communities Home Page. Retrieved on 13 February 2001 from *http://www.btrust.force9.co.uk/fsc/menu.html*.

FSF (2004) Football Supporters Federation Home Page. Retrieved on 27 April 2004 from *http://www.fsf.org.uk*.

Funtowicz, S. and Ravetz, J. (1996) 'Risk Management, Post-Normal Science, and Extended Peer Communities', in C. Hood and D. Jones (eds.) *Accident and Design: Contemporary Debates in Risk Management*, pp. 172-181. London: UCL Press.

Gaskell, G. and Hampton, J. (1982) 'A Note on Styles in Accounting', in M. Douglas (ed.) *Essays in the Sociology of Perception*, pp. 103-111. London: Routledge and Kegan Paul.

GG-CT (1999) Grid-Group Cultural Theory Home Page. Retrieved on 07 February 2001 from *http://www.frw.uva.nl/ggct*.

Giddens, A. (1986) *Sociology: A Brief But Critical Introduction* (Second Edition). Basingstoke: Macmillan Education.

Giulianotti, R. (1994) 'Social Identity and Public Order', in R. Giulianotti, N. Bonney and M. Hepworth (eds.) *Football, Violence and Social Identity*, pp. 9-36. London: Routledge.

Glaser, B. and Strauss. A. (1967), *The Discovery of Grounded Theory: Strategies for Qualitative Research*. Chicago: Aldine.

Gold, R. (1958) 'Roles in Sociological Field Observations', *Social Forces* 36:217-223. Reprinted in G. McCall and J. Simmons (eds.) (1969) *Issues in Participant Observation: A Text and Reader*, pp. 30-39. Mass: Addison-Wesley.

Goldberg, A. and Wagg, S. (1991) 'It's Not a Knockout: English Football and Globalisation', in J. Williams and S. Wagg (eds.) *British Football and Social Change - Getting into Europe,* pp. 239-253. Leicester: Leicester University Press.

Hall, C. (2001) 'Campaign to Persuade Parents that the MMR Jab is Safe', *Daily Telegraph,* 23 January 2001, p. 5.

Hall, M. and Almond, P. (2000) 'MoD Bungles Cost Taxpayer £6bn in 10 Years', The Sunday Telegraph, 27 February 2000, p. 15.

Hamil, S., Michie, J., Oughton, C. and Warby, S. (2000) 'Recent Developments in Football Ownership', *Soccer and Society,* 1(3): 1-10.

Hammersley, M. and Atkinson, P. (1995) *Ethnography: Principles in Practice* (Second Edition). London: Routledge.

Hampden-Turner, C. (1996) 'Schon, Donald (1930-)', in M. Warner (ed.) *International Encyclopedia of Business and Management*, pp. 4399-4402. London: Routledge

Harrington, J. (1968) *Soccer Hooliganism: a Preliminary Report*. Bristol: John Wright.

Hart, C. (2000) *Doing A Literature Review.* London: Sage.

Haynes, R. (1995) *The Football Imagination: The Rise of Football Fanzine Culture.* Aldershot: Arena.

Health and Safety Commission (1993) *Guide to Health, Safety and Welfare at Pop Concerts and Other Similar Events.* London: HMSO.

Health and Safety Executive (1988) *The Tolerability of Risk from Nuclear Power Stations.* London: HMSO.

Health and Safety Executive (1989) *Quantified Risk Assessment: Its Input to Decision Making.* London: HMSO.

Health and Safety Executive (1996) *Use of Risk Assessment Within Government Departments.* Sudbury: HSE Books.

Health and Safety Executive (2000) *Managing Crowds Safely* (Second Edition). Sudbury: HSE Books.

Health and Safety Executive (2003) *Five Steps to Risk Assessment.* Sudbury: HSE Books.

Hibberd, M. (1990) *Research and Evaluation.* London: The Police Foundation.

Hinde, J. (1997) 'Why Talk of Risk is Full of Hazards', *The Times Higher Educational Supplement*, 14 March, pp. 18-19.

HM Treasury (2001) *Management of Risk: A Strategic Overview.* London: HM Treasury.

Hoare, M. (1997) 'The Case For: Theories of Risk Are Relevant to Practitioners', *International Journal of Risk Security and Crime Prevention*, 2(2): 133-135.

Hobbs, D. and Robins, D. (1991) 'The Boy Done Good: Football Violence, Changes and Continuities', *The Sociological Review*, 39(3) 551-579.

Holdaway, S. (1983) *Inside the British Police – A Force at Work.* Oxford: Basil Blackwell.

Holland, B. (1993) 'Colour Field', *When Saturday Comes*, February 1993, pp. 16-17.

Home Office (1924) *Committee of Inquiry into the Arrangements Made to Deal with Abnormally Large Attendances on Special Occasions, Especially at Athletic Grounds - Report by the Rt. Hon. Edward Shortt KC.* London: HMSO.

Home Office (1946) *Enquiry into the Disaster at the Bolton Wanderers Football Ground on 9 March 1946 - Report by R Moelwyn Hughes KC.* London: HMSO.

Home Office (1972) *Report of the Inquiry into Crowd Safety at Sports Grounds (by the Rt. Hon. Lord Wheatley).* London: HMSO.

Home Office (1985) *Committee of Inquiry into Crowd Safety and Control at Sports Grounds - Chairman Mr Justice Popplewell - Interim Report.* London: HMSO.

Home Office (1986) *Committee of Inquiry into Crowd Safety and Control at Sports Grounds - Chairman Mr Justice Popplewell - Final Report.* London: HMSO.

Home Office (1989) *The Hillsborough Stadium Disaster 15 April 1989 - Inquiry by the Rt Hon Lord Justice Taylor - Interim Report*. London: HMSO.

Home Office (1990a), *The Hillsborough Stadium Disaster 15 April 1989 - Inquiry by the Rt Hon Lord Justice Taylor - Final Report*. London: HMSO.

Home Office (1990b) *Guide to Safety at Sports Grounds*. London: HMSO.

Home Office (1991) *Charges for Policing Football Matches,* Home Office Circular 36/1991.

Home Office (1994) *Dealing With Disaster* (Second Edition). London: HMSO.

Home Office Police Department (1994) *The National Strategy for Police Information Systems*. London: HMSO.

Hood, C. (1996) 'Where Extremes Meet: 'SPRAT' Versus 'SHARK' in Public Risk Management', in C. Hood and D. Jones (eds.) *Accident and Design: Contemporary Debates in Risk Management*, pp. 208-227. London: UCL Press.

Hood, C. and Jones, D. (1996) 'Introduction', in C. Hood and D. Jones (eds.) *Accident and Design: Contemporary Debates in Risk Management*, pp. 1-9. London: UCL Press.

Hoppe, R. (2002) 'Guest Co-Editor's Introduction: Cultural Theory's Gift for Policy Analysis', *Journal of Comparative Policy Analysis*, 4(3): 235-241.

Horlick-Jones, T. (1996a) 'The Problem of Blame', in C. Hood and D. Jones (eds.) *Accident and Design: Contemporary Debates in Risk Management*, pp. 61-71. London: UCL Press.

Horlick-Jones, T. (1996b) 'Is Safety a By-Product of Quality Management?', in C. Hood and D. Jones (eds.) *Accident and Design: Contemporary Debates in Risk Management*, pp. 144-154. London: UCL Press.

Hornby, N. (1992) *Fever Pitch*. London: Gollancz.

Hougham, M. (2000) *Syllabus for the APMP Examination* (Second Edition). High Wycombe: Association for Project Management.

House of Commons Home Affairs Committee (1991a) *Policing Football Hooliganism -Volume One - Report together with the Proceedings of the Committee*. London: HMSO.

House of Commons Home Affairs Committee (1991b) *Policing Football Hooliganism - Volume Two - Memoranda of Evidence, Minutes of Evidence and Appendices*. London: HMSO.

House of Lords (2000) Cultural and Recreation Bill, Part I: Safety at Sports Grounds – Explanatory Note. Retrieved on 22 December 2000 from *http://www.parliament, the-stationery-office.co.uk/pa/ld200001/ldbills/007/en01007x--.htm.*

Hudson, M. (1997) 'Business Continuity Planning', *International Journal of Risk Security and Crime Prevention*, 2(2): 95-105.

ICAEW (1999) *Internal Control: Guidance for Directors on the Combined Code*. London: Institute for Chartered Accountants in England and Wales.

ILGRA (1996) *The Use of Risk Assessment Within Government Departments*. London: Health and Safety Executive.

Inglis, S. (1987) *The Football Grounds of Great Britain*. London: Collins Willow.

Inglis, S. (1990) 'Grounds For Complaint', *New Civil Engineer*, 7 June 1990, pp. 24-26.

Inglis, S. (1996) *The Football Grounds of Great Britain* (Third Edition). London: Harper Collins.

Irving, B., Faulkner, D., Frosdick, S. and Topping, P. (1996) *Reacting to Non-Major Crime: The Management of Police Resources*. London: Home Office Police Research Group.

Irwin, A. (1995) *Citizen Science: A Study of People, Expertise and Sustainable Development*. London: Routledge.

ISE (1991) *Appraisal of Sports Grounds*. London: Institution of Structural Engineers

Jaquiss, K. (2000) 'Mutualism Rules: The Community in Football', *Soccer and Society*, 1(3):51-56.

Jasanoff, S. (1990) 'American Exceptionalism and the Political Acknowledgement of Risk', *Daedalus*, 119(4): 61-81.

John, G. and Campbell, K. (1993) *Handbook of Sports and Recreational Building Design, Vol. 1: Outdoor Sports* (Second Edition). Oxford: Butterworth Architecture.

Johnes, M. (2000) 'Hooligans and Barrackers: Crowd Disorder and Soccer in South Wales, *c.* 1906-39', *Soccer and Society*, 1(2): 19-35.

Johnson, G. (1992) 'Managing Strategic Change: Strategy Culture and Action', in D. Faulkner and G. Johnson (eds.) *The Challenge of Strategic Management*, pp. 202-219. London: Kogan Page.

Johnson, G. and Scholes, K. (1999) *Exploring Corporate Strategy* (Fifth Edition). Hemel Hempstead: Prentice Hall Europe.

Johnston, A. (1996) 'Blame, Punishment and Risk Management', in C. Hood and D. Jones (eds.) *Accident and Design: Contemporary Debates in Risk Management*, pp. 72-83. London: UCL Press.

Joint Working Party on Ground Safety and Public Order (1991) *Ground Safety and Public Order - Report Number One of the Joint Executive on Football Safety*. Association of County Councils Publications.

Jorgenson, D. (1989) *Participant Observation*. Newbury Park CA: Sage.

Jupp, V. (1996) *Methods of Criminological Research*. London: Routledge.

Kasperson, R. and Kasperson, J. (1991) 'Hidden Hazards', in D. Mayo and R. Hollander (eds.) *Acceptable Evidence: Science and Values in Risk Management*, pp. 9-28. Oxford: Oxford University Press.

Lacey, M. (1992) 'The End of Something Small and the Start of Something Big', in D. Bull (ed.) *We'll Support You Evermore: Keeping Faith in Football*, pp. 87-96. London: Duckworth.

Law Commission (1996) *Legislating the Criminal Code: Involuntary Manslaughter*. London: HMSO.

Lomax, B. (2000) 'Episode One: May the Force Be With You!', *Soccer and Society*, 1(3): 17-23.

Lowi, T. (1990) 'Risks and Rights in the History of American Governments', *Daedalus*, 119(4): 17-40.

Luder, O. (1990) *Sports Stadia After Hillsborough - Papers Presented at the Sports Council and Royal Institute of British Architects Seminar,* RIBA and the Sports Council in association with the Football Trust.

Lundberg, C. (1996) 'Argyris, Chris (1923-)', in M. Warner (ed.) *International Encyclopedia of Business and Management*, pp. 238-243. London: Routledge.

Malcolm, D., Jones, I. and Waddington, I. (2000) 'The People's Game? Football Spectatorship and Demographic Change', *Soccer and Society*, 1(1):129-143).

Mamadouh, V. (ed.) (1999) *GeoJournal* (Special Edition on Grid-Group Cultural Theory), 47(3): 395-500.

Margerison, C. (1995) *Managerial Consulting Skills: A Practical Guide*. Aldershot: Gower.

Marris, C., Langford, I. and O'Riordan, T. (1996) *Integrating Sociological and Psychological Approaches to Public Perceptions of Environmental Risks: Detailed Results from a Questionnaire Survey*. Norwich: The Centre for Social and Economic Research on the Global Environment.

Marris, C., Langford, I. and O'Riordan, T. (1998) A Quantitative Test of the Cultural Theory of Risk Perception: Comparison with the Psychometric Paradigm, *Risk Analysis*, 18(5): 635-647.

Mars, G. (1994) *Cheats at Work: An Anthropology of Workplace Crime* (Second Edition). Aldershot: Dartmouth.

Mars, G. (2000) 'Introduction', in G. Mars and D. Weir (eds.) *Risk Management - Volume I*. Aldershot: Dartmouth.

Mars, G. and Frosdick, S. (1997) 'Operationalising the Theory of Cultural Complexity: a Practical Approach to Risk Perception and Behaviours', *International Journal of Risk, Security and Crime Prevention*, 2(2): 115-129. Reprinted in G. Mars and D. Weir (eds.) (2000) *Risk Management - Volume II*, pp. 207-221. Aldershot: Dartmouth.

Mars, G. and Mars, V. (1993) 'Two Studies of Dining', in G. Mars and V. Mars (eds.) *Food Culture and History*, pp. 49-60. London: London Food Seminar.

Mars, G. and Mars, V. (1996) *Household Worlds: The Creation of Domestic Cultures*. Unpublished research carried out by the authors on behalf of Unilever.

Mars, G. and Nicod, M. (1983) *The World of Waiters*. London: Allen and Unwin.

Mars, G. and Weir, D. (eds.) (2000a) *Risk Management - Volume I*. Aldershot: Dartmouth.

Mars, G. and Weir, D. (eds.) (2000b) *Risk Management - Volume II*. Aldershot: Dartmouth.

Marston, D. (2001) 'Vehicles Regularly Stray on to Rails', *The Daily Telegraph*, 2 March 2001, p. 4.

Martin, P. and Turner, B. (1986) 'Grounded Theory and Organizational Research', *The Journal of Applied Behavioural Science*, 22(2): 141-157.

Mason, C. and Robins, R. (1991) 'The Spatial Externality Fields of Football Stadiums: The Effects of Football and Non-Football Uses at Kenilworth Road, Luton', *Applied Geography*, 11(4): 251-266.

Mayo, D. and Hollander, R. (1991) Introduction to Part II, 'Uncertain Evidence in Risk Management', in D. Mayo and R. Hollander (eds.) *Acceptable Evidence: Science and Values in Risk Management*, pp. 93-98. Oxford: Oxford University Press.

McCarra, K. (1999) 'Violence a Sign of the Drinking Times', *The Times*, 14 May 1999, p. 30.

McCracken, G. (1988) *The Long Interview.* London: Sage.

McGibbon, E. (1996) Unpublished MA Thesis, University of Leicester.

Merton, R. (1957) *Social Theory and Social Structure.* Free Press: New York.

Ministry of Housing and Local Government (1969) *Report of the Working Party on Crowd Behaviour at Football Matches (Chairman John Lang).* London: HMSO.

Moore, G. (2002) 'Violence Mars Cardiff's Day of Delight'. *The Independent*, 7 January 2002, p. S1.

Moran, R. (2000) 'Racism in Football: A Victim's Perspective, *Soccer and Society*, 1(3):190-200.

Murphy, P., Williams, J. and Dunning, E. (1990) *Football on Trial – Spectator Violence and Development in the Football World.* London: Routledge.

Muspratt, C. (2003) 'Counting the Cost of the Year's Disasters Around the World', *The Daily Telegraph*, 29 December 2003, p. 26.

NASUWT (2004) 'NASUWT Reaffirms Advice to Members to Avoid Taking School Trips'. Retrieved on 21 April 2004 from *http://www.nasuwt.org.uk/Templates/internal. asp?NodeID=70431.*

National Audit Office (2001) *Why IT Projects Fail,* United Kingdom Lead Paper, INTOSAI EDP Committee Performance Audit Seminar, Slovenia, 14-16 May 2001.

National Audit Office (2003) *Ministry of Defence: Major Projects Report 2003.* London: Stationery Office.

Ney, S. (2003) 'New Developments in Cultural Theory', *Innovation – the European Journal of Social Science Research*, 16(4): 315-317.

NSPIS (1995a) *High Level Strategy Statement.* Home Office Police Advisory Group IT. London: HMSO.

NSPIS (1995b) *Programme Definition Statement*. Home Office Police Advisory Group IT. London: HMSO.

O'Riordan T. (1996) 'Exploring the Role of Civic Science in Risk Management', in C. Hood and D. Jones (eds.) *Accident and Design: Contemporary Debates in Risk Management*, pp. 182-192. London: UCL Press.

O'Riordan T. (1997) 'Images of Science Underlying the Public Perception of Risk'. Paper presented at the Royal Society: *Science, Policy and Risk*, 18 March 1997, London.

OGC (1999) *Managing Successful Programmes*. London: Stationery Office.

OGC (2002a) *Managing Successful Projects With PRINCE2* (Third Edition). London: Stationery Office.

OGC (2002b) *Tailoring PRINCE2*. London: Stationery Office.

OGC (2002c) *Management of Risk: Guidance for Practitioners*. London: Stationery Office.

OGC (2004) *Successful Delivery Toolkit* (Version 4.5). London: OGC.

Okely, J. (1994) 'Thinking Through Fieldwork', in A. Bryman and R. Burgess (eds.) *Analysing Qualitative Data*. London: Routledge.

O'Neill, S. (2000) 'Geldof Fury As Can't Do Culture Kills New Year Fireworks', *The Daily Telegraph*, 21 November 2000, pp. 1-2.

Olli, E. (1999) 'Rejection of Cultural Biases and Effects on Party Preferences', in M. Thompson, G. Grendstad and P. Selle (eds.) *Cultural Theory as Political Science*, pp. 59-74. London: Routledge.

Osborn, A. (1953) *Applied Imagination: Principles and Procedures of Creative Thinking*. New York: Scribners.

Osbourne, A. (2002) 'Atkins Blow Shakes Confidence in PFI', *The Daily Telegraph*, 2 October 2002, p. 35.

Pareto, V. (1971) *Manual of Political Economy*. New York: August M. Kelley.

Pearce, D. (1985) 'Cost Benefit Analysis' in A. Kuper and J. Kuper (eds.) *The Social Science Encyclopedia*, pp. 165-166. London: Routledge and Kegan Paul.

Perrow, C. (1984) *Normal Accidents: Living with High Risk Technologies*. New York: Basic Books.

Phillips (2000) 'Report of the Inquiry into BSE and variant CJD in the United Kingdom'. Retrieved on 12 February 2001 from *http://www.bseinquiry.gov.uk/report.*

Pidgeon, N. (1992) 'The Psychology of Risk', in D. Blockley (ed.) *Engineering Safety*, pp. 167-185. Maidenhead: McGraw-Hill.

Pidgeon, N. (1997) *Risk Communication and the Social Amplification of Risk - Phase I Scoping Study*, Report to the Health and Safety Executive. Bangor: University of Wales.

Pettipher, M. (1992) 'Seated Areas Miss Goal', *New Builder*, 6 February 1992, p. 5.

Pidgeon, N., Turner, B., Toft, B. and Blockley, D. (1991) 'Hazard Management and Safety Culture', in D. Parker and J. Handmer (eds.) *Hazard Management and Emergency Planning: Perspectives on Britain*, pp. 243-254. London: James and James.

Pook, S. and Eden, R. (2000) 'Silverstone's Name is Mud With Soggy Fans', *The Daily Telegraph*, 24 April 2000, p. 3.

Power, M. (1999) *The New Risk Management*, Inaugural Professorial Lecture and Launch of the Centre for the Analysis of Risk and Regulation (CARR), London School of Economics, 9 December 1999.

Priest, G. (1990) 'The New Legal Structure of Risk Control', *Daedalus*, 119(4): 207-28.

Punch, M. (1986) *Politics and Ethics of Field Work*. Beverley Hills, Sage.

Rahilly, H. (1996) *Environmental Policy and Practice in Premier League Football*. Unpublished BSc thesis, Liverpool Hope University College.

Rayner, S. (1992) 'Cultural Theory and Risk Analysis', in S. Krimsky and D. Golding (eds.) *Social Theories of Risk*, pp. 83-115. Westport: Praeger.

Redfern Consultancy Ltd (1997) Risk IT. Retrieved on 16 May 2000 from *http://www.redfern-consultancy.co.uk.*

Redhead, S. (1991) 'Some Reflections on Discourses on Football Hooliganism', *The Sociological Review*, 39(3):479-488.

Rippl, S. (2002) 'Cultural Theory and Risk Perception: A Proposal for a Better Measurement', *Journal of Risk Research*, 5(2): 147-156.

Rose, G, (1982) *Deciphering Sociological Research*. London: Macmillan

Rothschild (1978) 'Risk', The Richard Dimbleby Lecture, *The Listener,* 30 November, pp. 715-18.

Royal Academy of Engineering and British Computer Society (2004) *The Challenges of Complex IT Projects.* London: The Royal Academy of Engineering.

Royal Society Study Group (1983) *Risk Assessment.* London: The Royal Society.

Royal Society Study Group (1992) *Risk: Analysis, Perception and Management.* London: The Royal Society.

Royal Society (1997) *Science, Policy and Risk.* London: The Royal Society.

Royal Society (2000) *A Code of Practice for Scientific Advisory Committees: The Royal Society's Response to the Office of Science and Technology,* 6 December 2000. London: The Royal Society.

Ryan, M. (1999) 'Penal Policy Making Towards the Millennium: Elites and Populists; New Labour and the New Criminology', *International Journal of the Sociology of Law,* 27: 1-22.

Scarff, F., Carty, A. and Charette, R. (1993) *Introduction to the Management of Risk.* London: HMSO.

Schrader-Frechette, K. (1985) *Risk Analysis and the Scientific Method: Methodological and Ethical Problems in Evaluating Societal Hazards.* Dordrecht: Reidel.

Schrader-Frechette, K. (1991a) 'Reductionist Approaches to Risk', in D. Mayo and R. Hollander (eds.) *Acceptable Evidence: Science and Values in Risk Management,* pp 218-248. Oxford: Oxford University Press.

Schrader-Frechette, K. (1991b) *Risk and Rationality: Philosophical Foundations for Populist Reforms.* Berkeley: University of California Press.

SCIF (1992) *Code of Practice for the Assessment, Specification, Maintenance and Operation of Sound Systems for Emergency Purposes at Sports Grounds and Stadia in pursuit of approval by Licensing Authorities.* Marlow: Sound and Communication Industries Federation.

Scott, M. (2004) 'West Ham Suffer Day of Shame'. *The Guardian,* 22 March 2004, p. F11.

Scottish Education Department (1977) *Report of the Working Group on Football Crowd Behaviour.* London: HMSO.

Silbergeld, E. (1991) 'Risk Assessement and Risk Management: An Uneasy Divorce', in D. Mayo and R. Hollander (eds.) *Acceptable Evidence: Science and Values in Risk Management*. pp 99-114, Oxford: Oxford University Press.

Sj★berg, L. (1997) Explaining Risk Perception: An Empirical Evaluation of Cultural Theory, *Risk Decision and Policy* 2(2): 113-130.

Slovic, P. (1991) 'Beyond Numbers: A Broader Perspective on Risk Perception and Risk Communication', in D. Mayo and R. Hollander (eds.) *Acceptable Evidence: Science and Values in Risk Management*, pp. 48-65. Oxford: Oxford University Press.

Smallman, C. (1996) 'Challenging the Orthodoxy in Risk Management' *Safety Science* 22(1-3): 245-262.

Smith, M. (2000) 'Izzet Has the Answer to Racist Tormentors' *The Daily Telegraph*, 10 April 2000, p. 52.

Strauss, A. and Corbin, J. (1990) *Basics of Qualitative Research: Grounded Theory Procedures and Techniques.* Newbury Park: Sage Publications.

Strutt, J. (1993) *Risk Assessment and Management: the Engineering Approach*. Unpublished paper. Cranfield Centre for Industrial Safety and Reliability: Cranfield University.

Tait, E. and Levidow, L. (1992) 'Proactive and Reactive Approaches to Risk Regulation: the Case of Biotechnology', *Futures*, 24: 219-231.

Tansey, J. and O'Riordan, T. (1999) 'Cultural Theory and Risk: a Review', *Health, Risk and Society* 1(1): 71-90.

Tavistock Institute (2002) 'About Us'. Retrieved on 27 May 2005 from *http://www.tavinstitute.org/index.php.*

Taylor, I. (1991) 'English Football in the 1990s: Taking Hillsborough Seriously?' in J. Williams and S. Wagg (eds.) *British Football and Social Change - Getting into Europe*, pp. 3-24. Leicester: Leicester University Press.

Taylor, R. (1991) 'Walking Alone Together: Football Supporters and Their Relationship with the Game', in J. Williams and S. Wagg (eds.) *British Football and Social Change - Getting into Europe* pp. 111-129. Leicester: Leicester University Press.

Taylor, R. (1992) *Football and its Fans – Supporters and their Relations with the Game, 1885-1985*. Leicester: Leicester University Press.

Thompson, M. and Wildavsky, A. (1986) 'A Cultural Theory of Information Bias in Organizations', *Journal of Management Studies*, 23(3): 273-86.

Thompson, T. (1997) 'The Case Against: Theories of Risk Are Not Relevant to Practitioners', *International Journal of Risk Security and Crime Prevention*, 2(2): 136-137.

Thompson, M. and Rayner, S. (1998) 'Risk and Governance Part I: The Discourses of Climatic Change', *Government and Opposition*, 33(2): 139-166.

Thompson, M., Ellis, R. and Wildavsky, A. (1990) *Cultural Theory.* Boulder CO: Westview Press.

Thompson, M., Grendstad, G. and Selle, P. (1999) 'Cultural Theory as Political Science', in M. Thompson, G. Grendstad and P. Selle (eds.) *Cultural Theory as Political Science*, pp. 1-23. London: Routledge.

Thompson, M., Rayner, S. and Ney, S. (1999) 'Risk and Governance Part II: Policy in a Complex and Plurally Perceived World', *Government and Opposition*, 33(3): 330-354.

Tilley, N. (2001) 'Evaluation and Evidence-Led Crime Reduction Policy and Practice', in R. Matthews and J. Pitts (eds.) *Crime, Disorder and Community Safety*, pp. 81-97. London: Routledge.

Toft, B. (1992) 'The Failure of Hindsight', *Disaster Prevention and Management: An International Journal*, 1(3): 48-59.

Toft, B. (1993) 'Safety Culture', paper presented to the Cranfield MSc in Safety, Risk and Reliability Management, 13 January 1993, Cranfield Centre for Industrial Safety and Reliability: Cranfield University.

Toft, B. (1995) 'Limits to the Mathematical Modelling of Disasters', Keynote address, *The Risk Society,* 26-28 February 1995, Liverpool: University of Liverpool Business School.

Toft, B. (1996) 'Limits to the Mathematical Modelling of Disasters', in C. Hood and D. Jones (eds.) *Accident and Design: Contemporary Debates in Risk Management*, pp.99-110. London: UCL Press.

Toft, B. (1997) 'Protecting the Organisation', *International Journal of Risk, Security and Crime Prevention*, 2(2): 85-94.

Toft, B. and Reynolds, S. (1997) *Learning From Disasters: A Management Approach* (Second Edition). Leicester: Perpetuity Press.

Toft, B. and Turner, B. (1987) 'The Schematic Report Analysis Diagram: a Simple Aid to Learning From Large-Scale Failures', *International CIS Journal*, 1(2): 12-23.

Trist, E. and Bamforth, K. (1951) 'Some Social and Psychological Consequences of the Longwall Method of Coal Getting', *Human Relations*, 4(1).

Trompenaars, F. (1993) *Riding the Waves of Culture: Understanding Cultural Diversity in Business*. London: The Economist Books.

Tuan, Y-F. (1974) *Topophilia.* Englewood Cliffs: Prentice-Hall.

Turner, B. (1978) *Man-Made Disasters*. London: Wykeham Press.

Turner, B. (1983) 'The Use of Grounded Theory for the Qualitative Analysis of Organisational Behaviour', *Journal of Management Studies*, 20(3): 333-348.

Turner, B. (1991) 'The Development of a Safety Culture' *Chemistry and Industry*, 01 April 1991, pp. 241-243.

Turner, B. (1994) 'The Future of Risk Research', *Journal of Contingencies and Crisis Management*, 2(3): 146-156.

Turner, B. and Pidgeon, N. (1997) *Man-Made Disasters* (Second Edition). Oxford: Butterworth-Heinemann.

Walley, L. (1997) 'The Changing Face of Criminal Liability', in S. Frosdick and L. Walley (eds.) *Sport and Safety Management*, pp.41-55. Oxford: Butterworth-Heinemann.

Walvin, J. (1986) *Football and the Decline of Britain*. London: Macmillan.

Warner, F. (1993), 'Calculated Risks', *Science and Public Affairs*, Winter 1992, pp. 44-9.

Weir D. (1996) 'Risk and Disaster: The Role of Communications Breakdown in Plane Crashes and Business Failure', in C. Hood and D. Jones (eds.) *Accident and Design: Contemporary Debates in Risk Management*, pp. 114-126. London: UCL Press.

Weir, D. (1997) 'Communication Behaviour in Risky Systems Operating in Degraded Mode', Paper Submitted to the Second International Stockholm Seminar on Risk Behaviour and Risk Management.

Wells, C. (1996) 'Criminal Law, Blame and Risk: Corporate Manslaughter', in C. Hood and D. Jones (eds.) *Accident and Design: Contemporary Debates in Risk Management*, pp. 50-60. London: UCL Press.

Whyte, W. (1961) *On the Evolution of 'Street Corner Society'*, (Appendix to *Street Corner Society,* Sixth Impression). Chicago: University of Chicago Press.

Wildavsky, A. and Dake, K. (1990) 'Theories of Risk Perception: Who Fears What and Why', *Daedalus*, 119(4): 41-60.

Wilde, G. (1982) 'The Theory of Risk Homeostasis: Implications for Safety and Health', *Risk Analysis*, 2(4): 209-25.

Williams, J. (1991) 'Having an Away Day: English Football Spectators and the Hooligan Debate', in J. Williams and S. Wagg (eds.) *British Football and Social Change - Getting into Europe* pp. 160-186. Leicester: Leicester University Press.

Williams, J., Dunning, E. and Murphy, P. (1989a) *The Luton Town Members Scheme: Final Report.* University of Leicester: Sir Norman Chester Centre for Football Research.

Williams, J., Dunning, E. and Murphy, P. (1989b) *Football and Football Supporters After Hillsborough: A National Survey of Members of the Football Supporters Association.* University of Leicester: Sir Norman Chester Centre for Football Research.

Williams, T. (1995) 'A Classified Bibliography of Recent Research Relating to Project Risk Management', *European Journal of Operational Research*, 85: 18-38.

Wilmot, D. (1993) *Policing Football Matches.* Manchester: Greater Manchester Police.

Winter, H. (2000) 'Fans on Their Feet 'An Accident Waiting to Happen'', *The Daily Telegraph*, 14 November 2000, p. 44.

Wootton, G. and Stevens, T. (1995) *Into the Next Millennium: A Human Resource Development Strategy for the Stadia and Arena Industry in the United Kingdom.* Swansea Institute of Higher Education Stadium and Arena Management Unit.

Wyllie, R. (1992) 'Setting the Scene', in *Lessons Learned from Crowd-Related Disasters,* Easingwold Papers No. 4. Easingwold: Home Office Emergency Planning College.

Yin, R. (1994) *Case Study Research: Design and Methods* (Second Edition). London: Sage.

APPENDIX A:
CASE STUDY PROTOCOL/CODING FRAME

100 **Organise the Project**
110   Initial contact with client
120   Determine which activities and tasks meet the client's specific needs
130   Prepare and submit proposal
140   Client agreement to proceed
150   Agree timescales/project plan

200 **Produce Risk Strategy Document**
210   Produce draft Risk Strategy Document
220   Circulate for comments
230   Produce Risk Strategy for Client's Project Initiation Document

300 **Undertake Stakeholder Analysis**
310   *Business*: commissioned and support the client's project
320   *Advisory Groups*: opposition or concerns about the client's project
330   *User Community*: neither supportive nor opposed
340   *Commercial*: potential tenderers, trade bodies or consultants

400   *Prepare for Risk Assessment Interviews*
410   Identify stakeholder interviewees
411   Identify *Business* stakeholder interviewees
412   Identify *Advisory Group* stakeholder interviewees
413   Identify *User* stakeholder interviewees
414   Identify *Commercial* stakeholder interviewees
420   Prepare briefing note for interviewees
430   Prepare interview schedule
440   Appoint liaison officer
450   Arrange appointments for interviews
460   Circulate briefing note to interviewees

500   *Risk Assessment Interviews*
510   Undertake risk assessment interviews
520   Write up risk assessment interviews
530   Interview coding and analysis
540   Draft risk assessment

600   **Prepare for Risk Assessment Workshop**

610   Agree date, time and location of assessment workshop
620   Identify source documentation
630   Prepare assessment workshop agenda
640   Identify stakeholder participants for assessment workshop
641   Identify *Business* stakeholders for assessment workshop
642   Identify *Advisory Group* stakeholders for assessment workshop
643   Identify *User* stakeholders for assessment workshop
644   Identify *Commercial* stakeholders for assessment workshop
650   Prepare briefing note for assessment workshop participants
660   Prepare attachments to briefing note
670   Circulate documentation to assessment workshop participants
680   Book assessment workshop accommodation, visual aids and catering
690   Prepare assessment workshop support materials

700   Hold Risk Assessment Workshop
710   Introduce process and brief participants
720   Identify hazards, threats or weaknesses – process?
730   Estimate risks – process?
740   Participation of stakeholder representatives
741   *Business* stakeholder participation
742   *Advisory Group* stakeholder participation
743   *User* stakeholder participation
744   *Commercial* stakeholder participation
750   Write up risk assessment
760   Circulate for comments
770   Amend risk assessment as necessary

800   Prepare for Risk Evaluation
810   Arrange risk evaluation meeting
820   Prepare risk evaluation tools

900   Complete Risk Evaluation
910   Brief Project Director/Manager
920   Obtain risk evaluation decision
930   Write up risk evaluation
940   Circulate for comments
950   Amend risk evaluation as necessary

1000   Prepare for Risk Management Workshop
1010   Agree date, time and location of management workshop
1020   Prepare management workshop agenda
1030   Identify stakeholders to participate in management workshop

1031   Identify *Business* stakeholders for management workshop
1032   Identify *Advisory Group* stakeholders for management workshop
1033   Identify *User* stakeholders for management workshop
1034   Identify *Commercial* stakeholders for management workshop
1040   Prepare briefing note for management workshop participants
1050   Prepare attachments to briefing note
1060   Circulate documentation to management workshop participants
1070   Book workshop accommodation, visual aids and catering
1080   Prepare management workshop support materials

1100   Hold Risk Management Workshop
1110   Introduce process and brief participants – process?
1120   Select priority risks
1130   Determine countermeasures/contingency plans
1140   Allocate responsibilities
1150   Participation of stakeholder representatives
1151   *Business* stakeholder participation
1152   *Advisory Group* stakeholder participation
1153   *User* stakeholder participation
1154   *Commercial* stakeholder participation
1160   Produce draft Risk Log
1170   Circulate for comments
1180   Amend Risk Log as necessary

1200   Prepare for Quality Review
1210   Agree date, time and location of quality review
1220   Prepare quality review agenda
1230   Identify stakeholder representatives to participate in quality review
1231   *Business* stakeholder participants
1232   *Advisory Group* stakeholder participants
1233   *User* stakeholder participants
1234   *Commercial* stakeholder participants
1240   Prepare briefing note for quality review participants
1250   Prepare attachments to briefing note
1260   Circulate documentation to quality review participants
1270   Book quality review accommodation, visual aids and catering
1280   Prepare quality review support materials (slides, hand-outs, etc.)

1300   Hold Quality Review
1310   Introduce process and brief participants
1320   Errors/comments by reviewers
1330   Additions from reviewers

1340   Participation of stakeholder representatives
1341   *Business* stakeholder participation
1342   *Advisory Group* stakeholder participation
1343   *User* stakeholder participation
1344   *Commercial* stakeholder participation
1350   Amend Risk Log as necessary

1400   Undertake Risk Monitoring
1410   Produce Risk Management Progress Report Template **or**
1420   Produce Risk Management Database
1430   Agree report-by dates with persons allocated responsibilities
1440   Audit progress against Risk Management Plan
1450   Update Risk Management Progress Report **or**
1460   Update Risk Management Database and Produce Progress Report
1470   Schedule Management of Risk Review

1500   Organise Management of Risk Review
1510   Initial contact with client
1520   Determine which activities and tasks meet the client's specific needs
1530   Prepare and submit proposal
1540   Client agreement to proceed
1550   Agree timescales/project plan

1600   Prepare for Review Workshop
1610   Agree date, time and location of review workshop
1620   Identify documentation to be reviewed
1630   Prepare workshop agenda
1640   Identify stakeholder representatives to participate in workshop
1641   *Business* stakeholder participants
1642   *Advisory Group* stakeholder participants
1643   *User* stakeholder participants
1644   *Commercial* stakeholder participants
1650   Prepare briefing note for workshop participants
1660   Prepare attachments to briefing note
1670   Circulate documentation to workshop participants
1680   Book workshop accommodation, visual aids and catering
1690   Prepare workshop support materials (slides, hand-outs, etc.)

1700   Hold Review Workshop
1710   Introduce process and brief participants – process?
1720   Review existing priority risks
1730   Review existing action plans

1740   Review existing residual risks
1750   Identify new risks
1760   Review risk evaluation decision
1770   Assess new risks
1780   Devise action plans for new priority risks
1790   Participation of stakeholder representatives
1791   *Business* stakeholder participation
1792   *Advisory Group* stakeholder participation
1793   *User* stakeholder participation
1794   *Commercial* stakeholder participation

1800   Prepare Reports
1810   Produce draft revised Risk Log
1820   Circulate for comments
1830   Amend Risk Log as necessary
1840   Produce revised Risk Management Progress Report
1850   Produce revised Risk Management Database

INDEX

A

accident investigation, 15, 19, 264
ACPO (Association of Chief
   Police Officers), V, 106, 110,
   213, 216, 217, 219
action science, 3, 72, 80
ALARP (as low as reasonably
   practicable), V, 26, 27
APM (Association for Project
   Management), V, 155, 157
arousal, 19, 21

B

blame, 10, 11, 12, 13, 27, 42, 43,
   47, 56, 82, 93, 94, 111, 114,
   118, 122, 124, 131, 135, 170,
   217, 230, 231
business continuity planning, 36,
   38, 39

C

Case Study Alpha, 2, 19, 194,
   202, 213, 236, 237, 240, 241,
   243, 251
Case Study Amber, VIII, 195,
   222, 223, 230, 236, 238, 239,
   240, 241, 243, 244, 245, 250,
   251, 252, 255
Case Study Apple, 195, 230, 236,
   238, 240, 242, 253
Case Study Bluegrass, VI, VII,
   VIII, 172, 195, 226, 227, 229,
   231, 232, 236, 237, 240, 241,
   243, 244, 245, 247, 253, 254,
   255, 260
Case Study Bravo, 194, 204, 209,
   236, 238, 240, 242

Case Study Broadway, 194, 201,
   202, 210, 235, 237, 238, 241,
   242
Case Study Central, 15, 195, 206,
   221, 236, 238, 240, 242
Case Study Charlie, 194, 203,
   205, 208, 213, 236, 238, 239,
   240, 242, 250
Case Study Delta, 194, 200, 207,
   235, 238, 241, 242, 252, 253
Case Study Echo, 194, 201, 202,
   235, 238, 241, 242, 249, 250,
   253
Case Study Foxtrot, 194, 201,
   235, 237, 238, 240, 241
Case Study Golf, 195, 214, 236,
   238, 241, 242, 250, 253
Case Study Harvard, 195, 229,
   236, 238, 240, 241, 242
Case Study Hotel, 195, 214, 216,
   217, 236, 238, 240, 242, 252
Case Study Hunter, 195, 213, 236,
   238, 239, 240, 241, 244, 250
Case Study India, 195, 215, 236,
   238, 241, 242, 250
Case Study Juliet, 194, 202, 210,
   235, 238, 241, 242, 253
Case Study Kilo, 194, 200, 201,
   202, 210, 235, 238, 241, 242
Case Study Lima, 98, 194, 204,
   236, 238, 240, 242, 244
Case Study Mike, 194, 196, 198,
   199, 202, 235, 237, 240, 242,
   243, 250, 253
Case Study November, 71, 81, 83,
   108, 113, 162, 180, 194, 196,
   206, 211, 220, 235, 237, 239,
   240, 241, 243, 244, 245, 250,
   251, 252, 253, 254, 267, 268,

271, 273, 274, 276, 288, 290, 294

Case Study Orange, VII, 173, 195, 223, 236, 238, 240, 241, 243, 244, 251, 259

Case Study Oscar, 194, 196, 198, 199, 201, 202, 204, 205, 206, 220, 235, 238, 239, 240, 242, 243, 248

Case Study Papa, 194, 207, 236, 238, 241, 242, 243, 244

Case Study Peter, 195, 232, 236, 238, 240, 242, 250, 253, 254

case study protocol, 71, 72, 73, 74, 84, 86, 193, 197, 259

Case Study Purple, 195, 213, 236, 238, 240, 242

Case Study Quebec, VII, 194, 205, 206, 213, 236, 238, 240, 242, 243, 250, 252

Case Study Ranger, VII, VIII, 171, 172, 195, 219, 220, 224, 226, 229, 231, 236, 237, 238, 240, 241, 243, 244, 248, 252, 254

Case Study Romeo, 194, 207, 236, 238, 240, 242, 244, 250

Case Study Royal, VII, VIII, 2, 6, 8, 9, 12, 13, 14, 21, 23, 24, 25, 28, 31, 32, 40, 42, 45, 56, 58, 60, 146, 160, 162, 174, 195, 229, 230, 236, 238, 240, 241, 243, 244, 245, 250, 253, 254, 264, 265, 267, 271, 275, 285, 288, 290

Case Study Sierra, VIII, 99, 195, 216, 236, 238, 240, 241, 243, 244, 252

Case Study Tango, 195, 217, 223, 236, 237, 240, 241, 243, 244, 251, 254

Case Study Trojan, 195, 210, 236, 238, 239, 240, 242

Case Study Uncle, VIII, 195, 224, 226, 227, 228, 229, 230, 231, 232, 236, 237, 240, 241, 243, 244, 255

Case Study Uniform, VIII, 195, 211, 212, 236, 238, 240, 241, 243, 251, 252, 253, 254

Case Study Victor, 194, 197, 235, 238, 239, 241, 242, 243, 244

Case Study Whisky, VII, 194, 197, 198, 200, 235, 237, 240, 241, 244, 245, 254

Case Study X-Ray, VII, 194, 199, 202, 208, 235

Case Study Yankee, VII, 195, 208, 236, 237, 238, 240, 241, 244, 251, 255

Case Study Zebra, 195, 231, 236, 237, 238, 239, 240, 241

Case Study Zulu, VII, 195, 209, 210, 236, 237, 240, 241, 252

case study/studies, VI, VII, VIII, 3, 4, 51, 53, 59, 66, 67, 69, 71, 72, 74, 75, 76, 80, 82, 83, 84, 86, 89, 90, 152, 153, 155, 159, 162, 165, 166, 171, 172, 173, 174, 179, 192, 193, 194, 196, 197, 198, 199, 200, 201, 202, 203, 204, 205, 206, 207, 208, 209, 210, 211, 212, 213, 214, 215, 216, 217, 219, 220, 221, 222, 223, 224, 226, 227, 229, 230, 231, 232, 233, 235, 237, 239, 240, 251, 255, 256, 258, 259, 260, 261, 262, 265, 294

CCTA (old acronym for Office for Government Commerce), V, 15, 75, 77, 162, 164, 180, 181, 192, 200, 201, 264, 269

CCTV (closed circuit television),
V, 99, 100, 104
certifying authorities, 109, 114
checklists, 15, 16, 244
coding frame, 71, 72, 73, 84, 85,
86, 193, 239, 295
commercial (risk) perspective,
137, 139, 143
consultancy, III, 50, 52, 53, 55,
57, 66, 69, 70, 71, 72, 74, 75,
76, 77, 81, 82, 83, 84, 85, 86,
87, 90, 163, 190, 213, 218, 219,
229, 258, 259, 260, 263, 264,
265, 289
cost benefit analysis, 27, 28, 31,
288
COTASS (club-oriented ticketing
and authorisation system for
stadia), V, 146
CPSMR (Centre for Public
Services Management and
Research), V, 67, 81, 82, 83, 84
CRAMM (CCTA Risk Analysis
and Management Method), V,
200, 201, 202, 204, 209, 210,
232, 246, 249, 269
cross case report, 52, 73, 85, 153,
257, 258
cultural bias, 19, 20, 30, 32, 33,
34, 35, 47, 55, 59, 61, 63, 111,
120, 131, 176, 255, 270, 271,
288
Cultural Theory, V, VI, VIII, 1, 2,
3, 4, 5, 32, 33, 34, 35, 41, 44,
45, 47, 48, 49, 50, 54, 55, 56,
57, 58, 59, 60, 61, 62, 63, 66,
67, 68, 69, 70, 71, 72, 73, 74,
76, 77, 80, 81, 82, 83, 85, 86,
87, 89, 93, 105, 107, 111, 114,
115, 118, 119, 120, 122, 127,
128, 129, 130, 134, 136, 151,
152, 155, 164, 166, 169, 170,

171, 172, 173, 174, 175, 176,
179, 181, 192, 193, 196, 197,
198, 199, 200, 201, 202, 203,
205, 207, 208, 211, 213, 215,
216, 217, 218, 219, 223, 224,
226, 229, 230, 231, 235, 236,
239, 241, 242, 243, 244, 249,
251, 252, 254, 255, 256, 257,
258, 259, 261, 263, 264, 265,
267, 268, 271, 272, 273, 275,
280, 283, 285, 286, 287, 288,
289, 291, 292
cultural web, VI, 64, 65, 66, 120,
176, 257

D

disaster(s), 2, 3, 7, 19, 21, 38, 39,
43, 45, 56, 64, 72, 80, 93, 94,
95, 96, 98, 99, 100, 101, 102,
103, 105, 107, 111, 118, 119,
130, 131, 132, 134, 138, 142,
162, 166, 167, 168, 169, 252,
264

E

egalitarian, 3, 30, 45, 56, 60, 93,
115, 116, 118, 130, 135, 137,
151, 165, 171, 194, 196, 198,
201, 202, 203, 204, 205, 206,
207, 209, 210, 211, 213, 215,
217, 218, 219, 221, 222, 223,
224, 228, 229, 231, 235, 256
egalitarianism, 34, 59, 61, 67, 107,
199, 205, 208, 209, 216, 218
event tree analysis, 18
external disruption (risk)
perspective, 138, 142, 144

F

fatalism, 34, 107, 199, 201, 202, 203, 205, 209, 213, 216, 218, 229

fatalist, 3, 45, 56, 93, 115, 117, 118, 128, 135, 137, 151, 165, 194, 196, 198, 201, 202, 203, 204, 205, 206, 207, 208, 209, 210, 211, 213, 215, 217, 218, 219, 221, 222, 223, 224, 225, 228, 229, 232, 235, 244, 256, 258

fault tree analysis, VI, 17, 18

FLA (Football Licensing Authority), V, 69, 96, 100, 103, 106, 109, 111, 270, 272

FMECA (Failure Modes and Effects Criticality Analysis), V, 15, 16, 18, 19, 20, 26

football grounds, III, IV, VII, 1, 67, 82, 94, 96, 98, 99, 101, 102, 103, 105, 110, 114, 115, 139, 146, 264, 267, 268, 272, 273, 274, 278, 279, 284

football organisations, 108

FSA (Football Supporters Association), V, 107, 116

FSADC (Football Stadia Advisory Design Council), V, 96, 106, 108, 109, 113, 140, 280

FSC (Federation of Stadium Communities), V, 107, 115, 280

FSF (Football Supporters Federation), V, 116, 280

FSOA (Football Safety Officers' Association), V, 106, 110

G

generalisability, 263

grounded theory, 1, 3, 4, 50, 51, 52, 72, 73, 76, 77, 79, 80, 152, 153, 179, 233, 235, 254, 257, 259, 263, 264, 281, 286, 291, 293

H

HAZOPS (Hazard and Operability Studies), V, 15, 16, 18, 19, 147

heuristic, 59, 65, 66, 70, 165, 169, 239, 254, 255, 257, 258, 261, 263

hierarchical, 3, 10, 20, 34, 45, 67, 93, 111, 115, 120, 129, 134, 136, 151, 164, 170, 171, 175, 194, 196, 197, 198, 201, 202, 204, 209, 210, 211, 213, 214, 215, 228, 230, 232, 235, 256, 260

hierarchy, 10, 34, 59, 60, 63, 67, 107, 111, 130, 135, 170, 174, 175, 176, 179, 196, 199, 200, 202, 203, 204, 205, 207, 209, 211, 212, 213, 214, 215, 216, 217, 218, 219, 221, 222, 224, 226, 229, 231, 251, 256, 263

hindsight, 15, 19, 20, 38, 70, 111, 201, 255, 292

HMIC (Her Majesty's Inspectorate of Constabulary), V, 216, 217, 218, 219

HSE (Health and Safety Executive), V, 9, 26, 29, 31, 267, 281, 282

I

ILGRA (Interdepartmental Liaison Group on Risk Assessment), V, 41, 164, 264, 284

impossibility theorem, 35

individualism, 10, 34, 59, 61, 67, 107, 135, 170, 175, 198, 199,

203, 204, 206, 209, 210, 216,
218, 222, 229

individualist, 3, 10, 34, 45, 56, 93,
114, 115, 127, 134, 136, 151,
170, 175, 194, 196, 198, 201,
202, 203, 204, 207, 211, 217,
223, 224, 231, 235, 256

inspections, 15, 16, 101, 120, 141

IPCC (Independent Police
Complaints Commission), V,
264

ISE (Institution of Structural
Engineers), V, 110, 284

isomorphism, 19, 111, 152, 169

IWI Associates, III, 81

K

Kick It (Racism) Out, 145

M

management of risk, III, VI, VII,
1, 3, 4, 5, 7, 15, 25, 30, 46, 53,
63, 64, 66, 71, 72, 73, 74, 93,
95, 119, 131, 135, 145, 146,
147, 150, 151, 152, 155, 164,
165, 166, 171, 180, 181, 187,
188, 189, 190, 208, 212, 226,
227, 232, 235, 237, 239, 254,
255, 256, 257, 258, 259, 260,
262, 263, 264, 265, 267, 273,
274, 275, 276, 277, 282, 288,
290, 298

match officials, 108

N

NASUWT (National Union of
Schoolmasters and Union of
Women Teachers), V, 11, 287

natural history (of research), 3, 51,
66, 79

NFFSC (National Federation of
Football Supporters Clubs), V,
107, 115

NSPIS (National Strategy for
Police Information Systems), V,
VI, VII, 70, 71, 81, 82, 89, 90,
155, 159, 160, 161, 165, 169,
171, 179, 180, 181, 182, 183,
189, 190, 193, 196, 244, 245,
250, 251, 252, 255, 275, 276,
277, 287, 288

O

OGC (Office for Government
Commerce), V, 15, 75, 77, 158,
162, 164, 232, 264, 288

P

PAGIT (Home Office Police
Advisory Group IT), V, 182,
183

participant observation, 3, 51, 52,
53, 66, 67, 68, 74, 76, 80, 104

PITACSA (Police IT and
Communications Suppliers
Association), V, 182, 186, 189

police programme and project
management, 155

police service, 1, 52, 53, 59, 70,
80, 81, 83, 85, 106, 121, 152,
160, 163, 166, 174, 180, 188,
190, 217

policing costs, 114

PRINCE 2, V, 75, 269, 288

probability theory, 23, 38

programme management, 190

programme risk, VII, 189, 190,
227, 269, 279

project initiation document, V,
196, 199, 202

project management, III, 1, 64, 72,
    75, 77, 152, 155, 156, 157, 159,
    162, 165, 169, 175, 180, 190,
    252, 254, 261
project risk, VIII, 4, 52, 53, 56,
    59, 77, 81, 119, 152, 180, 192,
    198, 201, 227, 257, 259, 261,
    262, 264, 269, 294
psychometric approach, 25, 28,
    30, 32
Public Assembly Facilities, V,
    VII, 1, 2, 3, 4, 44, 50, 51, 52,
    53, 66, 67, 69, 70, 71, 74, 75,
    80, 81, 82, 83, 85, 91, 93, 94,
    95, 104, 118, 119, 120, 121,
    134, 135, 136, 137, 142, 143,
    145, 146, 147, 148, 151, 152,
    153, 155, 162, 169, 175, 179,
    222, 254, 255, 256, 257, 259,
    263, 264, 265, 274, 275, 276
public safety, 80, 101, 102, 103,
    106, 110, 135, 148, 210, 273

Q

quality and usefulness (of
    research), 49, 73
quality review, 75, 89, 211, 218,
    252, 297
quantification, 21, 22, 25, 31, 42,
    239
Quantified Risk Assessment, V,
    21, 30, 31, 32, 42, 43

R

Redfern Consultancy, 71, 83, 84,
    276, 277, 289
reflexivity, 51, 79, 83
reliability, 21, 22, 23
requisite variety, 35, 36, 86
research approach, 49, 52, 70

research design, 49, 50, 51, 69, 75,
    82, 152, 219, 224, 226, 264
research methods, 3, 51, 81, 82,
    270, 273
research problem, 3, 49, 66, 213,
    254, 257
research setting, VII, 1, 2, 3, 4, 48,
    52, 53, 54, 69, 70, 76, 77, 79,
    81, 82, 91, 93, 95, 103, 104,
    118, 119, 145, 152, 153, 155,
    166, 176, 179, 222, 254, 255,
    256, 259, 263
risk analysis, V, 14, 15, 25, 32, 36,
    37, 76, 87, 88, 89, 90, 136, 147,
    180, 190, 192, 197, 198, 200,
    201, 202, 204, 207, 210, 231,
    243, 244, 261, 272, 275, 286,
    289, 290, 294
risk assessment, V, VIII, 3, 5, 14,
    16, 21, 24, 25, 27, 29, 32, 33,
    36, 41, 47, 54, 55, 56, 63, 66,
    67, 69, 71, 76, 87, 89, 139, 147,
    149, 150, 151, 152, 171, 172,
    173, 174, 181, 182, 184, 186,
    189, 192, 197, 199, 203, 204,
    205, 208, 211, 212, 213, 216,
    217, 218, 219, 220, 221, 222,
    224, 226, 230, 232, 243, 251,
    253, 254, 261, 262, 264, 281,
    282, 284, 290, 291, 295, 296
risk avoidance, 36, 37
risk communication, 36, 39, 40,
    41, 43, 190
risk compensation theory, 28
risk criticality, 26
risk estimation, 2, 5, 14, 15, 21,
    22, 87, 147, 148, 183, 223, 232,
    244, 255, 258, 263
risk evaluation, VI, 2, 5, 14, 25,
    26, 27, 29, 30, 31, 32, 37, 89,
    148, 149, 181, 184, 185, 207,
    220, 221, 223, 225, 232, 244,

249, 250, 251, 255, 258, 262, 296, 299

risk homeostasis theory, 28

risk identification, VIII, 2, 5, 14, 15, 16, 19, 20, 22, 87, 147, 164, 181, 182, 217, 223, 224, 227, 244, 247, 248, 255, 258, 263, 274

risk log, VII, 88, 89, 196, 197, 198, 199, 200, 201, 207, 213, 215, 218, 219, 220, 221, 226, 227, 229, 230, 232, 243, 253, 297, 298, 299

risk management, III, VI, VII, VIII, 2, 5, 6, 7, 8, 14, 15, 25, 29, 31, 32, 36, 40, 41, 42, 43, 44, 47, 48, 54, 63, 64, 74, 76, 80, 87, 88, 89, 90, 136, 147, 149, 150, 152, 156, 166, 167, 168, 180, 181, 184, 186, 187, 188, 189, 192, 197, 201, 203, 204, 207, 209, 211, 212, 214, 215, 217, 218, 219, 220, 221, 223, 225, 226, 232, 243, 247, 250, 251, 252, 253, 255, 258, 259, 261, 262, 264, 269, 270, 273, 276, 278, 279, 280, 283, 285, 286, 287, 288, 289, 290, 291, 292, 293, 296, 297, 298, 299

risk matrix, VI, 185

risk monitoring, 90, 147, 166, 167, 168, 180, 189, 190, 211, 226, 253, 298

risk perception, 1, 2, 3, 5, 10, 12, 19, 20, 25, 30, 32, 41, 45, 47, 54, 55, 56, 60, 63, 68, 76, 93, 111, 115, 151, 164, 169, 171, 174, 181, 182, 198, 200, 201, 206, 207, 208, 210, 214, 216, 218, 228, 232, 243, 244, 249,

253, 254, 255, 256, 257, 260, 263, 265, 268, 286, 289, 291

risk reduction, 10, 26, 27, 37, 38, 44, 149, 253

risk review, VIII, 90, 166, 167, 168, 211, 212, 217, 226, 244, 253

risk theory, 1, 2, 3, 5, 6, 8, 10, 12, 13, 20, 27, 28, 43, 45, 47, 48, 49, 54, 55, 57, 58, 63, 68, 72, 76, 89, 91, 255, 256, 261, 282, 289, 292, 294

risk transfer, 36

risk/risk comparisons, 27

Royal Society, 6, 8, 9, 12, 13, 14, 21, 23, 24, 25, 28, 31, 32, 40, 42, 45, 56, 58, 60, 264, 265, 267, 288, 290

S

safety and security (risk) perspective, 138, 141, 144

safety culture, VII, 3, 118, 119, 120, 121, 122, 125, 127, 131, 133, 146, 151, 175, 256, 273, 274, 275, 289, 292, 293

safety officer(s), III, IV, V, 68, 69, 100, 103, 106, 110, 114, 126, 135, 145, 206, 274, 278

sampling (of case data), 24, 49, 52, 67, 68, 71, 72, 193

scientific objectivity (myth of), 24, 31, 40, 244

SCIF (Sound and Communication Industries Federation), V, 110, 290

social amplification (of risk), 41

societal risk, 9, 29, 30, 32

spectator (risk) perspective, 137, 140, 143

stadia safety, VI, VII, 105, 106, 107, 273
Stadium Communities, V, 107, 115, 280
stadium designers, 110
stakeholder analysis, VII, 66, 70, 85, 86, 151, 171, 172, 173, 174, 197, 198, 208, 219, 223, 224, 226, 229, 231, 243, 254, 255, 257, 258, 261, 263, 295
stakeholders, 2, 3, 4, 69, 72, 76, 89, 119, 145, 155, 164, 165, 166, 169, 170, 171, 172, 173, 174, 175, 181, 182, 193, 202, 207, 211, 212, 213, 214, 216, 219, 220, 222, 237, 243, 244, 245, 249, 251, 256, 259, 261, 263, 264, 296, 297
steward(s), 110, 121, 125, 126, 127, 129, 130, 132, 135, 137, 138, 140, 142, 150, 279

supporter groups, 115
Supporters Direct, 145

T

television companies, 106, 108
training course, 77, 219, 227, 257, 258, 259, 261, 263
triangulation, 67, 75

U

UEFA (Union of European Football Associations), V, 106, 108, 109, 143
University of Portsmouth, III, IV, 68, 71, 83, 276, 277, 278, 279

V

virtual risk, 13, 41, 45, 46, 48, 63

Printed in the United Kingdom
by Lightning Source UK Ltd.
117514UKS00001B/1-45